AMERICAN GOTHIC

*The Story of
America's Legendary
Theatrical Family—
Junius, Edwin, and
John Wilkes Booth*

GENE SMITH

A TOUCHSTONE BOOK
Published by
Simon & Schuster
NEW YORK • LONDON • TORONTO
SYDNEY • TOKYO • SINGAPORE

TOUCHSTONE
Simon & Schuster Building
Rockefeller Center
1230 Avenue of the Americas
New York, New York 10020

Copyright © 1992 by Gene Smith

All rights reserved,
including the right of reproduction
in whole or in part in any form.
First Touchstone Edition 1993
TOUCHSTONE and colophon are registered trademarks
of Simon & Schuster Inc.
Designed by Edith Fowler
Manufactured in the United States of America

1 3 5 7 9 10 8 6 4 2

1 3 5 7 9 10 8 6 4 2 (PBK)

Library of Congress Cataloging-in-Publication Data

Smith, Gene.
   American gothic: the story of america's legendary
theatrical family—Junius, Edwin, and John
Wilkes Booth / Gene Smith

   p.   cm.
   Includes bibliographical references and index.
   1. Booth family. 2. Booth, John Wilkes, 1838–
1865—Family. 3. Booth, Edwin, 1833–1893—
Family. 4. Booth, Junius Brutus, 1796–1852—
Family. 5. Lincoln, Abraham, 1809–1865—
Assassination. 6. Actors—United States—
Biography. I. title.
PN2285.S543   1992
792'.028'092273—dc20
[B]   92-8497
                                                          CIP

ISBN 0-671-76713-5
      0-671-87301-6 (PBK)

Title page illustration: Edwin Booth as Hamlet.

AMERICAN GOTHIC

INTRODUCTION

A GREAT DEAL of time has passed since I first began asking
questions about the subject of this book. I can date the
moment quite precisely. It would have been in the spring of 1949.
In that long-ago year I received a June 20 letter from Philip Van
Doren Stern, author of *The Man Who Killed Lincoln*. He was kindly
responding to a letter of mine.

He addressed me as "Dear Mr. Smith," a usage to which I was
not much accustomed. I did not then realize that his book was
fiction—well researched, well grounded, but a novel, not history.
For this reason I cannot cite it in the Notes to this book. Yet I must
include it in the Bibliography. It was, I think, the first nonchildren's
book I ever read. In the early 1970s, when I was inducted into the
Society of American Historians, the first of my fellow members
whom I sought out was Philip Van Doren Stern. I reminded him
of our correspondence of a quarter century earlier. He said he
thought he remembered. A kid wrote asking about the exact location of where Lincoln's assassin died—wasn't that it?

Yes. That was it. And now, at an age that only with great
imprecision can be described as that of a kid, I return to the matter
that captured me so long ago. It is the story of an actor father whose
two actor sons cast themselves as regicides, the one on a stage as the
great Hamlet of the ages, the other on a stage as the American
Brutus. Here Theater meets History, with family figuring in, and
the events of 1861–65 known as the War of the Brothers, and
madness, fame, glory, and the posing of certain questions for which
there can be no answers.

Perhaps it is this last that drives researchers. Even now, so many years on, people still work, and work hard, to uncover new facts that will help explain or at least illuminate dark corners of a great classical drama. I must confess that when I contracted to write this book I did not know this was so. So I am indebted to those who with the greatest generosity directed me to new revelations and who with the greatest kindness shared their findings with me.

Mr. James O. Hall has been a student of the family Booth for decades. He accepts nothing on faith, makes no assumptions without proof. Nothing fuzzy or vague gets past him. He pointed me to many valuable sources I might otherwise have missed.

Michael W. Kauffman is a younger Mr. Hall. Our many long talks were always fruitful and always fun. Laurie Verge and Joan Chaconas of the Surratt House and Tavern offered me their insights and helped me through the large body of original research done by Surratt Society members over the years.

Raymond Wemmlinger of the Hampden-Booth Theatre Library made my months in The Players Club, which houses the Library, a delight. Our arguments about the motivations and relationships of the brothers, and their father and their mother and sisters, were of great value and great fun.

Frank Hebblethwaite of The Ford's Theatre National Historic Site was always ready to help and anxious to offer his views.

Now that this book is done, my more than forty years of working on the Booths are concluded. Full circle. I could almost wish I were starting out again.

PREFACE

By 1881 THE HOUSE on the sandy country lane two and a half miles out of Port Royal on the way to Bowling Green had turned streaked from need of painting and looked badly weather-beaten to the Massachusetts reporter. But then, he had found all of the Virginia of after-the-war desolate and run down. Port Royal's half a hundred rickety homes were brown and rusty. Lifeless Bowling Green, he thought, would not deserve a place on the map save for the county courthouse.

The house's cattle shed was crumbling into decay, the wooden mill for crushing sugar cane was idle, the servant quarters were almost tenantless, and the hands of the women who received him were roughened by labors performed by no southern lady, before. Everything was sterile and desolate. All around for miles stretched empty oak and pine forests.

There were no men. The oldest of the women remembered perfectly the visitor to what had been her parents' home, sixteen years earlier. "I thought he was the handsomest man I had ever seen," she said. "He had the most magnificent head and forehead I ever saw." He had adored her little sister, she said. The sister was Cora. He had called her his little blue-eyed pet. At the last meal he took with the family, Cora sat by him in her high chair. Her mother spoke sharply to her, and she burst into tears and he said, "What, is my little blue-eyes crying?"

The reporter was shown a charred post remainder of the vanished tobacco barn. The previous summer, he was told, the women learned a piece taken from it and tipped with gold was offered for sale in a Baltimore store. "Think of it, five dollars for a piece not

as big as your little finger!'' Fifteen years later a reporter for a
Philadelphia paper happened by. The thinly settled and somnolent
country along the way was made melancholy by the decaying tok-
ens of antebellum prosperity, he wrote, the crumbled post-Reconstruction economy, and the shabby crossroad stores and taverns.
None of the isolated little towns had regained the populations
known before 1861–65. By then, 1896, the house was approaching
the end of its use. By the 1920s it was empty and abandoned. The
walls sagged, the broken windows gaped, and the roof appeared
ready to collapse. Before the beginning of the Second World War
it had done so. Vines and weeds covered the rotting beams and
foundation stones, and the forest closed in. In 1965 the sandy
country lane become U.S. Route 301 was widened and made into
a high-speed divided highway. There is a thickly wooded little
hillock in the median strip; that is where the house once stood.
Down the road a few yards is a historical marker.

To the north, eighty-one miles away at 604 H Street, N.W.,
Washington, D.C., the outside entrance steps that the screaming
Elizabeth Susanna Surratt climbed on a summer day in 1865 are
gone. Hundreds of sightseers gathered on that occasion to see the
broken young woman alight from a closed carriage at what was her
home and what had been that of her mother. Soldiers were sent to
drive them away. On the neck of her mother's dress the girl hours
earlier had put a jet-black steel arrow pin through a black silk bow.
Though the hangman's rope had slashed the skin away, the pin was
seen still in place where the body was disinterred four years after
death. In 1904 the daughter was put by her hanged mother's side
in Washington's Olivet Cemetery. There is a plaque on the outside
of what was their house, put there by an Asian-American society,
for the executed woman's residence is now Go-Lo's restaurant,
Chinese cuisine. The alternately dusty and muddy paths of a
swampy and fly-ridden Washington where only Pennsylvania Avenue and part of Seventh Street were paved are hidden now under
the asphalt and concrete and roaring traffic and No Parking signs,
but the house is still recognizable from old photographs.

Far away the statue of John Parker Hale, twice Free Soil Party
candidate for the Presidency, congressman, U.S. senator, and minister to Spain, stands before the Capitol of the state of New Hampshire, and not one in ten thousand people passing by—if even
that!—knows who his daughter was, and what it meant to her that
once along a farm lane in Virginia a tobacco barn burned and on
the porch of the vanished median strip house a man died looking

at his paralyzed hands and murmuring, "Useless, useless." Farther
still away, a Hanover, Germany, cemetery became the last resting
place of the daughter and the son-in-law of one of John Parker
Hale's Senate colleagues. She was dead by her husband's gun, and
he, horribly wounded, by his own knife, was entirely insane and
destined to live out his days in a German mental institution before
burial at her side. A son of that fatal marriage grew up to be an
Illinois congressman successfully proposing in 1930 that the government establish in a former Washington theater at Tenth Street,
N.W., a museum commemorating what his mother and father had
seen and undergone there and what the father so frightfully du-
plicated, so horribly reenacted, with knife and gun in Hanover,
Germany, long after. Madness. He had never recovered from that
night in the theater, the feeling that he should have, could have,
averted all.

The museum in the late 1980s and early 1990s was visited by
no less than eight hundred thousand persons annually, the U.S.
National Park Service estimates, six thousand to eight thousand
people a day in the spring, when tourists flood Washington. Most
of the visitors know something beforehand of the exhibits they
study, but so many years have passed that old legends have faded
from public consciousness: that each April by the Hudson River
there came again a black crepe-hung train that once had gone
through vast crowds along the railroad right of way, under arches,
past weeping people, draped and lowered flags, past muffled drums
and minute guns sadly and slowly firing—that it came again, now
as a spectral pilot engine adorned with long black streamers and
pulling an open car with a band of unattended instruments playing
silent dirges, with behind the funeral train itself, skeletons sitting
by a coffin and vast numbers of blue-coated men, the ghosts of the
Union Army, bearing more coffins. That each April spots on the
brick pavement before the former theater glowed a brilliant, terrible red; that in the dark building a woman screamed and suddenly
all was lit up and the walls became as glass through which one saw
people rushing about and screaming with the woman; that the alley
behind became filled with black cats and howling dogs through
which came a galloping horse that bore a rider frantically lashing
his mount as voices cried, "Get him! Get him!" That then in a
twinkle all went dark and silent again.

Time has run its course and the legends have faded, and the
Victorian era's marble-topped tables, wax flowers under bell glass
and heavy lace curtains have vanished. The tufted haircloth uphol-

stery, ingrain or Brussels carpets, black walnut cabinetwork, red velvets, and gold clasps have given way to other things. In the seventies and eighties of the last century there were slaughter- houses where New York's Lexington Avenue ended at Gramercy Park, and Texas steers were brought there from the East River. A little north were horse markets whose proprietors used the avenue to show off the gaits of their mounts. All that passed, as did the old Gramercy Park Hotel, which catered to the Southerners visiting the city. With their broad hats and long frock coats they could be seen on the hotel piazza sitting with feet elevated. Once the New York theater area was in Park Row, below the Five Points. Then it moved to Union Square, then up to Madison Square, and in the end located at Times Square, Broadway. Now there is off-Broadway, and off-off-Broadway. Across the country a multitude of old fire- trap theaters have burned, or become storage houses or factory lofts. It is, of course, natural. Everything changes.

But not quite everything. On the third floor of Number 16 Gramercy Park South, above a black marble fireplace, an elaborate clock with a bronze bull beneath and a bronze woman above is set at the moment of the death of the only person ever to occupy this room: one-seventeen in the morning of a June night in 1893 when the lights went out momentarily as a woman screamed, "Don't let Father die in the dark!" When the electricity came back on, he was gone. His slippers are by the bed, whose patchwork spread is crumbling. The furnishings and pictures and books have never been changed or replaced. The faded wallpaper has never been touched. For one hundred years the sun has lit up the tops of Gramercy Park's trees reflected in the three-frame gilded mirror and lighted the skull of an executed horse thief that found a new career after the thief's hanging: It played Yorick to the Hamlet of the room's occupant.

In a corner is Macbeth's sword, outside in the halls are Lear's robes, and Shylock's, and those of Richard III. There are pictures of the occupant's daughter when she was a little girl in Civil War days, one on a rocking horse, and pictures of her children, the occupant's grandchildren. His pipes are in the room, for he smoked incessantly for years, long meerschaums when he did not have one of his twenty daily cigars in his mouth. Pens, pictures of his father, one of Elsinore Castle, his chairs and tables, a cast of his hand holding that of his daughter, the book he was reading when his last stroke took him opened at the last page he ever saw. Down below on the ground floor are his crowns of kings and helmets of warriors and his portrait done by John Singer Sargent before which even now, a century on, he is annually toasted as the greatest actor and the finest gentleman the American stage ever produced. Outside, in the center of Gramercy Park, stands his statue in bronze.

Above the sleeping alcove of his suite is carved in wood, *Now blessings on him that first invented this same sleep.* Facing the bed is the largest picture in the room, the wife of his youth he never ceased to love and for more than three decades longed to join in death. It is so placed that it would have been the last thing he saw at night before closing his eyes, and the first thing in the morning. Friends' pictures are on the walls; here are his writing box, scale, boot horn, statuettes, candlesticks.

In the room is a picture of one whose name, it was understood by all who knew this suite's occupant, must never be mentioned in his presence. He himself would not speak that name, not for nearly thirty years. Once on a Christmas night when he was talking of the days of his childhood, it slipped out. People stared at one another. He lowered his head and began to cry. Yet by the bed, none of the score of pictures closer, is a photograph of a superlatively handsome face. Johnny.

ONE

H<small>E WAS</small>, of course, quite mad, and well known for being so. <small>THE MAD TRAGEDIAN HAS COME TO OUR CITY</small>, newspaper headlines said. Once an old friend saw him ordering a barrel of flour in Baltimore. "How do you do, Mr. Booth?" asked Gabriel Harrison.

"Who the hell are you, sir? Don't you know who I am? I am Junius Brutus Booth, sir!" The barrel was hoisted into the wagon. "Get in there, sir!" Harrison did so, commanded by that thrilling voice and those flaming eyes that had commanded a thousand audiences in England, on the Continent, across the United States. The reins were handed to Harrison, and he got the wagon in motion.

"Faster!" The wagon's owner was waving a hatchet picked up from the floorboard. With it he smashed open the flour barrel. The tailgate was down. "Faster—faster!" Harrison laid on the whip. They shot down the street, a great plume of flour rising behind them. The hatchet swung and slashed through the air, sometimes coming, Harrison said later, within an inch of his nose. He crouched in terror, clutching the reins as howls resounded above him and clouds of flour streamed behind. Once the Mad Tragedian was on a ship heading south to Charleston and a theatrical engagement. They came to where an actor friend, William Augustus Conway, had committed suicide by leaping into the sea. He had a message for Conway, he said. He flung himself overboard. A lifeboat was hurriedly lowered and a traveling companion, the actor Thomas Flynn, joined the crew members rowing toward what could easily become the scene of a second suicide. They got there before that could occur, and hauled the potential victim into the boat. "I say, Tom, look out," were the rescued man's first words. "You're a heavy man—be steady. If the boat upsets we'll all be drowned." "Ah, Junius, Junius," his father used to say, "will you never have done with these mad freaks?"

The father, Richard Booth, had been born in London, the son of a silversmith said to be descended from a Spanish Jew named Botha who had been expelled from his homeland in the seventeenth century for speaking against the royalist government. Richard Booth continued in the family tradition, and when the American colonists revolted against George III, Richard and a cousin decided to join their cause. On October 28, 1777, the two young men wrote the king's perennial thorn in the side and leading parliamentary opponent of the war to ask aid for a journey to America so they could fulfill their duty to oppose tyranny. A stormy libertine, the author of pornographic works that at one time brought him banishment from England, but withal a genuine devotee of liberty and liberal reform, John Wilkes was a distant relative of the Booths. He turned the letter over to Richard's silversmith father, who had his son arrested and then arranged such restrictions as would make it improbable that Richard would be able to attempt the journey again. (The cousin made it out and became a captain in the Continental Army.)

With a silver presentation sent to John Wilkes by way of thanks for not encouraging the wayward son, the father put Richard to becoming a lawyer. In time he became a mildly prosperous one, with his home in Queen Street, Bloomsbury. Whatever his thoughts about what the hoped-for sponsor of his trip had done, they did not prevent him from marrying John Wilkes's niece. He never lost his regard for the colonies become the United States, and kept a portrait of George Washington in his parlor, requesting all who came before it to offer a bow.

Mr. and Mrs. Richard Booth had three children, the wife dying in childbirth when the last one, a girl, arrived. The would-be revolutionist kept his antimonarchial principles, with his first son named Algernon Sidney in honor of the antiroyalist sent to the scaffold for opposing the rule of Charles II, and the second, born in London's St. Pancras Parish on May 1, 1796, named for Junius Brutus, a remote ancestor of Caesar's assassin; hundreds of years before that event Junius Brutus had opposed the Roman monarchy and was a founder of the Republic. (The girl was unideologically named Jane.)

Richard Booth had been a trial to his father; now his younger son became no less—indeed, far more—of a trial to *his* father. Junius Brutus was very bright and very difficult. He early showed an embarrassing multiplicity of talents, said the American Council of Learned Societies' *Dictionary of American Biography* later, when he had become the most famous actor in the United States. The talents included "painting, poetry, sculpture and female seduction." It was this last quality, perhaps not previously itemized by Learned Societies among the fine arts, that caused the trouble. He was, said an 1817 book, "charged by a frail nymph with a deed of which she could no longer conceal the evidence."

The frail nymph was one of the Booth family's serving girls. Junius Brutus was defended in court by his lawyer father, whose contention that his son was too young for such an achievement was not entirely consistent with the father's earlier paying off of a similarly complaining young woman. Indicating his son's slight stature (for Junius Brutus was always short) and his youthful look (for he always looked young), Richard Booth charged the plaintiff with having entertained male callers at night in her room. One of them was responsible for the problem. His son was just a child. But the court did not agree. Damages were assessed. When officers came to collect, Junius Brutus went over a high brick wall and kept out of sight for months. Eventually he was caught. His father had to make good the money.

Richard Booth was understandably unhappy. He had tried to make of his son an artist, a printer. He had put him in his office to learn the law. He had secured for him an appointment as midshipman in the Royal Navy, and indeed the serving girl's bastardy charge had caused Junius Brutus to be yanked off the brig *Boxer* for his court appearance. (But as has been said, it is an ill wind that does not blow well for somebody: *Boxer* sank with all hands.) Now there was the making good for the court officers collecting on behalf of the frail nymph. Things were unpleasant at home. The wayward youth took his leave from the familial hearth.

He went to become an actor. Who can say why. In later years it was said of Junius Brutus Booth that if the stage had not existed, he would have created it; that he *necessitated* the stage. That his nature lay in Shakespeare's mind, and that when centuries after Shakespeare's death this interpreter of his words appeared it was as the destined and completed representative of the playwright's grandest creations. A great actor reflects his own self married to the portrait imagined by his character's creator, and makes us see inside the man we see behind the footlights. Junius Brutus Booth was sublime, supernatural, grand, reptilian and terrifying when such was called for—actresses playing opposite shrank away in fear and horror—devilish, hilariously funny, the purveyor of a dynamic and tortured power that left audiences deeply shaken. He filled up the stage with his personality. His blue eyes shone with a terrible light. Overwhelming power and splendor, said the critic William Winter, the portrayal of darker passions and fiercer moods super-lative. The tones of his voice were immense. He had the look of an uncaged tiger and seemed to snap with fire, said the great comedian Joseph Jefferson; his cheeks seemed to quiver and his lips pressed against his teeth. It was fearful.

Sinister, heartbreaking, horrific, stunning—the actor James E. Murdoch playing The Secretary to Booth's Sir Edward Mortimer in *The Iron Chest* felt a pistol held to his head: "Then for the first time I comprehended the reality of acting." Murdoch saw the "fury of that passion-flamed face" and felt a rigid clutch on his arm and looked again and saw the "scintillating gleam of the terrible eyes, like the green and red flashes of an enraged serpent" and was filled with dread and fell on the stage. Sir Edward Mortimer did not release his clasp on The Secretary's arm, and so also tripped and fell. He arose with his fingers still maintaining their grip. Murdoch lay prone, paralyzed, "stunned and helpless" as Booth carried on. When he fought onstage his fellow actors and actresses were terri-fied for what might happen.

It was quite amazing. An undersized youth who rehearsed in the most desultory fashion, running through his lines in mumbled or underdone fashion, whose physical presence offstage was, when he was sober, mild, modest, unpretentious, undemonstrative, and shy, and whose bowed legs made him, people said, a poor prospect to stop a running-away pig, seized the theater and made it his.

Those who saw him never forgot. "I can see again," the aged Walt Whitman wrote, "Booth's quiet entrance from the side, as with head bent he slowly walks down the stage to the footlights with peculiar and abstracted gesture, musingly kicking his sword, which he holds off from him by its sash. Though fifty years have passed since then, I can still hear the clank and feel the perfect hush of perhaps three thousand people waiting. A shudder went through every nervous system in the audience. It certainly did through mine.

"His genius was to me one of the grandest revelations of my life, a lesson of artistic expression. The words, fire, energy, *abandon* found in him unprecedented meanings."

He began his career on December 13, 1813, as Campillo in *The Honeymoon*, and trouped the provinces playing in tents on Market Day, from booths in fields where fairs were held. He competed with trained dogs, strongmen, jugglers, stilt-walkers, singers, prize-fighters. The footlights were tallow candles set on plates floating in a trough of water. The crudely painted backdrops scarcely differentiated between Bosworth Field and a drawing room. He was indifferent to his stage costumes, as he always would be.

He joined a troupe going out to Belgium, where the British were massing men to meet Napoleon at Waterloo, and saw three men guillotined in Brussels and five men and two women chained by their necks to a stake, pilloried. He noted that people kissed in the street, admired the needlework and churches, saw Wellington at the theater. He made alliances with girls and went to an Ostend costume ball as a bear. He acted. He was considerate of his fellow players, as he always would be, not worrying whether they came in from stage right or left—just appear, he said; "I'll find you."

At a Brussels lodging house he took up with the landlady's daughter. Adelaide Delannoy was four years older than he. She left home to troupe about with him. On May 8, 1815, they were married. He wrote pleasant letters to her mother in Brussels; the new Mrs. Booth wrote home that "I am as well as I can be and I am getting as fat as a great beast."

They went to London, where his playing was such as to make Edmund Kean, of whom Samuel Taylor Coleridge had said that to see him play was "as to read Shakespeare by lightning," fear for his laurels. Booth appeared at the Worthington Theatre for thirty shillings a week and then moved on to Covent Garden at five pounds. He made a sensation there. Edmund Kean came in a carriage to say that Booth should join him at Drury Lane. Here was a contract. They would play together. Booth signed as they drove in the carriage, forgetting he was signed for Covent Garden. When he read the fine print of his Drury Lane undertaking he learned he would be playing roles uniformly secondary to those of Kean. He would be supporting him. He threw up the contract and went back to Covent Garden.

The bouncing about of his allegiance upset the London theatergoing public. Egged on by Kean, who perhaps hired some of the demonstrators, an unruly crowd erupted when Booth came onstage at Covent Garden. Shouts and booing resounded. Nothing he said could be heard. A placard was raised onstage: *Grant silence to explain.* No silence resulted. A second appeal went up: *Can Englishmen condemn unheard?* Apparently they could. Men yelled, "No

Booth!" It was not a riot of the magnitude of New York's Astor Place disturbance centering on the question of whether Edwin Forrest was a better actor than William Macready, for that cost the lives of more than twenty people, but it was sufficient to demand police intervention. Constables invaded Covent Garden and began heaving the more obstreperous members of the audience into the street, where they continued to make known their views while pounding on the doors.

Finally a semblance of quiet was brought into being and Booth offered an apology and begged the pardon of all. (Ever after, he showed great distaste for addressing audiences in his own persona, and disdained curtain calls.) In succeeding days he took out newspaper advertisements to repeat his apologies in print. His career went on as it had begun. He played London and the provinces, showing enormous energy, sometimes performing three times in a day. In 1820 George III died. During his lifetime *King Lear* was forbidden in Great Britain, for Shakespeare's mad monarch was too uncomfortably remindful of the reigning royalty. With George's passing, Booth played Lear. Always at his best in tumultuous, frenzied roles, he was magnificent. Kean was said to be his only rival, and perhaps that was wrong, and that on his level there was no rival save himself, that he competed only with what he had done before and would do in the future.

His marriage seemed happy enough. The couple went out in society a great deal, or at least the part of society that would socially accept an actor. In 1819 Adelaide Booth presented her husband with a son, who was named Richard, for his grandfather. One day in a Bow Street Market flower shop near Covent Garden, Booth took note of a girl selling blooms. Mary Ann Holmes was six years younger than the twenty-five-year-old actor, who had been married for more than half a decade. Mary Ann Holmes was beautiful—one need only study the pictures of the children she would have to see it was so. Booth took up with her. As had his wife before their marriage, Mary Ann trouped about with him when he played the provinces. In 1821 he managed a trip with her to Madeira, taking with him also a piebald pony, Peacock, bought in Deal. It was at Madeira that she learned she was pregnant.

His wife, his father, and his child awaited him in London. But he loved Mary Ann, and indeed in the decades of life remaining never looked at another woman. Flight with her seemed the answer to his problem. America beckoned. For all of his youth, Junius Brutus had lived in a home whose owner—his father, Richard—

asked that all visitors bow to a picture of George Washington. And the clipper *Two Brothers* had put in at Madeira. Its next port of call was Norfolk, Virginia. They loaded Peacock on board and set sail.

The voyage lasted forty-four days. They landed in June of 1821. He wrote to Adelaide that he had run into some trouble with British stage people and so would play in America for a time; he would faithfully send money for her and Richard. The last was true.

He was at once engaged to play Richard III in Richmond, and then signed to repeat the role in Petersburg, where the theater manager placarded the city with notices heralding "the great tragedian J. B. Booth, from the London theaters Covent Garden and Drury Lane." Rehearsal was set for 10:00 A.M. He did not appear. The manager told the other cast members they would start without the star. They were into the fourth act when what looked to the actor Noah Miller Ludlow like a sixteen-year-old boy came running in. His jacket and cheap straw hat were covered with dust. He had missed the stagecoach from Richmond and had come the twenty-five miles on foot.

"Is it possible this can be," Ludlow asked himself, "the great Mr. Booth, 'undoubtedly the best actor living'?" He decided some sort of joke was on. The small man raced carelessly through the rehearsal, said a few things about the stage business he desired, ran through the swordplay of the last act twice, and said, "That will do." That night he came on and began saying his lines with what Ludlow thought was the indifference of a schoolboy reciting his lessons. The actors offstage and on looked at each other, and one of them said to Ludlow, "What do you think of him?"

"Think! Why, I think he is an impostor."

The play went on, Booth warming into the role of the sinuously evil king. When the point arrived for him to hint at the murder of the young princes, it came to Ludlow that it was given to Junius Brutus Booth to cast the kind of spell capable of creation only by a great actor. When the curtain came down there was applause such as Ludlow ventured to say Petersburg never knew before and would never know again.

Within a year Booth was the most prominent actor on the American continent. "He was followed as a marvel," said the critic William Winter. "His glance was deadly. His clear, high, cutting, measured tone was the note of hideous cruelty." He made stage monsters not only possible, but actual. "Mention of his name stirred an enthusiasm no other could awaken." He was, said Walt

Whitman, "beyond any of his kind on record, and with effects and ways that broke through all rules and all traditions."

Yet very shortly it was seen that he was difficult. More than difficult. He was the wildest drinker anyone had ever known. Nothing was beyond him when he was drinking. He could desert Ophelia to dash up a ladder where, perched among the overhead backdrops, he crowed like a rooster until the stage manager lured him down by promising to let him go back and stay there until the President of the United States was reelected, for those were the conditions he stipulated for continuing in his part. He could go up in his lines in Boston, jumble in bits of other plays, announce he did not know his part, and finally gibber, "I can't read, I am a charity boy, I can't read. Take me to the lunatic hospital." Carried to his lodgings, he escaped and was found walking entirely naked down a road.

He was capable of pawning himself for a drink, standing patiently in the pawnbroker's window until a friend redeemed him. Managers all over the country learned to lock him up before a performance, for otherwise he might head for a tavern where he could end up addressing the other patrons on the pressing need for volunteers to go to Texas to straighten out the troubles there; they would depart at once. He was adept at getting liquor despite all efforts aimed at prevention. He bribed hotel bellhops to bring a bottle and the stem of a long tobacco pipe to the keyhole of a locked door so he could use the latter to sip the former dry. Then at the theater it would be a great question of what might happen. Once he fell onstage and the audience booed. Another actor got him up and he staggered to the footlights to shake his fist at the people and shout, "Wait! Wait! I'll be back in five minutes and give you the goddamndest performance of King Lear you've ever seen!" He probably did.

In Richmond once the theater was sold out days in advance. Booth appeared in town and then vanished. For three days the house was dark as the management conducted a search. Finally staff member John Ellsler located, in a dilapidated shanty on the James River and surrounded by "ragged, besotted wretches, the greatest actor on the American stage."

"Mr. Booth, I think you had better come to the hotel." The response was a warning finger raised at Ellsler and a long shush. "I am discoursing with these learned Thebans."

But "the wrecks," hearing the "magic name of Booth, reacted noisily," for they had not previously known the identity of the man

who supplied them not only with liquor but also "jest and story."
They asked that he recite a piece. But while willing to be an anonymous boon companion, he could not fraternize with them as Junius
Brutus Booth. Gravely rising, he took off his hat. "Good night,
gentlemen." He went off arm in arm with Ellsler.

At the hotel the management people locked him in his room
and put a man on guard outside with orders not to let him out. His
appearance on the stage was announced for that night throughout
Richmond. In the evening Ellsler went to the room and was told by
the guard that the actor had several times tried the door and once
the transom, but when respectfully informed that he could not
come out had retired quietly. Ellsler opened the door. The room
was empty. The window was open. He looked out to see Junius
Brutus Booth perilously escaping down a water spout. The theater
was again dark that night.

Mary Ann Holmes—Mrs. Booth to everyone in America—
presented him with a son, Junius Brutus, Jr. There followed a
daughter, Rosalie. They lived on Exeter Street, Baltimore. He
rented and then purchased a cabin and some hundred fifty acres for
summer use in Bel Air, Harford County, Maryland, some twenty-
five miles from Baltimore. He called his place The Farm. All life on
his property must be sacred, he said, for it came from the Almighty. And he was a religious man although of indeterminate
denomination. Saying he was a Jew, he sought out rabbis in syna-
gogues and spent hours discussing the Torah with them; he "joined
in their worship in the Hebraic tongue," wrote one of his daughters, and "read the Talmud and strictly adhered to many of its
laws." On days when he was scheduled to play Othello he went
about with a crescent on his breast and passages from the Koran on
his lips. (That the Moor was a Christian he disregarded.) He knew
the Bible, and his recital of the Lord's Prayer was something that
once heard was not forgotten. Catholics took him for one of their
persuasion because he knew so much about their faith. No priest
or minister in any church found him to offer anything but the
greatest attention and respect for what went on.

Because of his feeling for the sacredness of life, he absolutely
forbade killing anything found on The Farm. He would not permit
the branding of his cattle and hogs, for it might pain them. They
were never consumed on his grounds, nor were his chickens, and
his children were brought up as the strictest vegetarians. No one
was permitted the use of firearms on vermin. Lizards, turtles, and
mosquitoes he regarded as deserving of life no less than himself. He

refused to own slaves, but leased those who were the property of neighbors, housing and nursing and burying them. He forbade the cutting of flowers, and only already fallen trees were used for the fireplaces.

He farmed seriously, subscribing to journals on the subject and advertising for ground bones to use as fertilizer. To the neighbors he was Farmer Booth. Often he hitched up Peacock, the pony brought on *Two Brothers* from Madeira, and with another horse also in harness drove a wagon filled with goods to Marsh Market in Baltimore. There one day John Ellsler was sent by the Front Street Theater manager to say that he wished to see Mr. Booth in his office. Ellsler found the individual he sought standing surrounded by potatoes, wearing a blue coat with brass buttons, flowered waistcoat, cassimere trousers, and a broad-brimmed hat. He felt such awe that he could barely speak, but made known the reason for his coming.

"My dear little man," Booth replied, "oblige me by telling Mr. Wymss that as soon as I have disposed of my remaining bushels of potatoes I will be with him but that I cannot leave until they are sold."

Ellsler delivered the message to the theater manager, waiting with another man who suggested the potatoes be purchased by the theater. That would expedite matters. Ellsler returned with the offer. "Very good," Booth said. "I am glad Mr. Wymss is going to try our potatoes. He will find them excellent. Here, my little man, jump into the wagon. We will drive to the Barnum Hotel, deliver all but two bags there, and then to the theater with what remains."

No greater opposite to the hustle and lights and glare and travel of an actor's life could be imagined than the remote and forestbound farm in Bel Air, a complete sanctuary for all living things and for peace. Some wondered how he endured it. "Gad," an actor friend asked after a troupe's wagon had broken down on the road and they took shelter at his place, "how can you exist in such a wilderness?" Yet he seemed happy there with Mary Ann and a growing family of children, ten in number eventually, of whom four died young, as children did in the 1820s and 1830s. But wreathed in glory, garnering immense sums of money, he suddenly applied for the full-time job of keeper of the light in North Carolina's Cape Hatteras lighthouse, enthusiastically talking about the vegetables he could grow and the firewood he might collect. The pay for the position was three hundred dollars a year. He could make that and more any week he appeared in a theater. Actors and managers argued with him and finally talked him out of the idea; and it was well that they did so, said one friend, for it would be wiser to douse the light completely and let the ships take their chances than to leave its running to Junius Brutus Booth. (A later writer remarked that his decision not to take the post could be seen as "performing a service to the American merchant marine which could hardly be reckoned.")

It could not have been said that he was drunk when he undertook to secure the lighthouse job, for he pursued the matter for many weeks, and even he could not stay steadily intoxicated over that period of time. Something deeper was involved, and it was soon said of him that he was the premier example of Plato's rule that for an artist of the very highest rank a dash of insanity, or what the world calls insanity, is indispensable. He was a kindly man, generous, almost childlike in his faith in the essential goodness of human nature, loving, sincere; and usually his seizures, spells, pranks, and illusions harmed nobody except possibly himself. That he sometimes painted his face and dressed as an Indian chief, that he entered churches wearing the robes used for playing Cardinal Richelieu, the minister and congregation assuming themselves honored by some religious figure come from far places—whom did it hurt? Or that dressed as Shylock he walked the streets flinging coins in the air? Or that he would howl "Murder!" in a restaurant each time a friend swallowed an oyster?

Of course he shocked people, as he did the Quaker who, addressing him as Friend, offered him beef and ham on a steamer. "Friend!" Booth said, "I only indulge in one kind of flesh—human flesh—and that I take raw." But only occasionally did he act in dangerous fashion, and when he did so it was under the delusion that he was doing something of value. Riding with friends in a St. Louis street he saw two Catholic priests walking along and, conceiving them to be the Inquisition fanatics of *The Apostate*, he shouted to his companions to go on the attack. "Ride them down! Down with them!" When he held a loaded musket on a ship captain, he did so for what he thought was the man's own good. He wanted the captain to down some medicine. "You're bilious and require physic; I know it by your eyes, I know it by your skin. Drink, sir, or I'll send you to another and better world." ("Pray, let me off," begged the captain. "Think of my wife and children. I've drunk six bowls of this damn stuff already, and a seventh will physic me to death." People came and talked the healer out of his musket.)

Well read and intellectual—his library contained works by
Shelley, Keats, Coleridge, Racine, Dante, Plutarch, Milton, and
Locke—he was a linguist capable of performing in French in New
Orleans and could converse in German. He knew Greek, Latin, and
Spanish, and worked on Arabic and Italian. He was said upon
occasion to play Shylock in the Jew's own language. But there was
always that madness that sometimes, not often, could turn poten-
tially lethal. There was a distinct danger to the well-being of Mary
Ann Holmes when, upon the pony Peacock's death, he forced her
to wrap herself in a sheet and sit on the body while he walked about
with a shotgun in his hand reading a funeral service. One of the
slaves he hired from neighbors ran for help and returned with some
men, one of whom engaged the grieving actor in conversation while
another got around behind him and pinioned his arms. He did not
struggle. "Well, you've got me. Come to the house and have a
drink." Later in the day he vanished, and when he turned up the
following day was entirely irrational and unbalanced. The death of
anything or anyone closer to him always had more than a normal
effect. Told at a theater in Baltimore that a daughter had died, he
flung himself on a horse and with his Richard III cloak streaming
behind him galloped for home, along the road slashing with his
stage sword at branches of trees that he took for enemies. He broke
into the vault, got out the child's body, and lay in bed with it,
crying and laughing. Once he attacked the graves of his dead children with an ax, chopping their marble slab stones to bits. Mary
Ann Holmes did not interfere or argue with him. She seemed to
understand that when at times he was not himself he could not help
it. She loved him, and he was very sweet when he was himself.

The only real violence he ever perpetrated was upon the actor
Thomas Flynn, who helped rescue him when he jumped into the
ocean to deliver a message to his friend the suicide Conway. Flynn
and he were playing Charleston, and when the performance was
over retired to their rooms in a hotel. Flynn was on the ground
floor. In the middle of the night he awakened to see Booth crawling
through the window. Booth took an andiron from the fireplace and
struck the prone Flynn, who managed to get up out of the bed.
Booth hit him again with the andiron. He had played Othello to
Flynn's Iago that night. Perhaps to his disordered mind Flynn was
actually the evil intriguer of Shakespeare's work. Flynn's life was in
real danger. He picked up a pewter pot and smashed Booth in the
face, breaking and permanently disfiguring his nose.

It would not have been like him to blame Flynn for what he

did, and they remained close friends. Booth had many friends,
Edgar Allan Poe, the son of an acting family, being one. The two
drank together and together seized a man who offended them after
a play and suspended him "by his breeches on the spikes of a
convenient area railing, where they left him kicking and howling
while they pursued their tortuous way in gladsome mood." He was
close to Sam Houston and while drinking they performed recitations of a kind, Booth crying out a line and Houston, in a roar,
echoing it. The hero of New Orleans, General Andrew Jackson,
had the actor as his guest at the Hermitage, his fabled home, for a
week. It was, Booth said, one of the most pleasant experiences of
his life, but that did not stop him a few years later from expressing
himself harshly in a letter to the then President of the United States
concerning two men, allegedly Spanish pirates, whom some said
had been falsely accused:

> You damn'd old Scoundrel if you don't sign the
> pardon of your fellow men now under sentence of death,
> DeRuiz and DeSoto, I will cut your throat whilst you are
> sleeping. I wrote you repeated Cautions, so look out or
> damn you I'll have you burned at the Stake in the City of
> Washington.
>   You know me! Look out!
>
>   Your Master

He was quite right in saying President Jackson *did* know him,
and so the letter was ignored and five months later his old friend
came to see him play Hamlet. His letters to his wife in London, or
when she stayed with her mother in Brussels, were, of course, of
quite a different character. They contained money for Adelaide
Booth and young Richard, and soothing assurances of an early
reunion. There was no mention of Mary Ann, nor of the children
he had by her. In late 1825, after more than four years of American
residence, he made good on his promises, returning for a visit to his
wife and six-year-old son. He did not mention that sequestered
away in London were Mary Ann, Junius Brutus, Jr., and Rosalie.
After a short tour of the Continent, where he acted to splendid
reviews in Brussels and Amsterdam, he and his American family
returned to Baltimore and The Farm. He would not see Adelaide
and Richard for nearly a decade more, and she continued to receive
letters and money, never dreaming of his American situation,
which saw new babies arriving almost yearly.

His drinking did not decrease, nor his peculiarities. In Louis-

ville in January of 1834 a young Unitarian clergyman, James Freeman Clarke, received a note from him on the stationery of the
United States Hotel. It requested the minister's assistance in finding a place in a churchyard for interment of Booth's friend. The
word "friend" appeared to be followed by an "s" but the minister
reasoned there had been a simple mistake in writing, "as we do not
usually find ourselves called upon to bury more than one friend at
a time." He went to the hotel to offer his services. He and Booth
had never met. Booth was found with another man in a private
parlor. The actor was short and with clear blue eyes, Clarke noted,
an unexceptional figure when contrasted with his stage presence of
animated expression, brilliant eye, and lively air.

He and his friend were at a table upon which was a decanter
of wine and some bread. The friend did not utter a single word
during the evening that followed. Clarke took a seat, reasoning that
Booth, a stranger to Louisville and unfortunate enough to lose a
friend there, needed consolation. And, of course, it was a clergyman's office to sympathize with the bereaved. He inquired about
the actor's reason for sending for him as opposed to another, more
mature minister—he had been ordained only six months earlier—
and Booth said that as of Jewish descent and a monotheist he felt
most comfortable with a Unitarian. Clarke turned to the object of
his visit and asked if the recent death was a sudden one.

"Very."

"Was he a relative?"

"Distant." He offered wine or a cigar, and when Clarke declined both, said, "Well, let me try to entertain you in another way.
Perhaps you would like to hear me read?"

"I certainly should."

"What should I read?"

"Whatever you like best. What you like to read, I shall like to
hear."

"Then suppose I attempt Coleridge's *Ancient Mariner*. Have
you time for it? It is long."

The clergyman assured him time was of no essence. Booth
began to recite. Over his life, Clarke remembered years later, he
saw the performers William Macready and Edmund Kean, Jenny
Lind and Fanny Kemple, and also Henry Ward Beecher, Daniel
Webster, Henry Clay, and Ralph Waldo Emerson. Nothing they
did or said touched the recital of Junius Brutus Booth in the hotel
room. "I forgot the place where I was, the motive of my coming,
the reader himself. I knew the poem almost by heart, yet I seemed

never to have heard it before. I was by the side of the doomed
mariner. I was the wedding guest, listening to his story, held by his
glittering eye. I was with him in the storm, among the ice, beneath
the hot and copper sky. The actual words receded into a dim,
indefinable distance." Booth ended. Clarke drew a long breath.

The actor asked if his guest had ever read Shelley's *Queen Mab*
argument against the use of animal food. Clarke had. Booth asked
his opinion and Clarke said, "Ingenious, but not satisfactory."

"To me it *is* satisfactory. I have long been convinced that it is
wrong to take the life of an animal for our pleasure. I eat no animal
food." He pointed to the bread on the table. "There is my supper."
He spoke of biblical sanction for his views, pointing out endorse-
ments of vegetarianism from Genesis to Revelation and saying that
it was only after the Deluge that men were permitted meat and that
it was "for the hardness of their hearts"; that in the beginning it was
not so, only herbs were then given to man for sustenance. He
quoted the Psalmist to show man's food came from the earth and
said the reason Daniel and his friends were fatter and fairer than
other children was that they ate only pulse, the seeds of such
leguminous plants as peas, beans, and lentils.

He continued in this vein, making his arguments in highly
intelligent fashion, Clarke thought, and then in the most solemn
tone asked, "Would you like to look at the remains?"

Clarke said he would. Booth took a candle and led the way
into an adjoining chamber. Clarke prepared himself to see a laid-
out corpse. But the bed in the room was empty. Spread out on a
sheet in a corner were a score or more of dead passenger pigeons,
Columbia migratoria. All week flocks of them had been flying over
Louisville, millions of birds, and bushels of them shot from the sky
were for sale at every street corner, ready for the city's dinner
tables. Booth was on his knees, pressing the dead pigeons tenderly
to his heart.

At first it came into the minister's head that this was some
hoax, a practical joke. He decided it could not be, not after the long
and elaborate biblical arguments. And it would be too poor a joke
in itself and unworthy of such a man as Junius Brutus Booth. He
realized the keening actor was expressing his belief in the sacredness of life and that he was sincere and convinced. "You see these
innocent victims of man's barbarity," Booth said. This was waste-
ful, wanton, it was murder. Clarke was sincerely touched, but in
reply to Booth's request for religious services said he must reply in
the negative. He could not officiate at funeral solemnities for birds.

The actor understood. "That is fair. I cannot ask anything more. I am obliged to you for coming to see me." In the morning he hired a hearse and carriage and buried the pigeons in a cemetery plot he purchased. "For several days he continued to visit the graves of his little friends, and mourned over them with a grief that did not seem at all theatrical."

His performances at the theater, nights, were brilliant, Clarke remembered; days he was seen going about giving apples to horses and urging drivers to treat them with kindness. A flood struck Louisville, and a river steamer was wrecked. It began to sink. There was a horse securely tethered on deck who must drown. Booth came and took out twenty dollars—a month's wages for the average worker—and offered it to anyone who would swim out and cut the halter. A man did so. A few days later word spread that Booth had vanished. The theater was dark. He was found wandering in snow, miles from the city. He left Louisville, leaving a letter for the Reverend Clarke:

> Allow me to return to you my grateful acknowledgments for your prompt and benevolent attention to my request last Wednesday night. Although I am convinced that your ideas and mine thoroughly coincide as to the real cause of Man's bitter degradation, yet I fear human means to redeem him are now fruitless. The fire must burn, and Prometheus endure his agony. The Pestilence must come again ere the savage will be taught humanity. May you escape! God bless you, sir!

Yes, of course, perhaps he was insane, Clarke reflected. "If an insanity, it was better than the cold, heartless sanity of most men."

TWO

By 1840, when his last child was born, the actor Junius Brutus Booth was master of a two-residence, three-generation family. His father, Richard, had come over to live with his son, Mary Ann Holmes, and their six surviving children. Ever since his abortive attempt to join George Washington's forces had been thwarted by the English firebrand politician John Wilkes, Richard Booth had longed to see America. The marriage of his last child and only daughter, Jane, had sent him on his way. She united herself with a brutal drunkard miles beneath her socially, for he was a bootblack and knife sharpener, and with her husband and passel of squalling children moved in on Richard. He took it for a time and then made for Baltimore and The Farm.

There he struck the few neighbors of the remote Bel Air countryside as an intellectual English gentleman of the previous generation who wore knee breeches, a queue, and buckled shoes. He spent his time translating classics from the Latin and seemed to fit into the life of his son and his son's family, although perhaps rural Maryland was not quite the America of which he had dreamed for so long. (His correspondence from Bel Air to friends back in London he datelined as coming from "Beggarsburg" and "Robinson Crusoe's.") When away on tour his son wrote him long and pleasant letters of a philosophical and advisory nature, including admonitions regarding the oldest child of the house:

> Tell Junius not to go opossum hunting, or setting rabbit-traps, but to let the poor devils live. Cruelty is the offspring of idleness of mind and beastly ignorance, and,

in children, should be repressed, and not encouraged, as
is too often the case, by unthinking beings who surround
them. A thief, who takes property from another, has it in
his power, should he repent, to make a restoration; but
the robber of life can never give back what he has wan-
tonly and sacrilegiously taken from beings perhaps innocent, and equally capable of enjoying pleasure or suffering
torture with himself. As respects our accountability to
animals nothing that man can preach can make me believe
to the contrary. Every death its own avenger breeds. God
bless you. I hope soon to see you again. Your affectionate
son.

Twenty years had passed since the actor and Mary Ann
Holmes left Madeira with Peacock the pony. During all that time
several letters a year and sufficient money for her to live on had
regularly been dispatched to the real Mrs. Junius Brutus Booth,
who had gone to live with her mother in Brussels. Twice the
husband had gone back to call upon the wife, taking with him but
carefully hiding Mary Ann and a growing number of children, one
of whom had fallen sick and died during an 1834 visit. Adelaide
Delannoy Booth's marriage was of a quarter century's duration and
she appeared to have accepted its long-distance nature, always expecting that one day her husband would return to her. Then she
found out everything.

What happened was that Mrs. Booth's son, reaching his middle
twenties, decided to visit his father in far-off Maryland. Young
Richard was a devout Catholic gifted in languages, something of a
scholar. He soon discovered that Junius Brutus Booth was a wild
drinker—several times, he wrote his mother in Brussels, his father
had narrowly escaped being run over by carriages—but soon he
discovered something infinitely more startling. Theater people told
him that his name could not legitimately be Booth. To them the
real Booths were the half-dozen children of Baltimore's Exeter
Street and The Farm. Richard's shock may be imagined. He wrote
his mother. Her reaction may also well be imagined. She took a
ship to America. The ship was wrecked. She survived, went back
to Europe, and booked passage on another. She arrived in New
York and made for Baltimore. It was October of 1846.

Her husband was away. He was beginning a winter tour, she
wrote her sister Therese, back in Brussels. "I don't want to do
anything to prevent him from making money, so I shall wait until

he comes to Baltimore, and as soon as he arrives my lawyer will fall on his back like a bomb.''

It was not only the lawyer who exploded upon the actor when he returned. His wife's detonation was even more violent. When he came to Marsh Market to sell his vegetables he was likely to find her there offering her opinion of him in tones audible to all who cared to hear. The eventual divorce petition pointing out that he lived with a woman "with whom he has been in the habit of adulterous intercourse" was mildly phrased when contrasted to the language Adelaide Booth employed to the errant husband's face. Sometimes she paraded in front of the Exeter Street house, shouting. Once she appeared at The Farm. In an age when to be illegitimate was to be a social leper, she defined, loudly, what she called "the Holmes set" as exactly what they were, all six of them, each and every one: bastards.

It was quite horrible. Mary Ann endured the insults silently and with what the neighbors felt was considerable dignity, considering the circumstances. It can only be guessed how she and Junius Brutus Booth explained the situation to their children, the oldest in his late teens and the youngest six years of age when the real Mrs. Booth invaded Baltimore. Booth appealed to his wife to return to Brussels; she would not. She took a flat to wait out the period of Maryland residency necessary before filing for divorce. So for five years the parents and children had to live through a state of matters with which all Baltimore was conversant. Their half brother Richard secured work as a teacher of Latin and Greek and so supported his mother, who found Maryland's heat terrible; another summer like her first on United States soil would kill her, she wrote her sister. But she did not die. For years her rage at her husband's decades-long deception gave her energy, that and her desire to make him and his inamorata and their children pay. Even after the divorce was finally granted she continued to abuse her ex-husband and all close to him. Years after he was gone and when she herself had died, her tombstone stood as a permanent reproach. In huge letters she arranged to appear there that here lay the Wife of Junius Brutus Booth, Tragedian.

The chaos and tension she stirred up was not the only affliction the actor had to suffer. His sister Jane and her drunken ne'er-do-well husband, James Mitchell, and their swarm of children also descended upon him. They took up residence at The Farm to everyone's discomfiture, with the young Mitchells running about in undisciplined fashion. It was arranged that they move to a house that, if not far away, at least was not on the property, but Mitchell's inability or disinclination to provide for them meant that the children often appeared, barefoot and hungry, to beg clothes and food from Mary Ann. Booth had always looked upon The Farm as his resting place from the rigors of the theater and the road. Now trouping seemed almost a vacation.

Yet when he was away he drank more than when he was at home, and when he drank, his madness intensified. For a time Mary Ann prevailed upon the oldest son, Junius Brutus, Jr., to accompany him as dresser and general help, but it did not work out well. June, as the family called him, was practical and business-minded, a brilliant athlete whose physical feats were remarkable. He was not suited to be a guardian, for that is what it amounted to, that was what was needed.

So the job was given to the second son, Edwin Thomas, Edwin for the actor Forrest, Thomas for the Flynn who had helped rescue at sea, and later broke the nose of, the boy's father. He was barely into his teenage years, born November 13, 1833, on a night of spectacular celestial display that saw star-shower rains of meteors shoot through the skies in such fashion that people thought the heavens were falling. He came into the world with a caul, which was carefully preserved. Such a child, the black workers on The Farm said, would be gifted to see ghosts and guided by a lucky star.

He grew into a frail-looking, withdrawn youth notably different from the vivacious and active surviving children, except for Rosalie, the oldest girl, and Joseph, the youngest boy, both of whom much of the time were abnormally silent and depressed. Edwin took up no sports, never laughed out loud, was always apart. Appearing gloomily mute and ill at ease in most situations, he froze at the approach of a stranger. He was slim and no taller than five feet seven. He had great dark luminous eyes.

His father during his childhood had largely ignored him, preferring the more amusing company of the others. On one occasion Edwin threw him into a rage. It was Junius Brutus Booth's lifelong rule that the theater, theatrical gossip, actors, and acting were not to be discussed in his home. He did not wish any of his offspring to know much of his profession, much less follow him into it. (Edwin, he decreed, must be a cabinetmaker.) When once Edwin and some playmates decided to put on a show in the basement of a Baltimore hotel near the Exeter Street residence, his father ordered the project halted. When he went away on tour it went forward. Posters appeared announcing the prices: "Boys, 3 cents;

little boys 2 cents." The public was "enjoined to come with its parents," to "come early and bring your fathers and mothers."

The costumes were largely supplied by Edwin—he had cut down and altered some of his father's things. The janitor of the hotel acted as doorman. Success attended the shows—sometimes more than a dollar a performance was taken in. Then Father returned from tour. Looking through his wardrobe, he discovered his losses. He demanded an explanation from one of Edwin's younger brothers, who upon occasion had been allowed to participate in the shows to the extent of being given a triangle to beat upon as an introduction for each new act, and to sing "The Heart Bowed Down." The child denied knowing anything about the missing costumes. Father administered a thrashing that ended with a full confession, including the information that a show was going on at that moment.

Booth rushed off to the hotel basement, to be halted by the janitor demanding three cents for admission. This impediment was loudly toppled over. Edwin was up on the improvised stage wearing armor lifted from his father's wardrobe and shouting for a horse, a horse, his kingdom for a horse, when the armor's owner roared in. King Richard made a dash for an open window. He got halfway through before getting stuck in such manner that he was perfectly positioned for the second spanking it fell to his enraged parent to administer that day. When the father laid on, King Richard's resulting shrieks attracted the attention of a passing policeman, who concluded a burglary was in progress. He grabbed the flailing arms and tried to pull the presumed malefactor out while the father batted away at the invitingly proffered rear. All performances were permanently canceled.

School was in session when it was decided that Edwin would replace his brother June as their father's dresser, aide, attendant, and guardian. He was taken out of class, never to return save for haphazardly spaced periods of a few weeks now and then when his father was between engagements. They set out, the strange pair, a brilliant actor who was also a madman, and a somber boy. Edwin entered a world of endless travel by springless stagecoach jolting over muddy roads, indifferently heated trains, swaying river- or coastline boats, and dismal hotels and hostelries. Ice could delay winter movement. Heated bricks were offered to warm one's frozen feet in horse carriages. Summer meant swarms of gnats on the road. There were cockroaches, flies, moths, and mosquitoes in the screenless hotel rooms.

He moved through a universe of scene painters and scene shifters, sound-effects men, stage managers, soubrettes and supernumeraries, of grease and paint pots, rouge with a rabbit's foot to apply it. In the upper tiers of the theaters were barrooms where, it was understood, the demimonde could be found congregated while seeking assignations for after the performance. In smaller towns the show was put on in dingy pillared hotel dining rooms. In such towns there were no daily newspapers, so the advance man stuck bills up in post offices and barbershops. Edwin helped his father dress, adjusted his wig, kept ready his sword, cap, cloak, was ready to dab him with bloodlike makeup as he went into the glare of the footlights, something terrible shining from his eyes, "his dramatic force and magnetism like a giant whirlwind sweeping all before it," wrote the theatrical historian Montrose J. Moses.

The pot boy raised and lowered on a windlass Palace, Center Door Fancy, Plain Chamber, Dark Wood, Light Wood, Kitchen, or Prison; people new to their parts stood just offstage "winging it"—learning their lines before going on; the earthbound scenery, the "tormentors," was shoved forward into place and hauled back; overhead were the "flies," and underfoot the stage sloped forward to where the orchestra, led by The Professor, blared away. The theater competed with carnivals, the circus, prostitutes; and to entice an audience, managers spread their nets as widely as was conceivable: A bill, beginning at seven and ending at midnight, could include a saucy dance by the resident stock company's soubrettes; the singing of a couple of ballads, a burletta—musical farce—Othello, a "fancy dance"; The Mayor of Garret, with the actor who had transfixed the audience earlier as Iago, or alternatively as the Moor, now showing as a henpecked husband with his eyes crossed throughout as he bumbled about sending people into paroxysms of laughter. Everybody in the street recognized the First Player of the American theater; "Father, who is that?" Edwin asked when, early on, a man greeted his father by name as they passed by. "Don't know." Another person offered a salute. "Who is that?" "Don't know." It happened again, and finally to the boy's question came, "My child, I do not know these people! But everybody knows Tom Fool."

They went up and down and across the country as the young, slim, pale, quiet, frail son attended a father whose frenzies on the stage could lead him so to attack Desdemona that when he pushed the pillow down on her face it became apparent that she must actually perish at his hands and was saved only when cast members rushed out and pulled Othello away. Actresses slid away in actual loathing from the vile Pescara, and Richard was capable of chasing Richmond off the stage and into an alley, slashing him into barrooms where drinkers massed together to get the sword out of his flailing hands. Junius Brutus Booth could go without sleep for long periods of time, Edwin trailing him and trying to get him back to the hotel. Very often the father would obey but sometimes he erupted into mad ravings, jumbling in his disordered mind memories of how, long before, his own father had gotten him a position on the Royal Navy's *Boxer*, from which he had been removed to face the bastardy charge of the serving girl whose child, the court had ruled, was his: "Go away, young man, go away! By God, sir, I'll put you aboard a man-of-war, sir!" Edwin would not go away. In Boston once the father after a performance declared that the hotel room, situated just over the stables, was too odoriferous to endure. "I won't stay here," he told Edwin. "I'm suffocating."

"You're not going out, Father." To go out meant he would find drink. They stared at each other. "You shan't go out." The older man turned and stepped into a closet and bolted the door. Edwin waited. He wondered if perhaps the amount of air available in the closet was limited, and banged on the door. There was no response. He kicked and smashed and rattled the handle, terrified that his father was unconscious inside and actually suffocating. He was about to run into the hall to scream for help when his father opened the door, came out silently, and got into bed.

Sometimes the actor could not be restricted to the indoors, and when that happened, Edwin simply stuck to him. In Louisville after a performance he felt he must walk the streets. He ended in a long, open, covered market, walking its length back and forth all night, Edwin behind him every step. At daylight he concluded his pacing and headed back to the hotel, Edwin alongside. In the course of the endless marching neither had spoken a single word.

Sometimes, of course, the guardian failed of his task. It happened once in Kentucky, where, Edwin remembered years later, a certain Fontaine was much discussed as the area's "most prominent figure in the appropriating of horseflesh." It was a capital crime. Upon his head "a heavy price was fixed." Escaped from his son and keeper, the father wandered along the Bardstown Pike. He saw a horse grazing in a field and led it out and got aboard. Deep in thought, he rode along. Two farmers came along, halted him, and asked where he had gotten the horse.

"I captured him."

"Indeed. And what might your name be?"

For Junius Brutus Booth there was only one logical answer: "Fontaine."

The farmers took him to the sheriff, who recognized him. "What does this mean, Mr. Booth?" the sheriff asked.

"I haven't the slightest idea. I met these two men with this horse, which they insisted on giving me. I think they stole him."

As the farmers sputtered their outraged protests, word was brought to the sheriff that Fontaine had just been taken into custody. The case interested Booth: He visited the horse thief in prison, found him an interesting fellow with many stories to tell of his exploits, brought him food and refreshment, hired a lawyer for him, and mourned when despite the lawyer's efforts, death by hanging was ruled his proper destiny. Some time after the execution, a package was delivered to The Farm. It contained Fontaine's head, severed from his body at his request and sent with a last-words note asking that Mr. Booth use the skull for Yorick when he played Hamlet and that when he held it in his hands he think of the "gratitude his kindness had awakened." The lady of the house asked a doctor to prepare the head for its new function. Before that could be done, Booth, out on the road, grew angry when presented by a theater manager with a skull made from a pumpkin, or perhaps of bread dough. He declared that if he could not have a real skull there would be no Hamlet trodding the boards.

Edwin discussed the matter with a local youth, who said he could supply the needed property if properly reimbursed. A bargain was struck, and that night the youth was at the theater with a grinning skull. All went well. At the end of the engagement Edwin noticed the boy continually following him about. He asked what the matter was. The return of the skull was requested. "Go to the property manager for it, perhaps he can find it for you," Edwin said. "If he can't, I'll give you a couple of dollars, and that will square it."

The boy agitatedly said he could not sell the skull. "Why not?" Edwin asked. "I'll pay you more if it's worth more. I don't know the market price of such commodities."

The boy repeated that he could not sell it, Edwin recalled years later. It was his father's. He had just borrowed it from the grave for the occasion. When he would tell the story, Edwin smiled. He might add a very quiet, sigh-like chuckle. Never a laugh. No one ever saw him laugh. The actor and his son went on their way, trouping. They were together more than six years. In their hotel rooms Edwin played his banjo—he wasn't bad. Once the actor Edwin Forrest, for whom he was named, came in. "Edwin," Forrest asked, "do you play 'Nelly Bly'?"

"Yes, sir." He picked it out on the strings, accompanying himself in a decent amateur's voice.

"Do you play a Negro jig, Edwin?"

"Yes, sir." He got into "Old Zip Coon," accompanying himself in the manner and accents of the plantation South. Forrest's foot began jumping up and down. Forrest got up and danced a jig. Junius Brutus Booth got up and joined him, doing a fancy heel-and-toe. They danced across the room. Edwin played on. There were other, more public entertainments soon in store. In September of 1849, in the building that in deference to Boston's Puritan traditions was not called a theater but The Boston Museum, the stage manager complained to Edwin about being slated to play Tressel to the Richard III of Edwin's father in addition to his regular duties. "This is too much work for one man. *You* ought to play Tressel."

The elder Booth had never wanted to have any of his blood play. But Edwin knew the few lines. That night the father sat with his feet on the table of his dressing room wearing his costume of long and belted purple velvet shirt ornamented with jewels, and armhole cloak trimmed in fur. "Who was Tressel?" he asked his son.

"A messenger from the field of Tewksbury."

"What was his mission?"

"To bear the news of the defeat of the king's party."

"How did he make the journey?"

"On horseback."

"Where are your spurs? Here, take mine."

Edwin unbuckled them from his father's heels and went out and played his brief part. When he finished, he returned to his father's dressing room to find him exactly as he had left him, with his feet still up on the table.

"Have you done well?"

"I think so."

"Give me my spurs."

Edwin was not yet sixteen. News of the modest debut got talked about in theatrical circles, but his father fought against any idea of a stage career for him, telling managers who offered to cast Edwin that the boy was a good banjo player and could play a few tunes between acts, if the manager in question so desired, but that was all. He listed him as his aide and agent, and ruled that in addition to his own fee of four hundred dollars for a week's performance, his son must have fifty dollars.

But he could not hold forever to his policy of forbidding the stage to Edwin. And perhaps he had seen something when for the first time Edwin went on at The Boston Museum. All his life Edwin believed that his father had watched his debut from the wings before running to his dressing room to put his feet back on the table. And the father had given his son gruel after the performance, his own inevitable after-theater supper, and made him put on the worsted nightcap he himself wore when the curtain went down so as to avoid, he said, head colds. He capitulated. Edwin began playing small parts opposite his father. But when Edwin was not onstage, Father forbade him to watch from the wings. He could listen but not see, for the elder Booth wanted his son's ear educated first. He could observe the visual stage business in good time. He offered no other suggestions, Edwin remembered, no "instruction, professional advice or encouragement in any form." This seeming indifference was very painful to the boy he had then been, he told his intimates decades later. But it made him think for himself. That was what his father must have wanted. "And for this he has ever had my dearest gratitude."

And, of course, simply appearing opposite Junius Brutus Booth meant lessons were learned. When Edwin Booth was older than his father ever lived to be, he still remembered and talked about an occasion when in John Howard Payne's The Fall of Tarquin he played Titus to his father's Brutus. It was in Richmond. The action called for Brutus to condemn his son Titus to die. Real tears poured from the father's eyes as he pressed Edwin's head to his bosom and told him he must be executed. The audience was breathless. Then an intoxicated man in the gallery created a disturbance. Junius Brutus looked up. The words were his, but it was the stern Roman of the play who spoke to the drunk: "Beware. I am the headsman, I am the executioner." "It was like a thundershock!" Edwin remembered. Such was the power of the elder Booth that it seemed not unlikely that he would treat with the drunk as his threat implied. The audience sat paralyzed. Then there was a brief roar of applause, and the scene went on to end with the people in tearful silence.

They were playing New York's National Theatre on Chatham Street in February of 1851 when one night at the hotel, for no apparent reason, the father announced he would not appear as scheduled. "Who can they substitute at the last moment?" Edwin asked. A carriage was waiting outside to take them to the theater.

"Go act it yourself." He refused to leave the room.

Edwin had himself driven to the theater and announced that his father would not be playing that night. "No matter," said Manager John R. Scott, "*you* act it."

"That is what my father said, but it is impossible. I cannot."

Others urged him to do the part, for otherwise the theater would be dark and all would suffer. So in his father's robes, which hung loose upon him, he went on. The audience had come expecting the great Junius Brutus Booth and got instead a seventeen-year-old impersonating King Richard III in oversized costumes. At first there was some grumbling. Then there was intent silence. Something was happening onstage. Edwin Booth was playing the first lead role of his life. He returned to the hotel, and his father coldly inquired how things had gone. As with the first time he appeared on a stage, as Tressel, Edwin was sure, or at least wanted to believe, that his father had gone to the theater and watched his Richard III while hidden in the rear of the audience.

Two months later the uncontested divorce suit of Adelaide Delannoy Booth was granted. Junius Brutus Booth and Mary Ann Holmes applied for a marriage license. They were wed on May 10, 1851, the thirteenth birthday of one of their children, the one named for their slight relative through marriage who had blocked old Richard Booth's proposed trip to join the American revolutionists, the English statesman John Wilkes.

THREE

JOHNNY BOOTH and his sister Asia were one another's best friend. Most of the time they lived out at the remote Bel Air place which reminded their grandfather of Robinson Crusoe's island. To no small extent this hiding away was due to the unsettling Baltimore presence of Adelaide Delannoy Booth and her tirades against the whoremaster, their father, and his low mistress, their mother. So there they were, miles from nowhere.

Their oldest brother, June, older by fifteen years, was away from home and out in the world. The oldest girl, Rosalie, older by more than a decade, was neurotically withdrawn. Edwin was perpetually on the road with Father. The youngest child, Joseph, was almost another Rosalie—strange. (In later years Joseph said he had first begun suffering from what he called "melancholy insanity" at the age of ten or twelve.)

But Johnny and Asia had each other. She was two and a half years the elder, but never played the role of big sister. That Johnny was the favored child of both parents, "his mother's darling," Edwin said, his father's "always preferred," did not bother Asia. Johnny was her best-loved brother, the perfect playmate and confidant.

Looking very much like brother and sister, each with long jet-black hair and the darkest of eyes, long curling lashes, and creamlike complexion, they played Christopher Columbus in their brook, leaping from stone to stone, carrying long poles, and landing onshore to erect a cross. There was an immense green bullfrog there, and hearing that such a one could live for a hundred years, they speculated on how it must have croaked to others in the past as it did to them. Indian children, perhaps, for sometimes they found what they were sure were Algonquin arrowheads. (Edwin always felt the frog was unspeakably ugly, but Father's unbreakable rule was that there must be no killing of anything on The Farm.)

Asia was named for that continent upon which, her father said, Man first walked with God. (He had originally thought to call her Alysha, after Mahomet's favorite wife.) When she had grown beyond the days of playing Christopher Columbus, she sometimes fell into dark moods of what she called "hours of self-inflicted torment" and what one of their servants, a slave rented from the slave's owner, termed "Missy's long sulks." She sat alone, not eating, and then went off to bed. Nothing could be done about it, Father said, no reasoning would aid her. "It must be left to silence."

Johnny wasn't that way. He was cheerful, joyful, full of fun, kinder, Asia said, than she, much more gentle. There was a cider press on The Farm, a swimming pond their father had caused to be constructed, great cherry trees to be climbed, sheep whose wool was spun into blankets, many horses and dogs, cattle with names— the cow Lady Parker, she recalled, was grand, dark, and dignified—and songs she remembered long afterward: "Oats, peas, beans and barley groves . . ." "Here come three gallants out of Spain, all to court your daughter Jane." Once a week the postboy rode down the rough coach road by The Farm to sound his horn and toss letters and newspapers and Father's agricultural magazines over the gate. There were no locks or bolts on any of the doors.

"Don't let us be sad," Johnny would say to her when she had her long sulks, adolescent broodings. "Life is so short, and the world so beautiful. Just to *breathe* is delicious." He liked to fling himself on the ground in their woods, sniffing what he called "the earth's healthy breath" and nibbling, "burrowing," he called it, at the sweet roots and twigs. Rabbit, she said. Both of them loved botany and geology, but he was tender of insects and butterflies, and lightning bugs. Once she caught a katydid and said she wanted it for her collection, but he said, "No you don't, you bloodthirsty female. Katy shall be free and shall sing tonight out in the sycamores." He kissed the little thing and put it on a tree leaf.

They loved music—he played the flute, somewhat—and reading aloud, mostly verse but also some Plutarch and Nathaniel Hawthorne, she remembered, and they sang together by the piano and with a guitar. They read aloud Fox's *Book of Martyrs* and from it perhaps he decided to sleep for a time on the hardest mattress, with a straw pillow, in the fashion of the Spartan king Agesilaus.

Their rented servant Joe, the property of a neighbor, who

stayed with them for years, wove baskets during winter evenings, and they dined, the family, off immense pewter platters and drank milk kept in the dairy by the spring. Together brother and sister churned cream to make butter. "Arithmetic is amusement for *great* brains," he said to her after school. "It nearly drives me mad." But she noticed that once he got something straight he never forgot it. He never had to restudy for tests: When he had it, he had it.

He was cheerful and merry, but he loved sad and plaintive songs. They liked to go riding by moonlight and sometimes before the sun was up, singing together as they went, and they noticed that when they sang a quick tune—"I love the merry, merry sun-shine"—their horses kept up a quick gait, and when they sang something slow the horses seemed to go in measure. Once he was lounging in a hammock and she announced a great discovery. "Another continent?" he asked, but she grabbed a guitar and rushed off, he following, to a knoll of moss at the spring, where she halted and strummed away. Out came a whole congregation of frogs as orderly and noiselessly, she thought, as Quakers entering a meeting. The creatures sat listening to her music until brother and sister spoke to one another, when with a gulping noise their little friends vanished.

"Well, what do you think of that?" she demanded.

"It is wonderful," he said. "When did you make this discovery?" She told him she had been singing there earlier when the frogs appeared, and she recalled the horses stepping in tune to songs, and so she kept it up. He said there was supposed to be a jewel in the toad's head—maybe it was musical appreciation. Often after that they put on concerts for the frogs.

He taught her to ride, with and without a saddle. For a long period earlier she had been afraid of horses. Their father helped conquer the fear by leading her up to quiet ones in the streets and inducing her to pat them; with his help and Johnny's she became what she called a reckless if not accomplished horsewoman. He himself, Johnny, had a horse of pure black with a mane and tail she braided in tiny plaits. He broke the colt and named it Cola di Rienzi, for the great Roman tribune. He would start Cola off by shouting Choctaw Indians were after them, they must ride for their lives, and taught him to stamp for "No" and bow and neigh for "Yes" and to lie down as if dead. Once Cola bit him. He burst into tears. "I could have stood anything but that, I love the creature so. For a pet horse to turn and bite is *vicious.*"

But he could not stay depressed for long, whatever the cause.

"How glorious it is to live!" he said to her. "How divine! To breathe this breath of life with a clear mind and healthy lungs!" They read aloud from Byron's poems as they sat together in a swing under the gum trees and hickories. Once by mistake they shot a neighbor's turkey. He wanted to own up to it; she did not. Eve-like, she remembered, she suggested they dispose of the victim, and generously told him, "You were not like Adam, throwing the blame on me."

"I pity Eve," he said, laughing. "Poor little first mother. But Adam was a skulk and a sneak, and deserved to have the apple core stick in his throat." On Halloween they carried gates from farms nearby and put them somewhere else, and wheeled off carriages and then loosened the wheels for good measure. They freed up cattle and then, returning home, found somebody—what's good for the gander—had taken one of their horses and tied him a distance away with a cabbage around his neck. As they went about they heard a shotgun blast. Johnny flung her down and covered her body with his own. It was a close call. His soft felt hat was riddled with shot. One of the children trailing them around howled that he was hit, but he lifted the boy and said, "You're not touched, you little black ape! Curl up on Johnny's shoulder, and go to sleep." They went along. The draped child fell asleep. "How that little monkey snores up there," he said in low tones so as not to awaken his burden.

It was a black man who had fired upon them, and when spring hiring time for hands came, Asia urged her mother not to take on any members of his family: "Remember Halloween." "Oh, no," Johnny said, "revenge is so mean, and against a darky, too!" He had long forgiven the shooter. "Do you know," he said to Asia, "I believe you have a tinge of Jewish blood. You always cry revenge, and I notice that it strains your heart to forgive." He had gotten that from knowing Junius Brutus Booth's portrayal of Shylock. "Much of the evil of us boys and girls," he said thoughtfully, "and some of the good as well, must have been engendered by power of the furious plays that our father enacts."

He might have been right, yet he had never seen their father on the stage. She saw him act once, sneaking into a Baltimore theater next door to the home of a schoolmate she was visiting. She was colossally impressed, and in imitation memorized some Shakespearean lines to shout out at the top of her voice from high on the school staircase; "Well done, little Booth," said one of the teachers. But Asia's real talent was for writing. She was infinitely better at it than Edwin, whose writing all his life was mostly nervous,

prissy, so determinedly refined that it approached vulgarity—
something like a pinkie rigorously held out from a cup. She was
also more capable than Johnny, whose written work tended toward
the overdramatic, filled with flourishes that might have fitted in at
the court of the prince of Denmark but that read a bit strangely
when seen in letters to friends. When she was eighteen Asia turned
her hand to poetry. Her poem told of a vision, as her mother called
it, that the mother had had when Johnny was born. She had looked
into a fire, wondering what the future held for the infant in her
arms when, she said, the flames formed a single word: COUNTRY.

She went to a girls' boarding school and he to boys' boarding
schools, where at various times he was known as Jack Booth and
as Billy Bowlegs, for he had inherited the limbs that made the
London theater audiences say it would be impossible for Junius
Brutus Booth to halt a pig if it ran straight for him. At the end of
the school year at a Quaker institution he gave a recitation from
The Merchant of Venice and was brought back on the outdoor stage
for a bow. He blushed and smiled, and a Quakeress sitting by Asia
said to her, "What is his name? He is a comely youth. Does thee
think . . ." and asked if Asia thought the Hebrews got their due.
    " 'Does thee think?' " Asia remembered years later. "Oh,
what could I know of the rights of nations, what did I care for any
other Hebrew than the one who was tugging at my sleeve?"
    Johnny was saying, "Get away from thees and thous and meet
me over there in the hollow." She did so, and he threw himself on
the ground and leaned his head back against her knees when she sat.
He took out a paper upon which he had written what a Gypsy
fortuneteller had said to him a few days earlier. Asia kept the paper
always. "Ah, you've a bad hand, the lines all cris-cras," the Gypsy
had said. "It's full enough of sorrow—full of trouble—trouble in
plenty, everywhere I look. You'll break hearts, they'll mean nothing to you.
    "You'll die young and leave many to mourn you, many to love
you too, but you'll be rich, generous, and free with your money.
You're born under an unlucky star. You've got in your hand a
thundering crowd of enemies—not one friend—you'll make a bad
end, and have plenty to love you afterwards. You'll have a fast
life—short, but a grand one.
    "Now, young sir, I've never seen a worse hand, and I wish I
hadn't seen it, but every word I've told is true by the signs. You'd
best turn a missionary or priest and try to escape it."

She was finished. "For this evil dose do you expect me to cross your palm?" Johnny asked. The answer was Yes. She took his money, he told Asia, and said that she was glad she wasn't a young girl "or she'd follow me through the world for my handsome face."

He laughed with his sister. If his destiny was in the stars, or written on his hand, he asked, how could he escape? It was his fate. At least he'd have a short life and not have to endure this bad fortune for too long a time. He laughed, but often in future days referred to the Gypsy's rambling words.

He took dancing lessons in the Highland fling, sailor's hornpipe, and, she remembered, a Polish step. He thought himself clumpy—"jerky and stiff and too awkward." Perhaps he had more faith in his singing, for he hadn't been shy earlier about appearing at Edwin's hotel basement productions, where he beat on a triangle to introduce each new act and sang "The Heart Bowed Down" before it was spanked out of him that a show in father's cut-down armor was going on even as the confession was extracted.

A son of America's most prominent actor, he naturally was interested in his father's work, even if he had never seen him perform. So with Asia he practiced elocution. For a time he declaimed in the woods each day in what she felt were deep, strident tones, now fierce with passion, now soft and mellow. His voice was a beautiful organ, she told him, with perfect music. He played Lady Macbeth in his sister's petticoat and long dress before the mirror, and once wearing her skirts and with a scarf over his shoulders and tiny bonnet on his head said, "I'll walk across the fields yonder, to see if the darkies can discover me." His experiment was a success. The field hands took off their hats when the presumed lady of fashion came up, and so did the barn workers. Another time the trick did not work. "Undress Marse Johnny, undress him!" the servants begged Asia.

In winter brother and sister walked through the snow, she once falling into and entirely disappearing in an enormous drift. "Where are you gone?" Johnny cried, choking with laughter before he dug her out. In hot weather they endured flies, which their father forbade them to swat.

Theirs was a happy home, Asia felt. ("This is a *home*, not merely a habitation," an elderly lady friend told them.) They were very healthy—"dyspepsia and heartburn were strangers to our abode," Asia wrote—which they attributed to getting up early (their barefoot and straw-hatted father could be found gardening at dawn when he was home), eating simple meals with no "cakes running over with golden butter, and rich pastry," and relying for illnesses upon home remedies of licorice and green figs, or chamomile, or sassafras, pennyroyal, marshmallows, and spearmint. "We were not friends of the doctors, and entirely unknown to chemists and druggists."

The head of the house detested anything approaching snobbery. When a tramp with an ugly wound in his leg knocked on their door asking for alms or food, Asia remembered, Father brought him in, and knelt to wash out the infected slash and put on medicine and a bandage. If any of the children sassed a black servant within his hearing, an immediate apology was ordered. On Sundays he dressed in the most modest fashion because he felt it unbecoming for churchgoers to attempt to outdo one another with finery. When the woodsman who came to saw large logs finished his work, Father invited him to have a drink of wine at the family's glistening sideboard stacked with flowers and fruits. "What an idea!" the mother might say. "To think of your father bringing in that dirty old man to eat and drink at the sideboard." But he offered his wine as respectfully, they saw, as he would have to Daniel Webster.

At a Baltimore spring whose waters were noted for their medicinal properties, they once saw a filthy hobo dressed in rags and with sores drink from the spring's metal dipper held to a rock outcropping by a chain. The fellow assumed a Junius Brutus Booth would require something different from which to drink and offered, "Shall I fetch you a mug, sir? I won't be a minute." "No, no, my friend," Father said, and drank from the dipper without washing it. Then he thoroughly rinsed it before letting his children drink, as if concerned with germs from his own lips, all the while speaking with the man about the lovely weather. "Could *you* do that?" Asia whispered to Rosalie. "*I* couldn't. If he'd been merely unclean; but he is Lazarus himself." Her father did not see it that way. It might have hurt the man's feelings to wash the cup before he drank.

Such was their childhood. Their father's concepts of what was due to all living things extended even to a snake injured by one of the men plowing a field. Booth took Mary Ann's bonnet out of her bandbox, wrapped the snake's wound, cut holes in the box's top for air, put in food, and tied down the top. The accident victim allowed itself to be tended as a sick dog would have done. It lapped up the milk he gave it. "For nearly three days," Mary Ann remembered, "that fearful reptile occupied my bandbox and our parlor." After it was let out to crawl slowly away she worried for weeks that it would come back to show appreciation for the kind treatment.

■

In 1848 gold was discovered in California. An enormous migration of fortune seekers headed West to dig into the colossal lode. In the spring Sacramento consisted of four houses; by the fall ten thousand people were encamped there. San Francisco became not a city but an assemblage of mining claims worked by argonauts, so the gold seekers were termed, who today might be penniless but who tomorrow might possess fortunes rivaling those of anyone in Boston or New York.

Among the new arrivals was Junius Brutus Booth, Jr., always June to the family, just under thirty years of age. He had married and had a child by his wife before taking up with Harriet Mace, whose brother Jem was the famed bare-knuckles prizefighter. Matters in the East were not pleasant for June and his paramour. Precisely as his father had aroused the wrath of his wife, so did June's activities enrage *his* wife. (The eventual divorce petition baldly termed Harriet "a prostitute.") As his father before him, June took his inamorata and headed West. The one had arrived in Maryland; the other, three decades later, landed in California.

June was a wonderful athlete who had taught Edwin and John to fence almost as masterfully as he did himself. He had picked up the rudiments of acting—his estranged wife was the actress Clementine De Bar—and had made himself into a reliable, if technical, player. But he knew he had no innovation or inspiration on the stage. What interested him was theater management. Gold Rush California was the proper place for him, for the miners were starving for entertainment of any type. Gambling and drinking and whoring were their first choices, but right behind came theater. In California the word was broadly interpreted, and included clog dancing, displays of magic, recitations, carnivals, wild animal shows, minstrels in blackface singing what were called coon songs, burlesque, contests to see how many rats a terrier could kill in a given time, pantomimes, and actual plays.

The amount of compensation that could be realized was unprecedented in the history of the performing arts. At a time and in a place where an apple could cost up to five dollars and a dozen eggs up to fifty, where the rent for a cigar store was one thousand dollars a week and interest rates 15 percent a month, the possibilities can be imagined. Miners were capable of tossing chunks of gold on the stage to display their approval of a production. (When the audience departed, actors swept the stage for grains.) June set up theaters in Sacramento and San Francisco. Often his jerry-built constructions burned to the ground, the most common of occurrences out on the

Coast. June built new ones. His productions were primitive and the actors hardly of the first rank. It came to June that if he could build a really first-class theater and induce a really first-class actor to come out to California, he could be rich.

The really first-class actor whose name suggested itself to June was, of course, that of his father. In early 1852 June and Harriet Mace made the tortuous trip to Maryland to find the head of the family engaged in remodeling and enlarging The Farm's main residence into a pseudo-Elizabethan construction of leaded windows and what was called the Romeo and Juliet Balcony. He had already picked out a new title for the Booth country residence: Tudor Hall. It was going to cost a lot of money. There was money to be made in California. In the spring of 1852, June and Harriet, accompanied by Father and Edwin, set out.

They sailed down the East Coast to Aspinwall (now Colón, Panama), an offshoot of the Gold Rush traffic named for the financier William Henry Aspinwall, who created it as a base for his railroad across the isthmus to the Pacific. It was said the deadly humid heat and searing sun and the fevers took the life of a man for every tie put into that railroad. Aspinwall itself was a hellishly steamy and falling-apart place filled with rum shops selling liquor and quinine to ward off or cure malaria. The travelers jolted to the railroad terminus on the Chagres River, where the line's twenty miles gave out, and then went through terrifying green jungle with masses of decaying vegetation at the roots of the unfamiliar trees.

Their fellow journeyers were soldiers, adventurers, escaped convicts, European second sons, bail jumpers, and prostitutes, all flowing toward the western gold fields. Natives poled them up the Chagres on flatboats, and when the water gave out they traveled on mules along thin trails whose paving stones were laid by the Spaniards centuries before and whose width was such that one had to duck the overhanging reaches of the encroaching forest. Their porters were one step removed from savagery. The travelers slept with pistols in their hands, the father and two brothers on blanket-covered wine casks and barrels, Harriet in a hammock. They watched the natives sharpening knives and heard unintelligible speech. The jungle was filled with strange plants and alive with the screaming of strange birds.

They made Panama City and sailed north to San Francisco to find people living in board shanties with muslin partitions, to see boats abandoned in the harbor because their crews had run off to seek gold. There were lice and bugs everywhere, mud, rats. The town was known as the wickedest place on the continent, and it was said there was not a country in the world not represented there by at least one prostitute. There were 743 bartenders listed in the city directory, approximately one for each 53 inhabitants, and a total of 21 clergymen.

They opened in June's Jenny Lind Theatre in San Francisco in July, 1852, with Father playing Sir Edward Mortimer in *The Iron Chest* and Edwin supporting him as young Wilford. The shaggy miners and courtesans, men of almost uniformly uncertain antecedents and women of dubious background, did not accord the great actor the reception to which he was accustomed. He went with Edwin to Sacramento, played for a time, returned to San Francisco, and appeared half a dozen times more. Then he was finished. He had been trouping a long, long time, and he was tired. He said he was going home, but Edwin should remain. Junius Brutus Booth told his son that if he was going to act, it was time he got out from under the shadow under which he had always labored. After four months on the Coast, Father booked sea passage to New Orleans.

They saw him to his ship in the harbor, where he asked a sailor to take his luggage to his cabin. "I'm no flunkey," the sailor said.

"What are you?" Booth asked.

"I'm a thief," the sailor replied with a growl. It was the kind of response for which Junius Brutus Booth had the right rejoinder: "Your hand, comrade. I'm a pirate."

"All right, my covey; where's your traps?" Edwin was alone and on his own, save for whatever June could try to do for an inexperienced junior whose entire career had consisted of being his father's son. He was nineteen. His childhood could be defined as being over—but, as he often said, he never had a childhood. At the ages when others were guarded and guided and shepherded, he had done these things for another, and now the ship of the other was dropping down over the horizon. He joined a troupe of strolling players going north up the Sacramento Valley, actors off Mississippi River showboats or from Bowery dives, opera singers, circus performers, or, they said, direct from starring roles in Paris or London or St. Petersburg. June's Sacramento theater had burned to the ground, and so all the older brother could offer was a piece of advice: "Put a slug in the bottom of your trunk." A slug was an octagonal fifty-dollar gold piece. "Forget you have it, and when things are at the worst, bring out the slug."

So began the life he lived for years, playing the so-called theaters of the mining camps consisting of a few huts, the auditorium a hall over a shop, the stage often a few billiard tables pushed together with a dozen candles for the footlights, Cock-Tail Cañon, Shirt-Tail Bend, Haytown, and Jackass Gulch. He blacked his face to thrum away in minstrel shows while the "bones" rattled instruments, and was the San Francisco Fire Boy gallantly shouting he would quench great flames—"I go to save the city from conflagration!" He played *The Marble Heart, The Iron Chest,* and *The Lady of the Camellias* and was Richard III, Othello, and Iago. Years before, the French traveler de Tocqueville had noted that even the rudest cabins of the American frontier almost inevitably contained two books, the Bible and the works of Shakespeare, and an astonishing number of the wild men in lawless California knew the king's lines, and the Moor's, and showed their irritation by discharging their revolvers if a player confused his part. Then there were those who, less subtle, took the entire play for being real. One such took umbrage at Edwin's portrayal of the sinister Iago, shouted that he was a sneaking, lying little varmint, and opened fire. Everyone on the stage fled, Edwin by rolling behind a piece of scenery and then, still rolling, off into the wings as bullets sang overhead.

He danced jigs and reels and went up the steep and narrow winding trails of the Sierras, passing Indians and pack trains and possible highwaymen while seeing far down below through the thin mountain air tiny figures panning gold out of the waters. The players rested an hour before coming into town so as to present as fresh and high-spirited an appearance as possible, and then made their entrance banging drums and ringing bells to make known that there would be theater that night on a stage of boards on top of sawhorses, amid smoked hams and crimson calico and canned meats when they were playing in a store.

One dismounted from a coach and helped push it up the almost perpendicular hills, bowed and smiled as the audience tossed American fifty-cent pieces and huge Mexican silver dollars when the show went over well, put on pantomimes, stayed at a filmy canvas boardinghouse or log hotel, studied a part while sitting a horse jolting through blue-green pines above dizzying drops down to tiny lake chains, was a troubadour, a European noble, lover, dancer, villain, black-faced plantation hand doing what were considered hilarious travesties of the classics: theater. In the winter of 1852–53 the troupe became stranded in Nevada City. Snowdrifts had completely isolated the town. The so-called theater was closed. The actors were hungry.

Through the snow Edwin saw a man he knew coming with a lantern. A courier had broken through, he said. "What news is there?" Edwin asked.

"Not good news for you, my boy." At once Edwin understood. He felt himself half crazed with guilt for letting his father go somewhere by himself, alone without his son for the first time in more than half a decade. Junius Brutus Booth had made New Orleans, played Sir Edward Mortimer in *The Iron Chest*, and then took a Mississippi River steamboat for Cincinnati. On board he grew feverish and drank of the river water. He grew worse.

He lay alone in his cabin. "Yes, yes, that was just what he thought right to do," said his companion of thirty years and wife for two, when she was told. "To endure patiently, to suffer without a complaint, and to trouble no one." At the end a ship's steward asked if there were any help he could offer. "Pray, pray, pray," Booth said. Those were his last words. He was fifty-six. "There are no more actors!" cried the statesman and orator Rufus Choate.

He lay in state in his Baltimore home for three days, the walls draped with white to cover the picture and mirrors, and all ornaments removed, save for a bust of Shakespeare, which seemed to gaze down on the body. People connected with the stage from Boston to New Orleans wore black crepe on their left arms for thirty days. Asia remembered that Johnny went off by himself and for hours sat alone in the woods. He would have to be the man of the house at fifteen, his mother said, writing to far-off California that neither June nor Edwin must think to rush home, that they should continue in their careers.

In snowed-in Nevada City, blaming himself over and over for his father's death, Edwin joined a group of men who determined to make their way out through the drifts. Otherwise they might slowly starve. They went fifty miles on foot, taking turns at being the first in line. He went on through the Sacramento Valley and to San Francisco. June had gotten his feet under him and built a third Jenny Lind Theatre in place of two burned earlier ones, and was able to offer work in blackface productions, comedies, musical extravaganzas, spoofing burlesques of local celebrities, and some Shakespeare.

Along with almost all of the San Francisco acting colony, June and Harriet Mace lived on Telegraph Hill at a point called The Cliff, where there was a communally owned horse who drank champagne out of a silver pitcher. Edwin elected to settle some distance away with the middle-aged character actor David Anderson, always Uncle Davy to him, in a two-room construction built on stilts and entered from below via a trapdoor. It sat on a plot of land seventy-five by two hundred feet among sandhills and chaparral. Nearby lived some Chinese who beat on gongs and played strange music. Uncle Davy and Edwin termed their place The Ranch, and in the city directory Edwin listed his profession as "Comedian and Ranchero." When he and his housemate were wanted for rehearsals, it was understood they could be summoned by blowing a bugle. Then they came down their trapdoor, Edwin thin and dark, his hair worn to shoulders over which was draped a serape in Mexican fashion. In the boom-and-bust manner of San Francisco life they went through lean times when they could afford only goat meat, the cheapest thing the butcher shop sold. They used to go by and from the road yell, "Kid?" If the butcher shouted an affirmative reply, they went in. When he yelled, "No kid!" they kept going.

Edwin drank, like his father and perhaps more than his father. No one not subject to that urge could understand its pull, he said. There were times, out there in California, he said later, when he would have sold his place in heaven, his chance for salvation, for just one drink. Once, entirely done in, helpless, he fell into a river. A passerby pulled him out. Otherwise he must have drowned.

He indulged himself with women. San Francisco offered sex untrammeled and raw. There were performances of women with other women or with animals, and in many dives a free-spending visitor was for a small fee allowed to strip any girl employee. Downstairs were cellar rooms, tiny and stall-like, cubicles with a cot or a pallet on the floor. Waitresses rendered unconscious through liquor or knockout pills—a San Francisco staple, along with hickory clubs, for putting people temporarily to sleep—were dragged to a bed, where sexual privileges were extended to all comers. The girl was by general agreement to be given half the money when she awakened. Sometimes three dozen men would partake before that occurred. "At twenty I was a libertine," Edwin remembered. "I knew no better. Sin was in me and it consumed me while it was shut up close, so I let it out and it seemed to rage and burn. All the vices seemed to have full sway over me and I yielded to their bestializing voices."

In late 1854 he and Uncle Davy and the British-born actress Laura Keene and some others journeyed out to Australia. The pickings there were said to be immense, and the Coast had hit one of its periodic theatrical slumps. For nine months they labored back and forth across the Pacific, playing Hawaii, the Samoan

Islands, Tahiti. In Honolulu the native they hired to paste up their bills around town took the paste for a delicacy and ate it, so Edwin, as the youngest member of the troupe, volunteered to go about nights after performances with a paste pot to slather and then stick up the bills for the next night's offering. (He was an honest man, he assured the others, and would not eat the pot's contents.) King Kamehameha IV came and said he wanted to see young Booth play Richard III, as he had seen his father play it in New York decades earlier. But the court was in mourning, so he could not be seen in a place of pleasure by the audience at the Royal Hawaiian Theatre. The actors let him sit in a throne backstage, ordering him out of it when it was needed in a scene.

They were renting the theater for $12.50 a week. Receipts were thin, so they slung up hammocks and were sleeping there to save on lodging costs when Laura Keene got into a huff and announced her immediate departure for California. Someone was needed to play Lady Anne to Edwin's Richard III, and the best they could come up with was a small and cross-eyed man with a Dutch accent. It was work, Edwin remembered, to keep a straight face when intoning " 'Divine perfection of a woman.' "

They made their way back to California. He played Claude Melnotte in *The Lady of Lyons*, Benedick in *Much Ado About Nothing*, Shylock, Lear. June had obtained a collection of handpainted great paper rolls, up to half a mile in length, showing the cities of the world. They were unrolled slowly while June offered a descriptive lecture and Edwin played appropriate melodies on his banjo. A panoramic play. It could follow *Richard III*.

He went North on tour again, competing with dog and monkey shows and with temperance lectures. Any kind of bad luck— losing your shirt at cards, being rolled by a bar girl of all your money, having your mule fall off a mountain—was in California slang known as "seeing the elephant." Edwin began seeing the elephant, for it was noted of him that every other place he played burst into flame shortly after his departure, often reducing the whole town to ashes along with the theater. Word got around that this fellow could well be termed The Fiery Star, in imitation of one of several child players who uniformly were billed as The Fairy Star. At Downieville it was suggested that he and his troupe leave without offering a performance. The recommendation was given added weight by the sight of three ropes hanging from trees, signs of recent displays of quick justice. The players decided not to dispute the issue. But the company manager owed some money in

Downieville that he was unable to pay. What passed for the authorities ruled the proper way to deal with the problem was to appropriate Edwin's horse. He trudged off to Sacramento on foot.

The fall of 1856 came. He had been away from home since the spring of 1852 and possessed five hundred dollars, a clear profit of more than a hundred dollars a year, he noted. At least he was solvent enough to afford passage East. He left the California where he had rutted with many women—one could hardly call it making love—and downed the contents of many bottles, whiskey, brandy, champagne, wine, all the fancy new mixed drinks for which the dives of what would later be called the Barbary Coast were famous. He had played every conceivable kind of theatrical role in front of audiences whose patience was limited and demeanor difficult. He had learned that, for some, acting was a trade or a craft, but that for others it was something higher that could not be taught or defined but was, as he was to say until he died, a gift whose bestowal was only within the power of God.

He went back to Maryland and the home of his widowed mother. Asia was twenty-one and Johnny eighteen. They found their brother older in experience only, Asia thought, for he looked like a boy still. His long black locks and dark eyes gave him an air of melancholy, Asia thought. Yet she saw him also as owning the inherent grace and dignity of a prince who sometimes, with the family, could be merry, cheerful, and boyish, something like, she thought, one would imagine Hamlet before the tragedy in the orchard. That was not the comparison that might come into the head of the average young woman, but Asia, after all, was an actor's daughter. She would marry an actor. She was a Booth. She would have children who would be of the theater. That is what they did, the Booths, her brother June, her brother Edwin, her brother Johnny.

FOUR

WHEN HER HUSBAND died in November of 1852, Mary Ann Booth's instinct was to continue farming. The oldest son at home would supervise the work. "John is trying to farm," Asia laconically wrote her lifelong Baltimore friend Jean Anderson.

He might try, but his heart wasn't in it. Mrs. Booth leased out the land and animals and use of the rented servants to a man who turned out to be a brute. He drove the blacks and the horses to their utmost limits. It was pitiable. Mrs. Booth had it out with him. Rosalie and Asia added their pleas. The man told them all to mind their own business. He added some unpleasant language.

Johnny was informed. He went to talk to the lessee and see if he could arrange set hours for people and horses. He began by saying that amends must be made for the manner in which the women of the family had been addressed. "Will you go up to my house this moment with me, and apologize to my mother and sisters for the abusive names you have called them?" he asked. He would not have the ladies insulted.

"First find your *ladies*," said the man with a sneer, and added, "Do you think I am going to lose my share of these crops just to save a lot of lazy dumb beasts and thick-skulled niggers from being tired? Apologize! Won't I!"

"Then I'll whip you like the scoundrel that you are!" Johnny cried, and banged a stick over the man's head. "I knocked him down, which made him bleed like a butcher," he wrote an old school friend to whom he signed his letters with his old nickname, Billy Bowlegs. "He then warranted me and in a couple of weeks I have to stand trial. For assault and battery. As you call it."

The trial consisted of a magistrate coming to The Farm, now Tudor Hall, to discuss the matter. He bound the family over to keep the peace, and Asia recorded the song the servants instantly composed:

We's bound over to keep the peace,
To keep the peace, to keep the peace,
We's all bound over to keep the peace,
Glory Halleluyah!

It wasn't all in vain. The tenant agreed to be reasonably tender of man and beast. So the farming went on, but Johnny said he didn't see how he'd ever get anywhere trying, as he put it, to scratch a living from the soil. Asia understood. Her brother was a good listener, deferential toward his elders and figures of authority, but he wanted to shine in the world. He was ambitious. Perhaps, she reflected, it came from reading dramatic plays.

School days were over, and the child in both of them gone forever, she knew, and now they must be serious and give up lighthearted poetry and music and what she called their long, aimless rambles on foot and horseback. So she drilled him in theatrical parts. Perhaps he never actually decided to be an actor; more likely he never thought of anything else. It seemed natural that when he saddled Cola and took a saber given Father by someone back from the Mexican War, he would spout Shakespearean lines as he galloped about flailing the weapon. He was critical of his own ability. "I can never be a nimble skip-about like Romeo," he said, "I am too square and solid." When, reciting from *Julius Caesar*, he confused his lines and a servant picked them up correctly, he lamented, "Hark to that darky! She has sharper wits than I!"

Asia felt he should think of politics, for he liked to discuss current events. Unlike their father, who said no actor should be involved in politics, that the stage and politics did not go hand in hand, and who on principle never voted, although he wore silk badges for both Henry Clay and Andrew Jackson, Johnny was involved to the extent of being a steward for a Know-Nothing Party meeting. He carried a flagstaff, and when he fell off Cola, used the staff as a pole vault to return glamorously to his saddle without touching a stirrup. He was in a dark claret cloth coat with velvet lapels, pale buff vest, and dove-colored trousers lightly strapped down under his boots. He wore a broad Guayaquil straw hat with a black ribbon band, and his sister was not the only woman to take note of the quality of the face it shaded. The forehead under the silky jet hair was what people termed noble, the brilliant dark eyes enormously expressive and full of fun, the nose perfectly formed, the lips full, and the chin strong. The teenage boy was growing into someone whom a thousand people of the theater, who after all knew about good looks, would soon say was the handsomest man they had ever seen.

He remained as good-natured and lighthearted as he had always been—"Give my respects to all who ask after me, and to those that don't, tell them to kiss my Bumblebee," Billy Bowlegs wrote his old schoolmate—and rarely lost a friend for any reason; many of the friends of his maturity he had known since boyhood days in Baltimore and Bel Air. He was physically the most similar to Edwin of all the brothers, both dark and with great dark eyes, but both leaving opposite-poles impressions. Edwin was somber, John exuberant. Edwin rarely smiled and never laughed aloud; John always had a bright smile for people, and his laugh was charming and full. Edwin never participated in any kind of sport; John liked to take part in local horse tournaments with lances where one competed at spearing rings hanging from a tree, and went to gymnasiums to do exercises and work with acrobatic equipment. Edwin was always quiet, and it was said of him that he suffered from stage fright everywhere but on the stage; John was an excellent raconteur, liked to talk, liked to listen. Edwin always wanted to be alone and off by himself; John liked to go to billiard parlors and shooting galleries with his friends, and to picnics at Deer Creek near Bel Air. At social gatherings Edwin sat in a corner and spoke to no one, or found a child with whom he could spend time making animal forms out of handkerchiefs. John danced and flirted.

One day in August of 1855, with Father dead and Edwin and June away in the West, John rode up to where Asia was gathering apples and berries with, she itemized, six little black children, seven dogs, and a couple of cats. He had been to Baltimore. He threw the children a bag of candy, as he always did when coming from the city, and said to her, "Well, Mother Bunch, guess what I've done!

"I've made my first appearance on any stage," he said in his happy way. "For one night only, and in big capitals." It had been in Richmond at the St. Charles Theatre, under the management of Laura Keene, the actress who left Edwin in the lurch in Hawaii. The event had been a benefit for the actor John Sleeper Clarke—born John Clarke Sleeper—a boyhood chum of Edwin's who had changed his name for obvious reasons when he went on the stage. Now he was on his way to becoming a noted comedian who would do very well and who in time would marry Asia.

For his benefit performance John had played Richmond, ath-

letically dueling with Richard III. Asia saw that his face shone with
enthusiasm when he described it, and the tone of his voice was
exultant. But in fact he had forgotten his lines at one point, and the
audience had hissed. His mother was not happy at his debut. They
had put him on, she said, for his name. He was seventeen years old
and completely without performing experience. By no means was
he ready for such a part in such a play. This was premature, Mrs.
Booth said. He had been used by others.

He took to heart his mother's opinion, and it must have come
to him what he had done, for that night sitting in a swing with Asia
he said he knew he could never be as great as Father, and did not
think to try to rival Edwin, but that he wanted to be a Southern
actor and be loved by the Southern people. He had always identified with the South, aped Southern mannerisms, been offended
when told to eat at the same table with hired white laborers. He
certainly never got that from his father. But it was in him.

He had stuttered and stammered on the stage when he went up
in his lines. He had assumed too much, been given too much. It was
because his name was Booth. So he said he would renounce that
name in order not to capitalize on it or be compared to anyone else.
He would seek acting assignments as J. B. Wilkes. When he made
a success of his own, he said, he would take back his name. As Mr.
Wilkes he soon failed frightfully in his lines as Petruchio Pandolfo
in Hugo's *Lucretia Borgia*, saying to the actress opposite, "Madame,
I am Pandolfio Pet—Pedolfio Pat—Pantuchio Ped—Damn it! What
am I?" There was a roar of laughter. For three years he was Mr. J.
B. Wilkes.

He did not become a stock actor who works steadily in a
particular theater, but went where opportunity arose, living at
home. But more and more he was away on the road playing engagements offered increasingly less because he was the son of his father
and more for the fact that managers saw something in him. They
saw, of course—one could hardly miss it—the remarkable physical
appearance that soon brought him piles of letters from women. But
that was not all. He had a raw, energetic, impassioned power. He
reminded people of his father, far more than Edwin ever did.
John's work was unrestrained, even wild—undisciplined. He was
young, still only in his late teens. But he had inborn feeling and flair
and instinctively and intuitively did things that worked. He was on
his way. Edwin came home.

As he had in California and Australia, as he had in the days with
Father, Edwin went trouping. *The Merchant of Venice* was put on

in a tobacco warehouse of inland Virginia. The weekly river steamer would take them down to Chesapeake Bay, the actors were told. They must be ready to leave the moment the performance was over. But in the middle of the court scene, word came that the steamer had put in at the landing and that its captain had come to say he was leaving in ten minutes.

"Get up some sort of impromptu finish and ring down," the troupe manager whispered. "Go right ahead, take your cue from Ned." Edwin went onstage. The Shylock of the night was sharpening his knife on the heel of his shoe.

"You're bound to have the flesh, are you?" Edwin asked.

"You bet your life," said Shylock.

"I'll make you one more dicker. In addition to this bag of ducats, I'll throw in two heads of Niggerhead tobacco, a shotgun, and a couple of the best coon dogs in the state."

"I'm blamed if I don't do it."

"And to show you there's no hard feelings," said Portia, turning up in her legal gown, "we'll wind up with a Virginny reel." The prompter struck up on his fiddle, they danced a couple of figures, and rushed for the steamer as the curtain fell to thunderous applause. The captain offered a hot supper once their things were stowed away. "I'd like to see the whole of that play sometime," he said. "I'm blamed if I thought that fellow Shakespeare had so much snap to him."

More experienced theatergoers echoed the substance of his praise for Edwin's playing, perhaps in different tones. He had gone to California nearly five years earlier as the son of Junius Brutus Booth. Within a few months of his return to the East he was seen as the heir to his father's position on the American stage. He had electrical, fiery genius; power, passion, spirituality, solemn beauty, tenderness, a sonorous and thrilling voice. His acting, it was said, was inexpressibly sweet. It was terrifying. When he looked at actors playing ghosts, there appeared in his eyes a horror that undid many of those actors. Backstage they spoke of that horror.

When he played Sir Giles Overreach in *A New Way to Pay Old Debts*, he seemed to saturate the theater with evil, to strip the villainous fellow's soul naked, to make people slink away looking at one another as though evil had seeped into them, into their veins. His stage fury was like the crescendo of a great orchestra; he was like a tiger. His Shylock ended the play dragging off, knees feebly bending, shoulders drooping, dying before the curtain fell. He played him as greedy, ignoble, and a malicious usurer, but he played him also as regally defiant and so made him seem part old-clothes dealer and part majestic Hebrew financier and lawgiver, frightening and pathetic. How did he do it? Edwin had energy, spirit, imagination, intuition, and tremendous charm—his Iago's bewitchingly devilment of smile and twinkle of eye were immensely entertaining. Of course, it was the playwright who wrote the words; but it was Edwin who produced in Othello what was proud and beautiful and laden with jealousy and tragedy, like a hot and heavy summer afternoon presaging a great thunderstorm. His Moor brought back the Middle Ages, Venice, the Adriatic, and his Lear was grandeur mixed with senility, feebleness mated to authority, a broken and mad old man who yet owned royal bearing. His Macbeth seemed physically towering, his Cardinal Richelieu a stately giant for all that Edwin was not tall and of fragile build.

He exemplified with exquisite emphasis the music and meaning of the lines he spoke, and showed innumerable diversities of interpretation, shadings, new delicacies, and potencies. Behind Iago's gay villainy was the shadow of evil filled with anguish and hate. Through him Pescara became bland and infernal at one and the same time, Sir Edward Mortimer suffering and somber while possessing yet the essence of concentrated will and formidable power. Edwin owned tremendous presence, strength, and grace. He offered gestures of astonishing meaning and brilliancy that made all clear, with enormous emotional fervor married to melancholy refinement, his eyes conveying with electrical effect solemnity, tenderness, piteousness, weariness, glee, wrath. No one who saw Cardinal Richelieu's imperial entrance into the garden of the Louvre ever forgot it, nor Iago in the dark street with his sword in hand above the prostrate Cassio, nor Bertuccio at the door of the banquet hall breaking into hysteria, nor Macbeth going to the murder of King Duncan, nor Lear's wild screams at the parting with Goneril and Regan. He showed onstage the secrets of the human mind and heart, Julia Ward Howe thought. "He possessed the faculty of pure tragic power such as I have never known equalled," said William Winter, the *New York World* drama critic for forty years; "No actor so completely filled the eye, the ear and the mind with an ideal of romantic tragedy," said the writer-actor Otis Skinner.

He remained precisely as he had always been and would always be: somber, formal, and remote with strangers, grave, even frigid. He seemed always solitary and shy, thought Otis Skinner; "Sometimes moving in the throng, but never of it," said the theatrical chronicler Margaret Townshend. She noted his reaction to the "notes of adulation almost by the bushel basket" that came from women; none was ever answered. He did not wish to be introduced to new people and stared out at the world through melancholy eyes and met it with silence. His real life was the stage, that was the substance. The occurrences of everyday existence were the shadows.

His playing reflected what he was. His father, Booth the Elder, had ranted, shouted. He had played Shylock as a roaring demon. Edwin Forrest was the same. But Junius Brutus Booth's son, and Forrest's namesake, was exactly opposite. He was the least extravagant actor imaginable. He seemed most to stir audiences not by the violence of his feelings but by the repression of them. He never did too much but always seemed to find the right measure. He never exaggerated or overstepped, but, the picture of quietude onstage, reflective, restrained, seemingly natural, as if in your parlor, said the critics, seemed to court rapturous silence rather than clamorous applause. By power of suggestion, by subtlety, the points he made turned even more thrillingly profound when he erupted in passion or sorrow. He showed weaknesses, deepest depression, madness, despairing dignity, all with an exquisite, never-seen sweetness of words and the sense of their relation to one another. He did it by indirection, mostly. Through intonation, cadence, pause, emphasis—all was made clear.

He seemed never to raise his voice, but it carried in its thoughtfulness, power, and purity to the extreme corners of every theater, and to the range and carrying power of that voice was added the impression of those dark eyes of extraordinary brilliance and depth and that remarkable physical being—the stately tread, begging stance, monstrous hunch. Vibrant, poetic, spiritual, his lines delivered with flawless elocution, the embodiment of grandeur when that was called for, repellent when that was called for, he studied stagecraft and the work of the actors but was in the end unable to define how he achieved what he did. "I am conscious of an interior personality standing back of my own, watching and guiding me," he told the World's William Winter. Asked by Skinner to compare himself with his father, all he could offer was, "I think I am a little quieter."

He remained deferential to all, was the last actor in the world to be flamboyantly stagy away from the theater, dressed in the quietest manner offstage, spoke to few people backstage, and deplored the SON OF THE GREAT TRAGEDIAN and MANTLE FALLING UPON WORTHY SHOULDERS with which managers pointed to his heritage on their pasted-up bills. ("Just simple Edwin Booth," he told one printer; and so there appeared all over town that performing that night would be SIMPLE EDWIN BOOTH. He laughed his noiseless laugh.) He drank. ("Oh, Charley, my boy," he told a man helping him up from a supreme effort as Othello, "there's no use talking. This part is a great provocation to drink!" But he needed no provocation.)

As he had in California and Australia, he indulged himself with women. Not emotionally. They were bodies, no more. Yet even in such matters he retained the prudishness he would show to the last day of his life. In his letters he would never write *hell* or *damn*; it was always "h———l" and "d———m." So it was not surprising that when on October 31, 1858, he wrote brother June in California of "a little sweetheart of mine," he said the girl, an actress, had thought to go out to the Coast where a theater manager made an offer for her services, "but I talked her out of it, and my p———k into her." He couldn't "brag on her acting," he added, "so much as what we do in secret." Six weeks later he wrote June he detected in himself the first signs of an unpleasant illness, but had no doubt he was mistaken, "for the woman is *virtuous*." (Someone, either this one or another, was perhaps not so virtuous, for he suffered from a venereal disease until pronounced cured in April of 1860.)

In May of 1857, half a year after returning from California, he opened in New York at Burton's Theatre in Broadway opposite Bond Street. (HOPE OF THE LIVING DRAMA, the playbills shouted against his will.) Among the people who came to see him as he filled the house night after night was a thin, pale, red-haired little man who wore glasses and had poor posture. Adam Badeau was an intellectual newspaper essayist of ambiguous sexual orientation. He believed the stage was the only truly representative art of American life, and soon he came to believe that Edwin Booth was the finest flower the American stage had yet produced. This actor was, he wrote, the "incarnation of passion and romance and poetry." Badeau could not keep away from Burton's Theatre. He came every night to marvel at Edwin and to see people rise and shout with delight when the final curtain rang down. He had never seen anything more tremendous than the picture presented and the passion displayed, Badeau felt. He arranged an introduction to the young star.

All his life Edwin would lament his lack of education. He was shy with everyone, but particularly was he shy with those who had been to college and knew Latin, knew books and art. "I have suffered so much from the lack of that which my father could easily have given me in youth," he said sadly. Here was someone who belonged to The Century Association, membership in which was reserved for men of culture and letters. And Adam Badeau hardly had a threatening persona. Edwin took him as the closest friend he would ever know. He went with him to the literary salons Adam frequented, to sit in awed and frightened silence while yet thrilled to be in such company. The two visited museums to see clothing of the time Shakespeare chronicled. Together they studied interpretations of Edwin's roles and argued the meaning of words and lines. Adam worked on him to give up liquor.

Adam worshiped Edwin. "My Prince," he wrote him, "the man I love best in the world. Pray stay a god." In return Edwin told him everything. Told him of, and showed him clearly, what he considered his vices. The sexless or asexual or homosexual Adam became his first confidant. There was no one else. Adam could feel that he was Edwin's one and only. That applied to women also. "Hundreds flung themselves at him in those days," Adam remembered. "They sent him notes in verse and prose, flowers, presents of jewels, shawls, feathers to wear on the stage; they asked for appointments; they invited him to their houses; they offered to go to him.

"But he cared nothing for any of them." And more than once, Adam wrote, Edwin "saved some foolish child from what might have been disgrace, and sent her home to her family. And he never injured a pure woman in his life." (Which may have explained the venereal disease.)

Always so reticent and withdrawn, he opened up with Adam. Evil hung over him, he said. He would not come to any good. In his future he saw a terrible fate. It was appalling for Adam to see such fits of sadness, this veil shrouding him from other mortals behind which he walked apart. He tried to tell Adam what it was like, this overriding, all-encompassing depression; but he could not. He was so old when young, Adam remembered. Able to express in superlative manner the emotions of others, he was completely incapable of expressing his own. When it fell to him to thank an audience for its applause, he stammered and shrank back and offered only inarticulate sounds while standing on the very boards upon which he had scored his triumphs and where alone he felt at home and where he had his being.

Only with Adam Badeau could he feel completely in contact with another human being. Then things changed as classically and dramatically as in any play. Enter Mary Devlin.

■

The actor Joseph Jefferson, whose relation to comedy was for forty years what Edwin Booth's was to tragedy, had been, like Edwin, born to the stage. His parents were actors. He had trouped from childhood on, acted the little Duke of York at age five to Junius Brutus Booth's Richard III, sailed down the Cumberland River on a barge rigged up with painted scenery used as a sail with a forest background on one side and a palace on the other, while on deck the leading man and the low comedian flailed at one another with broadswords. (The passing tableau was taken by people onshore or on other boats, Jefferson was certain, for a floating lunatic asylum.) Out on the frontier a troupe he was in arrived at an Illinois town where a religious revival found church fathers preaching against the stage and getting passed a new law calling for an extraordinary licensing charge to perform so unholy a calling. A young lawyer turned up to tell the actors he would lodge an appeal without fee. Perhaps the lawyer's wife put him up to it, for long before they met she had told a schoolmate that as far as her needs in a future husband went, "her choice should be willing and able to let her see as much of the theater as she wanted, and beyond that she did not expect to be too particular." When the schoolmate heard that she "had chosen a struggling young lawyer, the plainest looking man in Springfield," the issue of the theatergoing immediately came to mind. In any event, the work-for-free volunteer took up the exorbitant licensing fee before the city government, traced the history of the theater, got everybody laughing in high good humor, and saved the day for Joseph Jefferson's troupe by getting the tax rescinded. It was Abraham Lincoln.

In the late 1850s Jefferson was managing a theater in Richmond. His players included a young woman born in Troy, New York, in 1840. At age twelve she made her debut there, appearing as a danseuse under the billing of "La Belle Elise." Her family was not well off, and Jefferson and his wife had taken her into their home when she was fifteen. From then on Mary Devlin traveled with the Jeffersons to act in companies he managed or starred with. She was thin, and her face was regarded as more sensitive than beautiful. Her eyes were her best feature, very large and exuding keen intellectualism and great magnetism. Over the years the Jeffersons grew to see themselves as her informal adopted parents. She was an accomplished but not brilliant actress.

In Richmond Jefferson said to her, "Tomorrow you are to rehearse Juliet to the Romeo of our new and rising tragedian." At the end of the rehearsal Mary Devlin said, "He is the greatest actor

I have ever known. I was inspired and could act forever with him."
"I have seen and acted with a young woman who has so impressed
me that I could almost forget my vow never to marry an actress,"
Edwin wrote his mother.

When they had known one another for a week, Edwin presented Mary Devlin with a beautiful turquoise bracelet. That upset
Joseph Jefferson. Were the affections of his de facto young ward
being trifled with by a heavy-drinking and seven-years-older roué?
He was reluctant to permit her to accept the expensive gift. He
changed his mind when the couple came to him in the theater green
room, the traditional place where actors gathered, memorized
lines, and socialized, and in mock heroic style fell to their knees
before him. "Father, your blessing," they recited in chorus. "Bless
you, my children," Jefferson responded. He consented to an informal engagement.

Then Edwin reconsidered. He had, after all, said that he would
under no circumstances marry a woman of the stage. And his sister
Asia was strangely and unaccountably, almost madly, against this
affair. Edwin's "hereditary disease" of drinking, his "only fault"—
that she could accept, Asia wrote her friend Jean Anderson. But
not Mary Devlin. "I will not write the evil I invoke upon her. I
detest and despise the woman—an actress not even second rate.
She wants his money and his name, a grand position for a poor
obscure girl. Her family are of the lowest Irish class. Ned will have
them to support, no doubt."

Asia appeared to lose all grip on logic. Mary became in her
letters to Jean Anderson "a bold faced woman who can strut before
a nightly audience, who can allow men of all kinds to caress and
court her in a business way." She appeared to forget the legions of
women of all kinds who caressed and courted Edwin and John
when they were onstage. What she remembered, perhaps, were the
long years of hearing her father's real wife proclaim all over Baltimore that Mary Ann Holmes was a trollop and that her children
were bastards. "I have tried so hard to keep far from all taint of that
which is low and vulgar," Asia wrote Jean Anderson, "tried to be
worthy of the great name our father made for us, and now that my
good and noble boy should throw himself away so lightly is enough
to break my heart. Nothing can induce me to condescend to her
level. I cannot meet with her. I cannot stoop to that which I despise.

"Adam Badeau is here. He is about leaving for Spain and other
places."

So there by her side was Asia's ally in her fight against Mary.

The proposed marriage devastated Adam. "I wish to God I had never seen you," he wrote Edwin. "It is a frightful thing to live out of one's self, to be buried alive in someone else. To depend upon that body for your happiness." Hysterically jealous, he wrote slightingly about marriage and possible fatherhood, and worried in his letters about how he would have to travel in Mary's wake, waiting for a crumb of Edwin's affection "when you could spare a moment or a thought now and then. Damnation, damnation, damnation, damnation. Hell!"

Edwin crumbled. He broke off the affair. Shortly the renowned actress-manager Charlotte Cushman asked Mary to join her company in Boston. It would get her away from the situation and into new surroundings. She joined Miss Cushman and in Boston made the acquaintance of a wealthy lawyer. He was much taken with her. Miss Cushman urged her to marry him.

It seemed the wise thing to do. She wrote Edwin, playing in New York. "He became quite wild," wrote an observer, "and plunged into such dissipation that it was necessary to close his engagement at the theater." In Boston, Mary was told. She went to New York to nurse him, to quiet his anxieties, to accept his renewed offer of marriage, to offer and then give him what happiness he would know in life. She would, he wrote a friend, make "my heart a happy one, if aught on earth could make it so." He was correct. Asia would never realize that, Adam would in time, and Johnny had known it all along.

Johnny had been acquainted with Mary as long as Edwin had, for he had achieved his aim of becoming, at least at the start, a Southern actor. He was happy in Richmond. *I would have written you before this, but I have been so busily engaged, and am such a slow writer that I could not find time,* read a September 10, 1858, letter to Edwin. *I am rooming with H. Langdon, he has stopped drinking and we get along very well together. I called on Dr. Beal soon after I arrived here. He and his lady seem a very nice couple. I like them very much. I have played several good parts since I have been here. I believe I am getting along very well. I like the people, place, and management, so I hope to be very comfortable.*

One thing bothered him: It was that his stage name of J. B. Wilkes fooled no one. *I have heard my name—Booth—called for, one or two nights, and on account of the likeness*—for he did look like Edwin—*the papers deigned to mention me. How are you getting along. I had hoped to hear from you before this. Give Mother my love. For I may*

*not be able to write her this week as they are casting and I will have much
to study. Excuse this dull letter. God bless you, write soon, and believe me
ever your affectionate Brother. John*

Dr. and Mrs. James Beal became his good friends, and often
he went to their home for after-theater supper, always beginning his
visit by running up to the nursery to look at their sleeping little
daughter, Mary. He had always loved children. One night he temporarily kidnapped Mary from her bed and carried her downstairs
to drowse on a large silver serving tray, from which she was
removed by a slave who declared that actor folk were crazy. Once
the child woke up believing she had dreamed that he came to her
in the night and put a ring on her finger. But it was not a dream.
There in the bed was a ring. It was too large, so her parents put it
away for a couple of years until her finger fit.

There were two aspects to his theatrical performances that
combined to secure for him a greater success than Edwin had at the
same stage of Edwin's career. One was his appearance. Pescara in
The Apostate, Charles de Moor in *The Robbers*, Fabien and Louis in
The Corsican Brothers, Claude in *The Lady of Lyons*, Richard III,
Hamlet—"He was one of the best exponents of vital beauty I ever
met," said the journalist George Alfred Townsend; "The stage
door was always blocked with silly women waiting to catch a
glimpse, as he passed, of his superb face and figure," remembered
the outstanding player Catherine Winslow; "His head and throat,
and the manner of their rising from his shoulders, were truly
beautiful," said the renowned Clara Morris. "The ivory pallor of
his skin, the inky blackness of his densely thick hair, the heavy lids
of his glowing eyes were all Oriental, and they gave a touch of
mystery to his face when it fell into gravity—but there was generally a flash of white teeth behind his silky mustache, and a laugh in
his eye. In his case only, so far as my personal knowledge goes,
there was nothing derogatory to dignity or to manhood in being
called beautiful, for he was that."

"He was the idol of women," said the actor and later British
baronet Charles Wyndham. "His conquest embraced the sex, and
with no effort. They would rave of him, his voice, his hair, his
eyes." "Very handsome, lovely," said the famous leading lady Mrs.
Gilbert—Anne Hartley Gilbert. "A very handsome man, perhaps
the handsomest I ever saw," said Jennie Gourlay of the family
whose members sometimes numbered three and four at a time in
a play.

Beyond those looks—"Here comes the handsomest man in

Washington," said Henry C. Ford of the Richmond and Washington and Baltimore theater-owning Fords—there was something else. Edwin's acting in no way resembled his father's for while Edwin was contained, delineated, restrained, precise, Junius Brutus Booth onstage was explosive, fiery, barely under control, dangerous, liable at any moment to—to what? To tear apart, lose all restraint. That was John. He had never seen his father act. Yet "We have almost forgotten that the Elder Booth was not before us," said the *Washington Chronicle.* "This handsome, passionate boy as an actor had more of the native fire and fury of his great father than any of his family," said Catherine Winslow. "John has more of the old man's power in one performance than Edwin can show in a year," said John Ellsler. "He has the fire, the dash, the touch of strangeness."

He did not want simply to be a romantic actor of the type who soon would be called a matinee idol, but actively sought Shakespearean roles. He played them with the utmost emotional impact, and married to it his physical capabilities, for he was very strong and athletic. In the meeting with the weird sisters in *Macbeth,* he arranged to have constructed a ledge of rocks more than ten feet high, from which he leaped onto the stage with electrifying, swashbuckling effect. His Richard III owned a snakelike crawl, revolting, and he played the hunchbacked ruler as a pure villain, brutal, coarse, scowling as his hands rubbed together unpleasantly. He invented new bits of stage business for the king's final sword battle with Richmond, falling over a tree to be attacked on the ground before regaining his feet to rain down his own blows. People gasped at the intensity.

He was the complete opposite of the decorous Teapot School of acting, which involved keeping one hand on the hip, the other extended and moving in curved lines. "A veritable sensation," said the *New York Herald.* He could be "*the* actor of the country," said the *Boston Daily Advertiser.* "The coming man, an actor with the suddenness of a meteor now illuminates the dramatic horizon," said the *Baltimore Sun.* In Rochester he was hailed as "The most talented young man upon the American stage"; in Providence he was "a young tragedian of very superior genius"; in Cincinnati he claimed "the sceptre that genius alone inherits"; in Louisville the *Democrat* said of his Macbeth's battle with Macduff that "in all our recollection of the stage we have never seen anything to surpass it. The hackneyed word talent cannot be used in speaking of this young actor of such wonderful promise. It is genius."

His Romeo, thought Mrs. Gilbert, was "perfect, the finest I

ever saw." He played the role in his usual fiery and passionate manner. Catherine Winslow was frightened of appearing opposite when he held a dagger in his hand, fearful of her safety when dealing with someone who "told me that he generally slept smothered in steak or oysters to cure his bruises after *Richard III*, for though an excellent swordsman he constantly cut himself." So she would always lend him a dagger of her own, one whose blunt blade was forced back into its handle if it struck anything. That did not save her from exciting moments. "How he threw me about!" His Romeo once caught the buttons on his cuff in her Juliet's hair. Trying to free himself, he trod on her dress and ripped it apart, and in his last struggle shook her out of her shoes. "The curtain fell on Romeo with a sprained thumb and a good deal of hair on his sleeves, Juliet in rags, and two small white satin shoes lying in the corner of the stage." As the slain Desdemona, she remembered, "I used to gather myself together and hold my breath, lest the bang his cimeter [scimitar] gave me should force me back to life with a shriek."

Star actors do not always show the best sides of their characters at rehearsal, but John was different: "The gentlest man I ever knew," remembered the actor Edwin A. Emerson. "Not feminine, but gentle as a woman. In rehearsal he was always considerate of the other actors, and if he had a suggestion to make, always made it with the utmost courtesy, prefacing it with, 'Now, Mr. ———, don't you think that perhaps this might be a better way to interpret that?' " But he took rehearsals most seriously. "Come on hard! Come on hot!" he once cried to the Richmond who that night would oppose his Richard. "Hot, old fellow! Harder—faster!" In their practice he suffered a slight gash over the eye, but poohpoohed it. That night the Richmond lost count of the number of head blows he had struck, and when John expected a thrust, brought down his sword with both hands across his forehead. One of the eyebrows was cut clean through. Blood poured down and masked his face. "Oh, good God! Good God!" gasped the other actor. John wiped his eyes. "Come on hard, for God's sake," he whispered. "Save the fight!"

The stage manager ordered a curtain rung down early. Ice, vinegar paper, and raw steak were brought, enough, John laughingly said, to start a restaurant. A doctor put in stitches. The other actor apologized and explained, but John held out his hand, saying, "Why, old fellow, you look as if *you* had lost the blood. Don't worry. Now if my eye had gone, that *would* have been bad."

It sometimes seemed to Asia (Mrs. John Sleeper Clarke now,

against John's advice, for he frankly told her before the marriage the actor Clarke was marrying her for the dowry of her name) that perhaps he had gotten everything too easily. He had never known privation or want, had never been out of an engagement. He was not like Edwin, who had a far rougher schooling, had endured hardships in distant places, had a fiercer struggle with himself, had learned through the drudgery of art. But perhaps Asia was incorrect, for John was a student of the theater, filled with successful suggestions about revolving platforms, cutaway sets showing various rooms in the same house, new lighting and sound effects. He had songs put into plays that previously had no music, and rewrote *The Marble Heart* so it became one of his most reliable vehicles. He had directorial instincts, and Clara Morris remembered how kind and astute he was when offering instructions. One night she was assigned to play one of the three ancient statues who come to life in *The Marble Heart*'s first act. "Well," she said to the other two statues during the first reading, "it's a comfort to know we look so like the three beautiful Grecians."

There was a laugh behind her. "You satirical little wretch," John said, "how do you come to know these Grecian ladies? Perhaps you have the advantage of them in being all-beautiful within?"

"I wish it would strike outward, then," she answered. "You know it's always best to have things come to the surface."

"I know some very precious things are hidden from common sight, and I know, too, you caught my meaning in the first place," he said. Before the curtain rose for the play, the three statues gathered together against a black velvet background, marblelike in white wigs, white robes, and with powder on their lips. John came to inspect them, such a picture in his Grecian garments, Clara Morris remembered, as made even the men exclaim at the sight. Miss Morris felt she must look like "a personified simper," gazing at the floor with her hand on her breast with one finger touching her chin, and offered a protest. He told her to take care not to move, for she would sway the others leaning against her, and said, "I expected a protest from you, Miss, so I came prepared. Don't move your head, but just look at this." He held up a picture of Greek statuary. "This is you on the right. It's not so dreadful, now, is it?" When the curtain rose and the three white statues came to life and slowly turned and pointed their index fingers at him, the effect was stunning.

The next morning Clara Morris saw him running out of the theater toward the telegraph office with a message in his hand. A little boy crossed his path and they collided, with the child, a "little urchin" with "dirty paws," going down in a heap. "Oh, good Lord! Baby, are you hurt?" He picked him up. "Don't cry, little chap!" He bent over the boy, got out a handkerchief and wiped the running nose, kissed him, put some change in each hand, and continued his run to the telegraph office. "He knew of no witness to the act. To kiss a pretty, clean child under the approving eyes of Mama might mean nothing but politeness, but surely it required the prompting of a warm and tender heart to feel for and caress such a dirty, forlorn bit of babyhood as that."

He had kissed the little street Arab twice, she saw, "and squarely on the mouth. Let me tell you there were many handsome, well-bred and wealthy ladies, married as well as unmarried, who would have done many foolish things for one of those kisses. Booth's striking beauty was something which thousands of silly women could not withstand."

She was quite right, of course—although for all that he was, as the theatrical chronicler Francis Wilson put it, "one of the world's most successful lovers," perhaps the enumeration of thousands of silly women constituted an exaggeration. But there were women aplenty. Agreeable, vivacious, gallant, dressed in velvet-trimmed overcoat and resplendent velvet vest, possessed of flawless manners—"My! What a dashing, elegant fellow he was, with his perfectly formed figure, graceful in every movement," Clara Morris remembered—magnetically charming, winning—"So young, so bright, so gay, so kind," she remembered—he had more than his share of women. But he did not permit them to go into things with closed eyes. The journalist George Alfred Townsend traced one of his romances, this in Philadelphia:

A girl sent him bouquets, notes, photographs, "all the accessories of an intrigue." It was all "familiar to him, common to him," but at length he gave her an interview and met an eager admirer who was young, fresh, beautiful. He told her the consequences of pursuing him. "That he entertained no affection for her, though a sufficient desire, and that he was a man of the world to whom all women grew fulsome in their turn.

" 'Go home,' he said, 'and beware of actors. They are to be seen, not to be known.' The girl, yet more infatuated, persisted." He "became what he had promised" and what she had desired. So yet another soul, Townsend wrote, went to the Isles of Cyprus, to that place where Aphrodite was worshiped. The affair and the type of girl were alike unexceptional, for he was, Townsend wrote, so graceful and good-looking that regularly "other than the coarse and errant placed themselves in his way."

The newspaperman did not have, he ended, the space to "go into the millionth catalogue of Booth's intrigues"—thus exceeding Clara Morris's estimate by a factor of one hundred—"even if this journal permitted further elucidation of so banned a subject." It was all quite different from what existed between Edwin and Mary Devlin. "My youth began with my marriage," Edwin said. John was the sole family member present, and when the ceremony was over, he flung his arms around his brother and kissed him.

FIVE

ARY TO HIM, Edwin said, was "wife, mother, sister, child, guide and savior. Angel." They agreed she should give up the stage. She did so willingly. Any love she ever had for the art of acting, she wrote, was transferred to him that she might see her favorite playwrights made greater by his genius and talents. "What more could I wish for than to be at home to receive my husband weary from his professional duties with kisses and open arms?"

He had scheduled a protracted tour prior to their betrothal and so he went away, "my head full of," he wrote his friend Richard Cary, "marry Mary—marry—marriage." She stayed behind in a rented New Jersey suburban place. She knew, she wrote, that women of all types would throw themselves at him as he toured, but that perhaps the "humble daisy" would win out over the "exotic roses."

He seemed to seek for her what he had never had, and so outlined a course of study. While he would be on the road she would take up French and the piano and visit museums and read books. Her tutor would be Adam Badeau. The soul of tact, astonishingly knowledgeable and comprehending for a Victorian era maiden not yet twenty years of age, Mary understood the sexually ambiguous but very lettered and very literate Badeau, and appreciated his qualities even as she joked about him with Edwin. "How indignant Mr. Badeau will be at the receipt of the fruit-card you sent him," she wrote her fiancé. "I laughed heartily at the drollness of the idea. What a pity he is not like other men." But she knew what the two meant to one another. "He complains bitterly that you do not write him often enough. Do not neglect him, I pray you."

Adam made her feel, she wrote, the responsibility of the life and heart entrusted to her care. "He like myself would see you great and glorious." Adam escorted her to the theater when her intended played anywhere in the New York area, and afterward the three discussed his showing. Edwin told Mary—"Molly" to him much of the time—everything, what to others, he said, would seem "a silly batch of whinings," believing that for what bothered him she could "find the antidote." She could. "Edwin, dear," she wrote him, "forget your past life, which has taught you a sad and useful lesson, and in my bosom, every throb of which beats for you, find that joy and repose that your nature requires. All the clouds of your life *must* pass away, and let the sunbeam which your love has created in me fall on its threshold and brighten what is within."

That he had rutted with whores, gotten a venereal disease, been a drunk—she knew all, and wished to know more. "Write me of yourself—your *wishes*, your *hopes*, your inmost thoughts. They will find a sacred shrine in my heart, be assured. Study your own *heart*, learn its ways; this self-examination is necessary to us all! God bless you, my own Edwin."

She wanted him to hold nothing back, he whose heart had ever been, before her, constricted and fearful. But now it was her heart, she wrote. He had given it to her. "Don't fancy that your gloom annoys me," she wrote him. "Write me all that you do and hear. God bless. Ah, truly, Edwin, there would be no light were you lost to me. If you could only see into my heart, how full of hope and love it is."

His dead father spoke to her, she wrote him, away on tour, and gave her "the true nature of his son." She studied Edwin's picture when she wrote to him, gazed at it as her pen lowered to the paper. Soon they would be married. "At night when thousands of eyes look upon you in admiration my heart will beat faster still to take to my breast the weary artiste—'artiste' no longer—but *man*."

She practiced playing the guitar, accompanying herself in a good contralto voice. "If my love is selfish," she wrote, "you will never be great. Part of you belongs to the world. I must remember this, and assist in its blossoming if I would taste of the ripe fruit. That will prove a rich reward. Dear Edwin, I will never allow you to droop for a single moment; for I know the power that dwells within your eye."

In July of 1860 they were married in the study of the Reverend Samuel Osgood at 118 West Eleventh Street, New York City. The guests were her sister and her sister's husband, and John and

Adam. The bridegroom had been offered appearances in London, and a few months after the wedding decided to accept, and to make the trip a belated honeymoon. In Fulham, England, she gave birth to a baby girl, Edwina. It was a matter of great concern to him that his child would come into the world on foreign soil, and he hung an American flag over Mary's bed so it could be said that little Edwina was born under the Stars and Stripes. The war was on by then.

There was an Ohio tanner's son who grew up to believe that serving God was the main concern of his life. He believed the Almighty had destined him to free the black people of America. Half soldier and half man of God, warrior and priest, John Brown carried his crusade for the freedom of the slaves into the heart of the enemy's country. Armed with rifles purchased by Northern supporters and followed by seventeen men, he swept down on Harper's Ferry, Virginia, to raise a rebellion that would spread, he said, into Tennessee, Alabama, the Southern coastal states. When he was finished, slavery would be dead.

John Brown ended up barricaded in some government buildings that were successfully stormed the next day by troops under the command of Colonel Robert E. Lee, 1st U.S. Cavalry. Headlines all over the country screamed of insurrection and riot and rebellion. Brown was put on trial and condemned to hang. The execution would take place in Charlestown, Virginia, on December 2, 1859. No one knew if masses of his supporters might appear to try to save him from the gallows, and so thousands of troops of all types were ordered to Charlestown to hold themselves in readiness for any eventuality.

On the morning of November 24, John took a break from rehearsals in a Richmond theater and stepped outside for a breath of air. In the street he saw lined-up members of two city militia units, the Richmond Grays and the Richmond Blues. They were off for duty at Charlestown. The train would be loading shortly. He asked if he could join them; a uniform was found; and in a matter of moments he was a private of the Grays. He had always wanted to see what it would be like to be a soldier, Asia knew. It was a dashing role to play. And here was the opportunity. Someone asked who would take his part in the play that night, and he replied that he didn't know and didn't care.

Nights in camp the new recruit entertained his fellow soldiers with dramatic recitations and poems, and caught the attention of a correspondent for the *Richmond Enquirer* who came to report on the militiamen: "Amongst them I notice Mr. J. Wilkes Booth, a son of Junius Brutus Booth, who, though not a member, as soon as he heard the tap of the drum, threw down the sock and buskin, and shouldered his musket and marched with the Grays."

Mary Devlin, not yet married to Edwin, had a different response to the impulsive enlistment. "Your news concerning the mad step John has taken I confess did not surprise me," she wrote her fiancé four days after his brother joined the Grays. "Tis a great pity he has not more sense but time will teach him although I fear the discipline is hardly severe enough to sicken him immediately with a soldier's life. I hope nothing serious will occur there, for it would frighten your mother so."

On December 2 the troops lined up around the scaffold. John was less than fifty feet from it. The man about to die handed a note to a jailer: *I John Brown am now quite certain that the crimes of this guilty land will never be purged away but with Blood. I had as I now think vainly flattered myself that without much bloodshed it might be done.*

A moment later he swung at the end of a rope. His body seemed to jerk once and he tightened his bound hands, and then he was gone. Philip Whitlock of the Grays saw how extremely pale one of his fellow soldiers suddenly became, and asked what the trouble was. It was John, and he asked Whitlock if he had a flask with him, for he needed a good stiff drink. They went back to Richmond and at the theater John was told by the manager that for leaving without notice he was discharged. That did not sit well with the Grays, a number of whom called upon the manager and asked that he reconsider. He did. "A brave old man," John said of Brown when he talked to Asia about the hanging. "His heart must have broken when he felt himself deserted."

He went on with his career. "The genius of the Booth family has been bequeathed to this third son," said the *Detroit Advertiser*. "He would have flashes, passages, I thought of real genius," remembered Walt Whitman. "Without having Edwin's culture and grace and without that glittering eye, Mr. Booth has far more action, more life, and, we are inclined to think, more natural genius," said the *Philadelphia Press*. The *Boston Post* summed up: "Edwin has more poetry, John Wilkes more passion; Edwin is more Shakespearean, John Wilkes is more melodramatic; and in a word, Edwin is a better Hamlet, John Wilkes a better Richard III."

By then he had ceased to bill himself as J. B. Wilkes. He took back his name, and on his posters arranged to have printed a quote from *Richard III*: "I have no brother, I am no brother . . . I AM MYSELF ALONE."

SIX

*I*N NOVEMBER 1860, the Illinois lawyer who had gotten an excessive tax rescinded for Joe Jefferson's troupe of players became President-elect of the United States. Lincoln was then as he had always been and would remain: tall, plain, bony, gawky, plebeian, of sallow complexion, shabby-looking and untidy, scruffy in his dress and with clothing always appearing ill-fitting and puckered, careless in his manners, and often ungraceful in his movements. He was not a cultured person, and indeed apart from law books and newspapers never appeared to read anything but the Bible and his shabby old set of the complete works of Shakespeare.

He had no hobbies beyond going to theatrical performances of all types, plays, tent shows, concerts. Two months before the Republicans met to nominate him for President, an old circuit-riding companion, the lawyer Henry C. Whitney, told him he had been given two tickets to what Whitney called a "nigger show." Did Lincoln want to go with him? "Of all things I would rather do tonight that certainly is one," Lincoln said. At the minstrel performance he applauded more loudly than any other spectator. A new song was played, "Dixie." "Let's have it again! Let's have it again!" Lincoln called, clapping his hands. His enthusiasm did not surprise his companion. Years earlier Lincoln had come into a Danville hotel to wake Whitney at midnight and describe each and every feature of a magic lantern show he had just seen. The next night he went again. Lincoln could erupt with gargantuan laughter at a theater joke or a funny song. His law partner William Herndon remembered how a recitation of "Miss Flora McFlimsy with Nothing to Wear" left him helpless. The desire of his wife, Mary, to marry a man who would take her to the theater as often as she wished was fulfilled.

Their shared love of performances was one of the few traits the couple had in common. Save for bouts of uproarious laughing and occasional moods of deep depression, he was entirely unexcitable, calm, easygoing. She was an abnormally tense woman who became terrified if a child vanished for a moment. "Bobbie's lost! Bobbie's lost!" she would shriek if little Robert Todd Lincoln briefly wandered away, and "Bobbie will die! Bobbie will die!" if he ate something that might disagree with him. Thunderstorms paralyzed her, and at the first sign of one her husband would hurry from his Springfield office to go home and calm her. He spent nothing on himself; she was a ferocious spendthrift who wasted enormous sums. (He was a most successful lawyer, receiving once what was said to be the highest attorney's fee ever paid in his state—five thousand dollars for an Illinois Central Railroad case—but their financial situation was never comfortable because of her expenditures.) She was ashamed of his social origins, which were far beneath her own, and deeply concerned about the fact that both he and his mother were possibly born out of wedlock. The matter did not arouse his interest. He was quite content with his own company, while she hated to be alone, and hired people to stay with her when he was off riding the law circuit. She was a great reader, alternately gay and teary, quick-tempered, impulsive, and excitable.

On the evening of the day he was elected President, he went home and lay down to rest. Opposite the chaise longue there stood a swinging mirror. He looked up and saw himself reflected full-length but with two faces showing. "I was a little bothered, perhaps startled, and got up and looked in the glass, but the illusion vanished." He lay down again, and again saw his face doubly reflected, but with one image five shades paler than the other. "I got up, and the thing melted away, and I went off, and in the excitement of the hour forgot all about it—nearly, but not quite, for the thing would come up and give me a little pang as if something uncomfortable had happened."

That night he told Mary and in future days tried to bring back the two faces. He was unable to do so. The matter worried her. It was a sign, she said. It meant he would be elected twice, but "that the paleness of one of the faces was an omen that I should not see life through the last term." This omen, Mary Lincoln told their friend Noah Brooks, was a warning.

Within a few days her fears were given a focus. Abraham Lincoln was entirely a sectional candidate of the North and West. No one in the South wanted him. (In Maryland, the most northerly placed of the border states—"We are of the North," Asia Booth Clarke maintained, her brother John violently disagreeing—ninety-two thousand votes were cast in the 1860 election of which but twenty-three hundred were for Lincoln.) To the Southern states his election meant the imposition upon them of an impossible President, an abolitionist who was, their papers said, ape, buffoon, and gorilla, a poor white trash, illiterate, ill-bred rail-splitter unaccustomed to wearing shoes. Letters threatening his life poured into Springfield:

> Never expect to occupy the White House (when you get into it it will be a Black House) for that is only intended for Southern Gentlemen and not for Black Republicans and mulatto scamps.
>
> *Charleston, South Carolina*

> Your death would greatly benefit the whole country.
>
> *Robert Kemmeck, Carrollton, Georgia*

> Dear Sir: Caesar had his Brutus, Charles the First his Cromwell. And the President may profit by their example. From one of a sworn band of 10, who have resolved to shoot you in the inaugural procession on the 4th March, 1861.
>
> *Vindex, Washington, D.C.*

> Sir: You will be shot on the 4th of March by a Louisiana Creole. We are decided and our aim is sure.
>
> *A Young Creole*

> God damn your god damned old Hellfired god damned soul to hell you god damned old Abolition son of a bitch.
>
> *Pete Muggins, Fillmore, Louisiana*

"The first one or two made me a little uncomfortable," Lincoln said. "But I came at length to look for a regular instalment of this kind of correspondence in every mail. There is nothing like getting *used* to things!" He joked to a carpenter whose shop was in the basement of his law office's building that he wouldn't be needing shavings from the carpenter to start his morning fire; "I am using instead letters from some of those southern fellows. They make fine kindling."

It was different with his wife. She was seized with a terror that would never leave her. For all the qualities that would soon make the President's two principal secretaries term her the Hell Cat who daily grew more hell-cattical, and Her Satanic Majesty, Mary Lincoln deeply loved, revered in ways, her husband. From childhood on she had predicted she would one day be First Lady of the country. When he was an obscure small-town lawyer— "the plainest man in Springfield," her friend, the one who knew of her love for the theater, was told—she had said of him that he looked like a President, what a fine-looking President he would be. When the brilliant Stephen A. Douglas had pressed his suit with her, remarking that if she married him she might be a President's wife, she replied that indeed she would be a President's wife, but not Stephen Douglas's. Now her dream was within completion—if he lived until his inauguration. The authorities in Washington were worried. There were rumors President Buchanan would be kidnapped so his Southern vice president might seize power; there were predictions Lincoln would never take the oath of office. The chief of the army, General Winfield Scott, took serious alarm. It was suggested to Mary that she and her children not go on the four-car special leaving Springfield for Washington because of the danger that it might be blown up in transit. She received in the mail pictures of her husband with a noose around his neck, pictures of skulls and crossbones, threatening letters, and was beside herself with hysterical fear; but she said she and the children would go with her husband—"danger or no danger."

They left, he telling his townspeople from the rear car's open platform that here in their town he had changed from a young man to an old one, that here he had lived his life, that now he left them, not knowing when, or even if, he would return. Earlier he had gone to see the old woman who had raised him when his mother died. He had been a child when he came under her care, and had come to regard her as his angel mother. She would never see him again, she said now. They would kill him.

The train went East, stopping often so he could say a few words, crossing into New York State. He came to Albany. His carriage passed the Gayety Theatre, in which J. Wilkes Booth was playing Pescara in *The Apostate* with his right arm, injured, strapped to his side. He had managed to stab himself and so had to fight his stage duels left-handed. Yet the reviews were good: "Full of genius," said the *Albany Atlas & Argus* of his performance on the day the President-elect arrived. "Fine face and figure, a favorite, never fails to delight with his masterly impressions."

Lincoln stayed the night in the Delevan Hotel. John was boarding at Stanwix Hall, as was the actress Henrietta Irving. They were to one another "as tender as love without esteem can ever be," said the journalist George Alfred Townsend. But within a few weeks the affair had run its course for him, and when she came into his room and said she felt she had granted him her favors under false pretenses, as he did not intend marrying her, he told her they must conclude matters. He offered a good-bye. She refused to accept what he said, again accusing him of tampering with her affections. He reacted coldly. She continued to plead. He made as if to pass her by and leave, and she drew a knife and drove it toward his heart. He threw up his arm and deflected the blow. His face was slashed, not seriously. Henrietta Irving turned, ran into her own room, and turned the knife on herself. She was not badly hurt.

By then, when she stabbed John, President-elect Lincoln was gone from Albany to New York City, there to surprise the audience at the Academy of Music by appearing at a performance as the only man wearing black kid gloves while all others wore white. The two younger Lincoln sons, Willie and Tad, went with their nurse and a policeman to Laura Keen's Theatre to see *Seven Sisters*, with elaborate scenic effects, and *Uncle Sam's Lantern*, a historical tableau. The four-car special went on, the President-elect telling a Philadelphia crowd that he would rather be assassinated where he stood than give up the principles for which the Union had been born and by which it had lived. The assassination reference was not simply taken from the air, and indeed the air was filled with talk of plans to kill the traveler. General Scott almost despaired of making Washington secure for an inauguration, and thought of suggesting that the ceremonies be held in Philadelphia.

As bad as Washington might be, Baltimore was worse. The announced schedule called for the President-elect to reach the city at one in the afternoon and attend a luncheon and then depart for a three-o'clock train to the capital. But it would be enormously dangerous to move through the streets protected by a Baltimore police force and Maryland militia pro-Southern to a man in the midst of crowds that would, within a few weeks, express their sentiments by physically attacking armed Northern regiments coming through to defend Washington against the Confederate Army. Scott was dead against the proposed daylight move through Baltimore, the detective Allan Pinkerton told Lincoln it was rash beyond measure, and Senator William H. Seward of New York, soon to be secretary of state, told his son to get a train out of Washington, go North, find Lincoln, and tell him he would be slain if he appeared on the Baltimore streets.

The President-elect listened, and departed Harrisburg in an unlighted railroad car and with the telegraph lines cut behind him so that word of his coming could not be sent ahead. He went through Baltimore secretly and by night, accompanied only by detective Pinkerton and the former Lincoln law partner Ward Hill Lamon, a herculean figure carrying four pistols and two large knives. They arrived in Washington with the dawn and went to the Willard Hotel. Word spread that Lincoln had come in disguise, wearing a long cloak and a Scottish bonnet, which he had not, and cartoons showed a comical figure dancing a Highland fling, or peering out at the world with a terrified expression as he was smuggled into the capital in a tam-o'-shanter, with skirts and naked legs. When he went to call on President Buchanan, General Scott lined the rooftops along the route with sharpshooters and had light artillery placed to rake the streets. The Inauguration Day trip to the Capitol of unfinished construction, with bare ribs against the sky, was conducted like a military movement, or in the fashion of a patrol traveling enemy country, with Lincoln and Buchanan surrounded by double files of District of Columbia cavalrymen ordered to keep their horses erratically prancing so it would be difficult for any assassin to get off an aimed shot. Artillery batteries were strategically placed. "If any of the Maryland or Virginia gentlemen who have become so threatening and troublesome of late show their heads or even venture to raise a finger, I shall blow them to hell," Scott said.

It was perhaps the most welcome moment of President Buchanan's life. For weeks he had paced an Executive Mansion porch, weeping as he prayed war would not come while he still held office. "Not in my time, not in my time," he kept repeating. In his inauguration speech Buchanan's successor asked the South for peace. "We are not enemies, but friends. We must not be enemies. Though passion may have strained, it must not break, our bonds of affection. The mystic cords of memory, stretching from every battlefield, and patriot grave, to every living heart and hearthstone, all over this broad land, will yet swell the chorus of the Union, when again touched, as surely they will be, by the better angels of our nature." But soon Washington was filled with troops, wagon trains, mules, commission brokers seeking positions for clients, sutlers, liquor dealers, whores, gamblers, keepers of concert saloons with waiter girls, and Sanitary Commission and Christian Commission representatives carrying Bibles. All around were barracks, forts, guns, dealers in camp furniture, the noise of cavalry bugles and troops firing by platoon, and, when the guns began to sound and the soldiers to march, the zigzagging ambulances wending their way through the rutted streets as the drivers sought smooth going to avoid jolting mutilated and bloody occupants. There would be other wagons whose occupants no jolting would disturb. On the sides was written U.S. HEARSE.

Edwin was appearing in New York that April when the war began, and *Harper's* in that month said he was the sensation of the city, eclipsed only temporarily by the passing excitement of the President-elect passing through. "New York rings with his triumphs," said the magazine. John was in Baltimore, recuperating at the family's Exeter Street house from Henrietta Irving's knife. President Abraham Lincoln was, of course, in the Washington in which he would come to know the McClellans, the Popes, the Burnsides, the Hookers, Meades, Grants, in which he would oppose Davis, Lee, the two Johnstons, Stuart, Early, Jackson, in which he would tell stories of and parables about animals and farmers, children and Illinois shopkeepers, wagons and law courts, and come in time to be seen as a great and mysterious figure, a gigantic presence in history, wondrous, complex, subtle, in the Washington in which he would work and live and die.

Edwin and Mary, often "Molly" to him, went to England, he to remind old-time theatergoers of the days when they saw his father, and she to await the birth of little Edwina under their country's flag. For a time Mary worried that a baby would come between her and her husband, but it did not happen, and she wrote home that little Edwina made even more precious the hours husband and wife, now father and mother, spent with one another. (He was fearful of handling the baby, she wrote her close friend Emma Cushman, the actress Charlotte Cushman's daughter-in-law, afraid he might "break" her by mistake.)

The hearts of both the temporary expatriates were entirely

with the North in the great conflict at home. "The seeming stand-still of McClellan's army tortures us," Mary wrote a friend. "We await the arrival of every steamer to hear the cry of Victory." To her the war was "this vile rebellion," and she desired the "entire demolition of the Southern Confederacy." Her husband wrote Adam Badeau that he had given up reading the pro-South *Times* of London because it was "so very rabid against us." Adam had joined the Union Army. "May the God of Battles guard you, Ad, and may you persevere in the good work so well begun. 'Tis said the enemy is retreating. God grant it may be so, and that they may be squelched by 'Little Mac.' " Adam's career as a soldier was one of the world's wonders. The sexually ambiguous little intellectual found himself on the staff of Ulysses S. Grant. As Grant rose, promotion after promotion was handed out to his people, and so Adam ended up wearing a general's star on each of his slumped shoulders. Sitting with Grant and watching Sherman pace up and down, a battle impending, messengers coming and going, a candle burning on the table, it came to Adam how like all this was to when Edwin played the tent scene in *Richard III* and of how Edwin had done and conveyed all that the great Union commanders did with-out ever witnessing anything of war.

When the three Booths came back to America, they centered their activities principally upon Boston and New York, where they took rooms at the Fifth Avenue Hotel, which filled up the block between Twenty-third and Twenty-fourth streets. One day in late 1862, they were in the dining room when Mary's greyhound dashed in and, during the confusion, made the acquaintance of Miss Lillian Woodman, a young woman of about Mary's age, twenty-one, who was staying at the hotel with her family. She took to them and they to her, and she visited their rooms, where he would lie on a black bearskin rug, supported on his elbows and reciting his lines as Mary gave him his cue. They took Lillian about with them and soon she met their friend the poet-journalist-writer Thomas Bailey Aldrich, who in his day would be esteemed the superior of Walt Whitman and would edit the *Atlantic*. They knew Aldrich through Adam. Lillian loved both her new friends—and was privy to how upon occasion craving for alcohol would seize Edwin and how, later, Mary would have to say, "Alas, Mr. Booth is not well today." His pathetic pleas for forgiveness would follow.

He did not want to troupe anymore, writing the actor-impre-sario Lawrence Barrett that "starring around the country is sad work—my brother John, successful as he was, is sick of it"; and

that was understandable, for it meant the wretched hotels and
miserable stagecoaches and cinder-spewing trains Edwin had
known for so long. John's reaction was understandable also.
Trapped in a snowbound train headed for a Louisville star turn,
John at two in the morning got out and picked up a half gallon of
liquor in a tavern, hired a sleigh and a black mare named The Girl,
and set out to make his date. The Girl ran into a huge snowdrift and
the sleigh overturned. John's valet had drunk too much from the
jug. John got him up on his feet and they righted the sleigh and got
in. They heard footsteps. They saw the eyes of a wolf. John
smacked the wolf with the jug. The wolf let out a howl. It was
echoed by the pack behind. The Girl bounded up into the air,
started on the run, and never stopped until she got them to a
freed-up train. A hard business where one lodged, as the actor-
writer Otis Skinner said, in a dubious quarter of town with houses
of no uncertain character next door. Edwin had seen all that for
years. So he restricted himself primarily to New York and Boston,
where he and Mary became close friends with Julia Ward Howe, of
"The Battle Hymn of the Republic" fame. Mary to her was "Little
B" and Edwin was "Great B." Mrs. Howe's two young daughters
thought of him as similar to the sun and the moon in being far
above their sphere, almost like a supernatural being, and were
almost afraid to say a word in front of him. In later life they
reflected that to someone like Edwin, this silent homage must have
been a little trying, for he had not a particle of the coxcomb about
him, but was always perfectly natural.

He acted toward the girls, they remembered, without the least
touch of theatricality. "Impossible to conceive of his posing when
off the stage; he laid that off with the costumes when he stepped off
the boards." Their mother gave a party for him and Mary and
invited the brilliant Senator Charles Sumner, the great voice of
abolitionism. "Have you heard young Booth yet?" Mrs. Howe
asked Sumner, and received in lofty reply, "The truth is, I have got
beyond taking an interest in individuals." (Mrs. Howe wrote what
Sumner had said in her diary and added, "God Almighty has not
yet got so far—at least according to the last accounts.") At the party
Mary wore a light silk dress high in the neck and fastened with a
beautiful brooch containing a single large opal, a gift from her
husband. He spent most of the affair showing his hostess's daughters how he manufactured animals out of his handkerchiefs. Sometimes, alone with Mrs. Howe and the girls, away from strangers, he
could relax for a moment. He told them of what Charlotte Cush-

man had said when they appeared together in *Macbeth*: that his playing was too refined, that he should remember his character was "the grandfather of all the Bowery villains." During the scenes when she, as Lady Macbeth, incited him to violence, he longed to say, "Why don't *you* kill him? You're a great deal bigger than I am."

They were happy with each other and their little baby, the young marrieds, but Mary was delicate, subject to headaches and a perpetually exhausted feeling. They decided to take a house in Dorchester so she could be placed under the care of an eminent Boston physician who specialized in cases like hers. Edwin would be with her and the baby most of the time, absent only for performances in New York. Their place was comparatively modest, not as grand as the Philadelphia residence of John Sleeper Clarke and his wife, Asia. Clarke was managing theaters in several cities while acting on the side, and making a great success of it. Asia seemed happy in her marriage, writing her Baltimore friend Jean Anderson of her two babies and of how when her brother John Wilkes visited—so now she designated him to distinguish him from her husband, John—he "lays on the floor and rolls over with them, like a child." When he had an engagement in Baltimore, Asia wrote Jean that she should "kiss my old John Wilkes for me," hoping that perhaps Jean would add something on her own account. For years she played matchmaker for her favorite brother and dearest friend, but although John thought Jean very pretty, so Asia wrote the subject of his opinion, a real romance never took.

But John was hardly lonely for feminine companionship. Plentiful opportunities arose when he was not actually onstage or working with Asia on a biography of their father they intended to write. (Their mother did not approve of the project, and over their protests threw in a fire most of the letters her husband had received.) Laundry girls took extreme care with his collars and cuffs, and vied with one another to deliver them personally, and hotel maids made and remade his bed. Waitresses at depot restaurants who normally slammed plates and shot coffee cups down the counter made "swift and gentle" offerings to John, wrote Clara Morris, "crowding around him like doves about a grain basket, leaving other travelers to wait upon themselves or go without.

"It is scarcely an exaggeration to say the sex was in love with John Booth. At the theater—good heaven! as the sun-flowers turn upon their stalks to follow the beloved sun, so old and young turned to him." A theater manager's little daughter came each night in her best gowns and "turned upon him fervid eyes that might well have served for Juliet," while the manager's stern old wife fluffed her hair as her eyes filled with sparkles, and when, "uncovering his bonnie head," he kissed her hand, the "wanton blood" came "up in her cheek as if she had been a girl again."

Yet he was a gentleman, Clara Morris saw. Not all actors were. Women who sent a "burst of amatory flattery" to most stage idols would shrivel if they knew how their offerings were passed around and laughed at. She told an actor flaunting his day's collection, "No gentleman would betray a confidence," and got in return, "And no *lady* would so address an unknown man." But John was different, snipping off the signatures from all letters from women he did not know while saying of the notes that their sting lay in the tail. Once an actor picked up one such, asking, "I can read it, can't I, now the signature is gone?"

"The woman's folly is no excuse for our knavery," John answered. "Lay the letter down, please!"

His career was blooming. A Lexington, Kentucky, paper termed him "the greatest tragedian of the age," and a St. Louis one echoed, "the greatest tragedian in the country." "My goose does indeed hang high (long may she wave)," he wrote the manager of the Boston theater where Edwin was appearing, adding that he would honor a minor debt in person because he had not enjoyed good fortune in sending money by mail. "I have been waiting (with all the patience in the world) for over two weeks to hear of $800 I sent my mother."

There was little reason for the Boston manager to worry over the money, which was for costume expenses. In Chicago, from where he wrote the man, "My first week paid me near $900. And this week has opened better." He offered some thoughts on future Boston productions relating to scenery, painted backdrops, the position of a tent, where the archers should exit. "I am glad Ned is doing so well. Give my love to him. Excuse this hurried scrawl. Wishing you all that's good, I am to you now and ever the same."

Despite the laudatory reviews and the lavish financial revenues, he remained modest, good-hearted, happy, and amusing, something of a practical joker who, when called upon to slap other actors with a ham in *The Taming of the Shrew*, carefully coated its base with soot so that in a moment he was surrounded by actors suddenly in blackface. Yet he was not the kind of star who allows himself everything and all others nothing. Once in Cleveland the resident stock company supported him abominably. Everything that could go wrong, did. Everybody expected a storm when the curtain mercifully went down, but all he said was, "It's too bad, too bad. You must do better for me tomorrow." Those who heard his words said it took a kindly heart not to berate actors who did their best, even though what they did made the star appear at his worst.

In early 1863 he went to Boston for an extended stay. Edwin and Mary were in the audience to see *The Apostate*. The next day Edwin wrote the couple's friend Richard Henry Stoddard, "He played Pescara—a bloody villain of the deepest red, you know, an *admiral* of the red, as 'twas, and he presented him—not underdone, but rare enough for the most fastidious 'beef-eater.' Jno Bull himself Esquire never looked more savagely at us poor 'mudsills' than did J. Wilkes, himself, Esquire, settle the accounts of last evening. Yet I am happy to state that he is full of the true grit—he has stuff enough in him to make good suits for a dozen of such player-folk as we are cursed with; and when time and study round his rough edges he'll bid them all 'stand apart.' I am delighted with him."

After that Edwin was off for a series of New York appearances. "I have not dared to think of parting with him," Mary wrote Mrs. Richard Henry Stoddard—Elizabeth. "You know well enough how I will suffer." Edwin would be low-spirited without her, she wrote Elizabeth; would she and Richard not try to comfort him? The Stoddards understood her meaning. Mary had quenched the evil that possessed his soul, Edwin wrote Elizabeth Stoddard, almost completely. She had kissed away "dark stains" from his "blackened heart," he told Elizabeth—and he had been "full of sin, up to the top of all that dissipation, evil associations and sensuality could lead me to." But not even she, Mary, could utterly cleanse him. A libertine he was no longer, yet drink still drew him. It was, he said, a spark covered but still smoldering.

Now in New York, away from Mary, "Molly," the spark burst into flame. "What is Edwin thinking about?" a friend asked Elizabeth Stoddard. "Why does he give himself up in this way when he has everything to live for?" Richard Henry Stoddard and Thomas Bailey Aldrich appointed themselves to keep liquor out of his grasp, as Edwin had once kept it out of his father's. A servant bringing a filled glass found it taken by Aldrich to be flung out the window. But a drunkard can always find what he desires.

In Boston John played to great audiences and reviews. Mary thought him extremely talented but still raw. "Very much pleased with him—but he has a great deal to learn and unlearn," she wrote Emma Cushman. On February 12, 1863, she wrote Edwin in New York that a drawback of John's was that he could not transform

himself for a part. She had just seen him play in almost
"gladitorial" costume, with sleeves fully rolled up so that the audience could admire his muscular development. The sight, she wrote,
eclipsed everything else. " 'Look at his arm,' everyone exclaimed,
and highly delighted the audience seemed at his exhibition."

He stayed with her in the Dorchester house. When his engagement was about to come to an end she took a trolley into Boston
to fetch a friend who would replace him as house guest. It was
snowing. The trolley was delayed. When she got home she was
freezing. "Take me upstairs and put me to bed," she told a servant.
"I feel as if I should never be warm again."

Her doctor, Erasmus Miller, had stopped by and felt it was
just a cold, John reported to Edwin in New York. John was booked
for a Philadelphia stand but briefly broke his journey to be with his
brother and to impress Lillian Woodman as "young, handsome,
gay, full of the joy of life." But here was one heart he could not
conquer, for her romance with Thomas Bailey Aldrich was at the
serious stage.

Edwin's drinking was getting out of hand. John drank also,
usually brandy smashes, but he handled liquor far more easily. He
never got drunk in the legs, he said, never staggered. Edwin's
reactions to alcohol were erratic. He might do well onstage when
completely intoxicated one night, and in similar condition the next
completely lose his touch. "We have seldom seen Shakespeare so
murdered," said the *New York Herald* of one of his displays in that
February. A friend heard that Edwin had been seen in such condition that he was unable to negotiate the steps leading up into a
trolley.

Mary's cold got worse. But there was no cause for concern,
Dr. Miller wrote Edwin on February 18. He should not give himself
"any undue anxiety." Should the patient's condition worsen in any
way, "which I do not expect," Edwin would be instantly informed.
The next day the doctor wrote again, repeating that if all did not
progress satisfactorily, Edwin would be told at once. That night he
awoke from a drunken sleep, feeling a puff of cold air touch his
cheek. He wondered where it came from, he wrote Adam, and
turned in bed and felt it again, and then heard, "as plainly as I hear
this pen scratching over the paper, Mary's voice. *Come to me,
Darling. I'm almost frozen.*"

But the doctor's messages were uniformly encouraging, a total
of six of them over a period of two days, February 18 and 19. Mary
wrote herself and said that she was bothered by pain at night,
awakened by it, but that she would be all right.

His drinking was out of control, and finally Elizabeth Stoddard took the bull by the horns. "Sick or well, you must come,"
she wrote Mary. "Mr. Booth has lost all restraint and hold on
himself. Last night there was the grave question of ringing down the
curtain before the performance was half over. Lose no time.
Come."

From Dorchester Mary replied, "I cannot come. I cannot
stand. I am going to try and write him now." But that evening after
finishing the letter to Elizabeth she suffered a turn for the worse.
She asked Miller to speak plainly and he told her the illness was a
fatal one. The cold had turned into pneumonia. She begged him to
keep her alive long enough for her to see Edwin one more time, so
that she could tell him herself that she was dying. Edwin would be
at the theater. The doctor sent a telegram to his dressing room
telling him to come at once. He was too drunk to open it.

The doctor sent another. It joined its predecessor on his dressing room table. The doctor sent a third.

The play ended. Richard Stoddard was with him when the
theater manager came into the dressing room with a telegram Dr.
Miller had sent to him, the manager. *This is the fourth telegram. Why
does not Mr. Booth answer? He must come at once.*

At last he opened the three previous telegrams and realized
what was happening in Dorchester. The midnight train for Boston
had gone. He must wait for the seven o'clock. He went to the
Stoddards' and drank coffee, refusing one minute to believe Mary
was so ill, crushed and hopeless with grief the next. Gray dawn
came. Stoddard went with him, and they took the train.

He gazed out at the winter landscape as they headed for Boston. It was the twenty-first of February 1863. "I saw every time I
looked from the window Mary dead, with a white cloth tied round
her neck and chin," he wrote Adam. "I saw her distinctly, a dozen
times at least."

At the depot a friend waited with a carriage. When he approached, Edwin raised a hand and said, "Do not tell me. I know."
He got in with Stoddard, and the three drove to the Dorchester
house in absolute silence. Not yet twenty-three years old, Mary lay
in her room with a white cloth tied round her neck and chin. She
wore a gold chain with a miniature of her husband. He went in
alone and sat with her silently for hours. He never touched liquor
again.

On the playbill of the Philadelphia theater where John was scheduled to play there was printed what was termed "A Card to the

Public." The actor would not be making an appearance, for he "felt the necessity imperative upon him to join his afflicted Brother." With their mother, John stood by Edwin as Mary's coffin was lowered into a grave at Boston's Mount Auburn Cemetery. Then the mourners dispersed, and Edwin went back to the empty Dorchester house. It seemed impossible to him that she was actually gone forever. "One week's illness," he wrote Adam. "Can you believe it, Ad? I can't." Nights when he awoke he sought her in the dark, holding his breath, believing he heard her speak. "I think she is somewhere near me now," he wrote Adam. "I see her, feel her, hear her, every minute of the day. I call for her, look for her, every time the door opens."

He held her dresses in his hands, her sewing things, and black despair alternated with hysterical laughing, tears to follow. He was on the narrow line of insanity, thought Lillian Woodman; the borderland of his sanity was not far distant, thought Otis Skinner. He could not forgive himself for drinking away the last hours of her life while she waited for him, and decided that was why she would not come back to him in spirit. "The frightfullest thought that hurts me is the fear that, now she knows me, she has ceased to love me. Does she hate me?"

"Yes, it is right, it is just" that she had left him, he wrote Elizabeth Stoddard. "Mary's love was too deep, too holy for such a selfish, beastly being as I." His little daughter, hardly more than a year old, could not distract him from his guilt and agony. "Edwina's sweetness makes me sad rather than cheerful," he wrote the Stoddards. He longed for death, telling the minister who had married them that he wished only to rejoin Mary or for madness, and saw the future as a giant, empty pointlessness. His work he called a farce. "I wish to God I was not an actor; I despise and dread the d——d occupation; all its charms are gone and the stupid reality stands naked before me. I am a monkey, nothing more. The beauty of my art is gone—it is hateful to me."

He canceled all his engagements for the season, and rode alone in a horse-drawn sleigh along the Brighton Road where, seeing him, Julia Ward Howe and her daughters hoped that the winter sights and sounds might offer diversion. "A glance at his face and figure showed the utter futility of this hope." They had never seen such an image of sorrow. His long black hair a frame for the dark, melancholy face, he passed in his cutter seeing, they knew, none of the gay throng of people, only a face that others could not, and a grave in Mount Auburn.

The young Junius Brutus Booth. "His genius was to me one of the grandest revelations of my life, a lesson of artistic expression," Walt Whitman said.

Booth in maturity—the First Player of the American stage. Kindly, generous, an absolute vegetarian who forbade the slaying of any living thing on his property, including snakes, rats, and flowers, he was at the same time accounted as insane by all who knew him.

MICHAEL W. KAUFFMAN

Above left, Mrs. Junius
Brutus Booth, as the for[...]
Mary Ann Holmes becar[...]
after bearing ten childrer[...]
a man who had a wife an[...]
legitimate child elsewher[...]

Above, Asia. Devastated [...]
brother's crime, she fled [...]
England and returned on[...]
many years later for buri[...]
at John's side.

Booth and his son Edwin,
who acted for years as his
aide and companion—and
keeper.

John, perhaps the most handsome man the American stage has ever known.

The brothers Booth, costumed for *Julius Caesar* in November of 1864. From left, John, Edwin, and Junius Jr. Within half a year Edwin would play Hamlet for one hundred nights; and Abraham Lincoln would be dead.

Above left, Miss Lucy Hale, the object of the affections of Robert Todd Lincoln, future Supreme Court Justice Oliver Wendell Holmes, presidential aide and future Secretary of State John Hay—and the secret fiancée of John Wilkes Booth.

Above, Mary Devlin Booth, the light of Edwin's melancholy soul. When she died young he spent the remainder of his life wishing only to join her, which at last he did when he lay by her side—Hamlet leaping into Ophelia's grave after thirty years.

John. Decades later, those who had known him still wondered why.

Edwin,
"the Prince of Players."

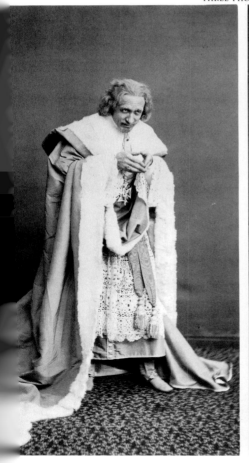

The boarding house of Mrs. Mary Surratt at 604 "H" Street, N.W., Washington, D.C., where the kidnapping of President Lincoln was planned. Today it is a Chinese restaurant.

Harper's Weekly. The assassination of President Lincoln at Ford's Theatre on the night of April 14, 1865.

The weapon that put a bullet of nearly half an inch in diameter more than five inches into Abraham Lincoln's brain.

Ford's Theatre, closed, guarded, and draped in mourning after the assassination. A century would pass before actors again performed on its stage.

Major Henry Rathbone and his fiancée, Miss Clara Harris, were guests of President and Mrs. Lincoln at an April 14, 1865, theater party. Severely injured during the assassination, Rathbone was haunted by the event. He eventually went mad, killing his wife and then attempting suicide.

Secretary of State William H. Seward and his daughter Fanny. "This must be a fearful dream," she thought when a man with a knife in one hand and a revolver in the other came bursting in upon her father.

Lewis Powell. His brutal rampage in the home of Secretary of State Seward left five people seriously injured. "I'm mad! I'm mad!" he shouted as he ran out into the street.

Opposite, Laura Keene. She played opposite Edwin many times, gave John his first part in a play, and emerged from Ford's Theatre the night of the assassination seeming to those who saw her as a blood-covered apparition.

The Surratt tavern/post office, thirteen miles from Washington, restored today and looking as it did when Lincoln's assassin stopped to pick up supplies after fleeing Ford's Theatre.

Dr. Samuel Mudd, who set the broken leg of Lincoln's killer.

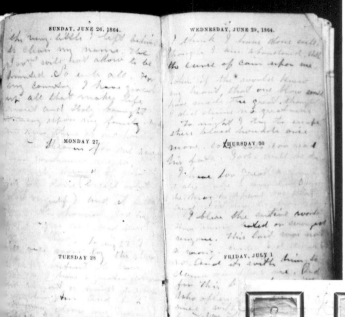

Two pages from the appointment book turned into a diary by John Wilkes Booth during the twelve days he was at large after assassinating Lincoln.

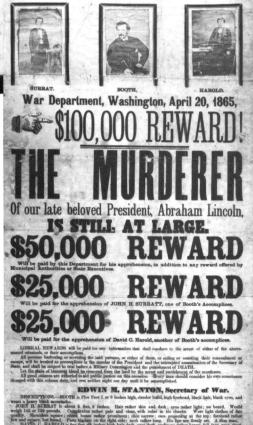

The first posters, inaccurate in many details. The reward money would shortly be increased.

The Garrett farmhouse upon whose porch John died, as it appeared circa 1930.

Sergeant Boston Corbett, the self-castrated religious fanatic who shot to death Lincoln's slayer. With him is Lieutenant Edward Doherty, commanding officer of the search party which included Corbett.

Opposite, Harper's Weekly. The dying Booth drawn from the barn where he had taken refuge, April 26, 1865.

Mrs. Mary Surratt, enigmatic leading woman of the trial of those charged with participating in the conspiracy to kill President Lincoln.

Davy Herold, the trifling boy who paid a heavy price for accompanying John Wilkes Booth to the Garrett farmhouse two-and-a-half miles south of Port Royal, Virginia.

On July 6, 1865, a verdict was handed down in the trial of the conspirators in the murder of Abraham Lincoln. This picture was taken at around two o'clock the next day. From left are Mrs. Surratt, Powell, Herold, and George Atzerodt, who had been assigned to kill Vice President Andrew Johnson.

Edwin with his daughter by his first wife sitting before him. Standing is his
second wife, whose madness almost destroyed him.

Booth's Theatre in New York City, the grandest playhouse of its day
anywhere. Building and running it sent Edwin into bankruptcy.

Edwin four years before his death.

The Players Club, New York City, today. Edwin bought the building and furnished it. The room there in which he died remains unchanged ninety-nine years later.

He thought of his dead, his father and his wife. He had loved his father, he wrote, but looked back upon him now without a tear, without a sigh. "And it is difficult at this time even to recall his features. Great God! Will this ever be the case with Mary?" The thought obsessed him. "One of the most agonizing of my tortures is the dread that I may live so long as to forget, not entirely, for that is impossible, but to be borne along by time into a misty recollection of something that has passed away, a dream of happiness I had when I was young. Oh Jesus! Spare me that!"

He gave up the Dorchester house, took one at 107 East Seventeenth Street in New York City, lived there with his mother and sister Rosalie, and went to spiritualists in an attempt to contact his dead wife. He said he would devote himself to making a life for Edwina, and would eventually return to the stage so he could give her all she needed. But nothing had changed from the moment on the train when it came to him that she was gone, and nothing ever really would. Two and a half little years of happiness, he said. Two and a half little years. Now? "Poor Molly is lying out at Mount Auburn, cold and lonely. Would to God I were there with her."

John was about to turn twenty-five, and of a theatrical stature to set himself up as a more or less permanent resident star in a leading city. He chose Washington. The wartime capital was bursting out of its seams with people, and entertainments of any type drew capacity crowds. He opened as Richard III at Grover's Theatre, on April 11, 1863, billed as THE PRIDE OF THE AMERICAN PEOPLE—THE YOUNGEST TRAGEDIAN IN THE WORLD—A STAR OF THE FIRST MAGNITUDE—SON OF THE GREAT JUNIUS BRUTUS BOOTH—BROTHER AND ARTISTIC RIVAL OF EDWIN BOOTH. President Lincoln attended. The National Republican said he scored a "complete triumph" and took "the hearts of the people by storm." A day later the paper added that his playing created a sensation. "His youth, originality, and superior genius have not only made him popular but established him in the hearts of Washington people as a great favorite." The National Intelligencer said he owned "that which is the grand constituent of all truly great acting, intensity. We have only to say that this young actor plays not from stage rule, but from his soul, and his soul is inspired with genius. Genius is its own schoolmaster; it can be cultivated but not created."

The extravagant billing and fulsome praise still did not turn his head, noted the Englishman Charles Wyndham, later a prominent theatrical figure in London, and later still, Sir Charles. Wyndham

had been hired to play minor parts at Grover's. At his first rehearsal he seated himself at an onstage table. John came by and
smiled at him pleasantly. The theater manager saw and rushed over,
all upset. This was the star's table, he told Wyndham; a supporting
player's place was back in the wings. Wyndham had gotten off to
a bad start. He apologized to John, who was perfectly nice about the
matter. The two became friends. "A marvelous man," Wyndham
remembered. "Lacked the quality of the student that Edwin possessed, but the artist was there." John had, Wyndham thought, a
"higher degree of inborn inspiration than Edwin." He had also a
"divine flash, amazing materials, extraordinary presence and magnetism." An "Adonis," he had "the most wonderful black eyes in
the world, living jewels. Flames shot from them." On the whole,
the Englishman concluded, "his gift was greater than that of his
wonderful brother." In addition he was witty, magnetic, a great
raconteur, a "brilliant, ready, enthusiastic speaker." The Englishman hardly needed to add: "He was the idol of women."

Accompanying President Lincoln and his wife to the theater one
night were the two daughters of Cassius M. Clay, U.S. minister to
Russia. Their mother was an old friend of Mary Todd Lincoln, and
when they sent in their cards to her she responded with this invitation. As the party drove, a piece of iron suddenly sprang up and
pierced the carriage seat between the President and his wife. For a
moment an alarmed Mary Lincoln thought it was an attack. Mary
Clay asked the President what measures he took to be guarded—no
czar of Russia would go through a St. Petersburg street without
cavalry escort and with police, detectives, and plainclothesmen
along the route, and for good reason—and the President said, "I
believe when my time comes there is nothing that can prevent my
going."

The star performer that night played a villain and twice "in
uttering disagreeable threats came very near" and appeared to
point to the President. "When he came a third time I was impressed by it, and said, 'Mr. Lincoln, he looks as if he meant that
for you.' "

" 'Well,' " he said of John Booth, " 'he does look pretty sharp
at me, doesn't he?' "

SEVEN

HE WAR dragged on, Shiloh, the Seven Days, Fredericksburg. Out West with Grant, Adam Badeau sustained a wound. He came to New York to recuperate at Edwin's house. John was there, staying for part of the summer, and the two brothers helped Adam upstairs and put him in Edwin's room. They took turns dressing his wound.

Just after he arrived, and just after Vicksburg was fought in the West and Gettysburg in the East, New York erupted into the worst riots of its history. The focus of the mobs was the military draft, and resentment against it found an outlet in slaying black men, women, and children. More than a thousand died. John took Adam's servant and hid him in the basement for days. The cruelties against the blacks enraged him.

In Washington the President turned ever more gaunt and haggard and careworn. For two years the Stars and Bars could be seen floating in the air just across the Potomac. Now it was gone, but the fighting was far from over. His only relief from the war and the hordes of people with demands upon his time, noted his old friend Noah Brooks, was the theater. Sometimes he went to a comedy just for an hour, "to take a laugh," as he put it. At least he could be alone in the darkness. There was little privacy at the Executive Mansion or his summer residence on the grounds of the Soldiers' Home three miles to the north, for anyone with the slightest of introductions, or no introduction at all, could reach him after business hours, and did. One entered the Executive Mansion (whose doorman went off duty in the early evening), passed a cleaning woman or two, knocked on doors, and found the President. A visiting Englishman who decided he would like to see the American leader found Lincoln casually dressed and was invited to sit down for a chat. But most people wanted more. An actor whose work Lincoln admired was invited to call and pained his host by requesting the position of U.S. consul in London.

But in a theater, Brooks said, the President could at least hope to escape office-seeker, petitioner, critic. Sometimes he might ask for a particular actor to be brought to his box between acts. (Brooks remembered with what diffidence Lincoln received John McCullough, dressed in rags and straw for Edgar in *King Lear*.) The President's little son Tad, mad for the theater, appointed himself a critic to recommend things for his father, and had him come for a Grover's Theatre patriotic spectacle Tad had previously seen a couple of times. Lincoln got a shock when, for the final chorus, Tad came onstage wearing wardrobe uniform, waving a flag, and singing in a childish treble, "We are coming, Father Abraham, three hundred thousand more, shouting the battle-cry of freedom!" A great laugh came from the Presidential box. Leonard Grover learned that Tad had it in mind to set up his own Executive Mansion theater, and gave him costumes and stage properties. His audiences were any servants who could be dragooned into attendance, and his parents.

Lincoln talked a great deal about the theater. The artist F. B. Carpenter, commissioned to do a large painting of the signing of the Emancipation Proclamation, heard Shakespearean recitations from the President as he posed, dozens of lines given from memory without mistake. At the end of the President's rendering of the opening soliloquy from *Richard III*, Carpenter put down his palette and brushes and, applauding, said he was not sure but that the President had made a mistake in his choice of professions. A more professional judge was the comedian Jeems Pipes, whose repertory included exaggerated stammering. Lincoln told him he had known a man who always whistled when he stammered, and he imitated the man's delivery. The comedian liked the concept, rehearsed it until he had mastered it to Lincoln's satisfaction, and added it to his act.

A still more polished performer was the scholarly actor James H. Hackett, who, learning from a Ford's Theatre official that Lincoln had particularly liked his playing of Falstaff, sent the President a book he had written, *Notes and Comments on Shakespeare*. He got back a letter containing Lincoln's views on the subject of Hackett's book: "Some of Shakespeare's plays I have never read; while others I have gone over perhaps as frequently as any unprofessional reader. Among the latter are *Lear*, *Richard III*, *Henry VIII*, *Hamlet*, and especially *Macbeth*. I think nothing equals *Macbeth*. It is wonderful."

He saw Edwin in *The Merchant of Venice*, *The Fool's Revenge*, and *Ruy Blas*, among other productions. When he saw John in *The Marble Heart* on November 9, 1863, Presidential secretary John Hay thought John gave a "tame" performance. The *Washington Evening Star* did not agree: "The romantic young actor by his earnestness, his vigorous grasp of genius, and his fervor of style, claims the most brilliant honors of his art." Once Lincoln "rapturously" applauded John's playing, said the reporter George Alfred Townsend; when told, John said he would rather have the applause of a black. Lincoln wanted to meet him, and told the actor Frank Mordaunt he had sent him an invitation to call. He had not responded. Mordaunt said he knew John Booth well and would arrange a meeting. He failed to do so.

For to John, as to the vast majority of Marylanders, Abraham Lincoln was an odious tyrant oppressing a Southern state. Maryland all but surrounded Washington; the capital's communications with the North flowed through Maryland. So the state had to be kept tamped down. To avoid the possibility—indeed, the likelihood—of assassination, President-elect Lincoln had been forced to sneak through Baltimore in the dead of night, and weeks later the 6th Massachusetts Infantry had to fire on mobs attacking it in the city's streets. The Constitution was suspended in the state, free speech was forbidden, arrests were made without warrant, people were imprisoned without trial, and newspapers were suppressed. For opening your mouth against the Union and Lincoln you found yourself in jail. No Russian czar had done worse, it was said. For doing less, Charles I lost his head.

A despot arbitrary, an absolute autocrat rode wild over them, Marylanders said. John Brown had been hanged for attempting to free the slaves whose condition was sanctified by the Constitution; for following in his footsteps Abraham Lincoln was given the endorsement of thirty million Northerners. But was he? Half of New York, the Draft Riots seemed to prove, was up in arms against the tyrant. Yet he went his way, ruling by bayonet and midnight arrest. That freedom of the individual against the Crown for which England's John Wilkes had fought—it was dead in America.

So reasoned John Wilkes's namesake, writing out his views in the manner of speeches he would deliver if ever given an opportu-

*nity. In a foreign war I too could say, "Country, right or wrong." But
in a struggle such as ours (where the brother tries to pierce the brother's
heart) for God's sake choose the right. A country like this spurns justice,
she forfeits the allegiance of every honest freeman. To love liberty and
justice, to strike at wrong and oppression, was the teaching of our fathers.
Oh, my countrymen, could you all but see the reality or effects of this
horrid war I know you would think like me, and would pray the Almighty
to create in the Northern mind a sense of right and justice.* Due process
of law was ended, the telegraph was censored, personal mail was
opened, the property of Confederate sympathizers was seized and
confiscated; as Caesar had said, in times of war the law was silent.

And who was this Caesar, emperor, king? "This man's appearance, his pedigree, his coarse low jokes and anecdotes, his vulgar
similes and frivolity, are a disgrace to the seat he holds," John told
Asia. Lincoln did his evil work with foreigners purchased in the
mean streets of European slums. There were entire regiments of the
Union Army where not a soldier was American-born. Like a Bona-
parte, John said, Lincoln saw himself with a future crown on his
head, put there by these foreigners. He was a false President. "If the
North conquers us—"

"If the North conquer us!" she interrupted. "We are of the
North."

"Not I, not I!" he replied. "So help me holy God! My soul,
life, and possessions are for the South."

Then why, she asked, did he not join the Confederate Army?
"I have only an arm to give," he answered. "My brains are
worth twenty men, my money worth a hundred." And his profession was such that he could freely travel. She began to understand.
Once a man had come to her Philadelphia residence asking for Dr.
Booth. "I am he," John told her, "if to be a doctor means a dealer
in quinine." He sent it through the Yankee lines in horse collars,
got through other things the South needed in other ways. With a
thousand others he was a smuggler piercing the North's blockade
of the South.

It was not only to Asia that he revealed his feelings, shared by
the population for a thousand miles south of Washington. Once
his emotions boiled over as he rode in a train with Asia's husband.
He did not care for John Sleeper Clarke, had opposed their marriage, and often urged her to get a divorce. Clarke in the train spoke
of the war. John frowned. Clarke went on. John drummed the train
seat with his fingers. Clarke spoke slightingly of the Confederate
leader Jefferson Davis, and John flung himself upon his brother-in-

law, seized him by the throat, and swung him from side to side.
"Never, if you value your life," he rasped, "never speak in that way
to me again of a man and a cause I hold sacred." Clarke let it go.
A "harmless temporary aberration," he told Charles Wyndham.
"Just another queer prank such as his father used to play."

To Edwin his brother's views were entirely mistaken. They
argued. But there was no great passion from Edwin's side. He
supported Lincoln and the Union. That was all there was to it. He
had other, more involving, concerns. After many months of stage
inactivity after the death of his wife, he returned to his profession.
He had a daughter to support. With John Sleeper Clarke he purchased Philadelphia's Walnut Street Theatre, and together they
took on the management of the Winter Garden in New York. He
thought of Mary, sitting daytimes alone in the darkened Walnut
Street Theatre. It was said of him that her funeral bell tolled forever
in his empty heart. On a packet of her letters to him he wrote: *Dear,
dear Soul! I was unworthy of so much goodness.*

Edwina was under the care of his mother and Rosalie in New
York, and in order not to be too far from her, he largely confined
his acting to no farther away than Philadelphia or Boston. In the
Jersey City railroad station he once saw a young man buying a
sleeping car berth from a conductor on the platform. There was a
crowd jamming in, and then the train began to move. The young
man was twisted off his feet. He dropped down between the platform and the car, helpless and in immediate danger of being
crushed under a rolling wheel. Edwin leaped forward, grabbed his
coat collar, and pulled him up to safety on the platform. The young
man looked up, recognized his rescuer at once, and said, "That was
a close call, Mr. Booth." Edwin always hated being recognized. He
went on his way. Weeks later he heard from Adam Badeau that the
young man had told the story around Washington and that word
had drifted down to Grant's headquarters. It was Robert Todd
Lincoln.

John went touring now and then out of Washington as opportunity offered, garnering splendid reviews. "The rush to see the
young tragedian last night was unprecedented," said the *Louisville
Journal* in early 1864. "A large number were compelled to go away
as the house was completely crowded at a very early hour. He is
Louisville's favorite." The *Philadelphia Press* said his Richard III
was "a piece of acting that few actors can rival, and is far above the
capacity of Edwin Booth."

But it was all beginning to pall for John. He was perhaps the most expensively outfitted performer of his day, his wardrobe replete with velvets, ermines, regal coats, and great wigs, including one fashioned from the tribute of a Richmond girl who shaved her head and sent him her hair; he had silver buckles, robes of East Indian shawls, black silk tights, slippers embroidered in gold, amulets, sabers, dirks, rapiers, heavy necklaces, rings, medallions. But did acting, he asked, really mean anything at all? It was different with Edwin, who said there was nothing else he could do, that this was what God intended for him, that if there was something else, perhaps he would try it. Edwin was right: there was nothing else. But often it seemed to John that the whole business was silly and ridiculous. Was it not unworthy, even humiliating, to play at war and combat when a couple of hours from the Washington theaters real soldiers were really dying?

What are actors, anyway? he asked. "Mummers, of the quality of skimmed milk. They know little, think less, and understand next to nothing." He began to talk of getting out. Sometimes his voice bothered him; he was tired of traveling. He thought of real estate, of the oil business. For real-estate investment he purchased lots on Boston's Commonwealth Avenue in his mother's name, and to look into oil possibilities went to the Pennsylvania fields, where fortunes were daily made by bringing in wells whose product was rapidly becoming indispensable as the Gaslight Era arrived. For weeks he lived in Franklin, putting away his usual attire of coat with velvet or astrakhan collar, high silk hat, gold stickpin and watch chain, kid gloves, walking stick with silver handle—"God damned spad," said the aging and on-the-way-out Edwin Forrest—in favor of slouch hat, flannel shirt, overalls, and boots. No one who had seen him onstage would have thought such a transformation possible. When he came to see about going in with John, John Ellsler cried, "Shades of Shakespeare! Look down in horror! Digging for the oleaginous, on the banks of the Allegheny!"

He took Ellsler to where he was living, a place that Ellsler said could only with courtesy be called a house. But John had fixed it up nicely, with reading material ready at hand, and engravings on the wall along with pictures of the family. He had a double-barreled shotgun and powder flask and fishing tackle, and on a shelf four well-colored meerschaums, a variety of clay pipes, and five pounds of Killikinick smoking blend. It was pretty cozy after all, Ellsler decided. They stayed there for weeks, looking into oil prospects. When one driller apologized for hands covered with oil and grease, John said, "Never mind, that's what we're after." They took their meals at a hotel near a harness shop, the little son of whose owner learned to wait for John to come along so they could play together and John could offer an improvised toy, a pocket knife, or a coin. In the end John put up six thousand dollars. The well proved a poor one, and so the money was gone. By late 1864 he was out of the oil business.

In November, Lincoln was reelected. He won with little help from a Maryland where there were counties in which fewer than half a dozen voters from a roll of thousands put down his name. Edwin was among the few, voting for the first and only time in his life. Back from California, June tried to smooth over the political arguments of his younger brothers by telling John that the war was simply a family quarrel on an immense scale. One day the matter would be resolved, and all would return to what had been. Later in November, theatrical placards in New York announced a great event. June, Edwin, and John had "come forward with cheerful alacrity to do honor to the immortal bard from whose works the genius of their father caught inspiration and of many of whose creations he was the best and noblest illustrator the stage has ever seen." The three brothers would appear together for a night in *Julius Caesar*. Proceeds would go for the erection of a statue of Shakespeare in New York's Central Park.

Two thousand people crowded the Winter Garden. Very high prices were charged for tickets, the public being reminded that the money went for a good cause. Seats went for up to five dollars. At the end the three brothers came onstage and together bowed to the box where their mother sat, June as Cassius, Edwin as Brutus, and John as Mark Anthony, with mustache shaved for the occasion. Applause rolled over them, "the eldest powerfully built and handsome as an antique Roman, Edwin with his magnetic fire and graceful dignity, and John Wilkes in the perfection of youthful beauty." It seemed to the watching Asia that Edwin had trembled for his laurels as he played opposite John. Never before had he beheld a being so perfectly handsome, Edwin told his sister. "Our Wilkes looks like a young god," she heard someone breathe from a seat near hers.

The following night, November 26, 1864, Edwin Booth began the stand that gained for him the position by which, for half a century and more, all other actors were judged. He became the standard to which all aspired and none reached. Prior to that night, few actors anywhere expected to appear in the same play for a week's time. Ten nights was considered a protracted run. Edwin that night began a stand of one hundred nights as Hamlet. History would remember him for what he had been in that run, statues would be erected of him as then he was, as Hamlet in late 1864 and early 1865, the Prince of Players.

In other roles, Adam Badeau thought, Edwin's nature was cloaked in the character he played. He was no Richard III, nor Iago. His inner being, perhaps, Badeau thought, was suggested at times by Othello and Lear. But Hamlet, moody, dreamy, melancholy, tender, at odds with himself and his world—it was Edwin. When wearing a miniature of Junius Brutus Booth on a chain, he called the Ghost "Father," there was an inescapable pathos in his voice. When he wandered between thoughts of action and revulsion for action, when he mourned Ophelia, when, indecisive, he showed the prince's inner meaning, the prince's inner feelings, sadly distant from all about him, fearful of a terrible future, he was Hamlet no more than he was Edwin Booth. Here, indeed, and only here the substance and the shade merged.

Princely in his performance, he cast a spell from which you could not escape. Of the one hundred nights George William Curtis wrote in *Harper's:* "His playing throughout has an exquisite tone, like an old picture. The charm of the finest portraits, of Raphael's 'Julius' or 'Leo,' of Titian's 'Francis I' or 'Ippolito di Medici,' of Vandyck's 'Charles I,' is not in the drawing, nor even the coloring, so much as the nameless, subtle harmony which is called tone.

"So in Booth's Hamlet it is not any particular scene, or passage, or look, or movement that conveys the impression; it is the consistency of every part with every other, the pervasive sense of the mind of a true gentleman sadly strained and jarred. It is not so much what he says or does that we observe; for under all, beneath every scene and word and act, we hear what is not audible, the melancholy music of the sweet bells jangled, out of tune, and harsh."

Once the actress Clara Morris heard some people praise John Booth's Hamlet. "No!" John said. "No, no! There's but one Hamlet to my mind, that of my brother Edwin.

"You see, between ourselves, he *is* Hamlet."

EIGHT

*I*N LATE 1864 as night after night Edwin Booth transfixed New York, his brother John went about lower Maryland just south of Washington. He told people he wanted to buy land there.

He did not wish to buy land.

The Civil War was three and a half years old. The Confederacy was still in the field, its army a gathering of heroes to John Booth's thinking—"a noble band of patriotic heroes. Hereafter, reading of their deeds, Thermopylae will be forgotten."

And what had he done while men died and epic battles were contested? Once he had been arrested in St. Louis for making known his hope that "the whole damned government would go to hell." Fined and forced to swear allegiance to the Union, he went on his way. He had slung his brother-in-law around in a railroad car for speaking ill of Jefferson Davis. On a window of an oil region hotel in which he frequently stayed, the proprietor found inscribed in the glass: *Abe Lincoln departed this life August 13th, 1864, by the effects of poison.* Who knew what that meant? The President was perfectly well on that date. Once in the oil region as he crossed the Allegheny River, a fellow boat passenger defined a remark he made about Lincoln as a lie. "I will never allow a man to call me a liar," John said, and pulled a revolver. The other man grabbed a boat push-pole with a metal-tipped spike.

The ferry pilot wrenched the pole away. The revolver was returned to the pocket from which it had emerged. That was the end of the matter. He had a spat about the war with Edwin—"The old feeling aroused by our loving brother has not yet died out. It's only for dear Mother that I have gone there at all when in New

York," he wrote June—but what did it all amount to, what did it count against the deeds of the chivalrous Southrons, so they were called, of the Confederate Army as they marched to glory behind Marse Robert, Uncle Robert, General Lee at the head of his fellow knights and heroes? Once John developed a fibroid tumor on his neck. He went to Washington's Dr. John Frederick May and was told it could easily be removed but that then the area of the minor operation must not be disturbed, for if left alone the edges of the surgical wound would draw together and leave little scar, but if irritated in any way they would gape and the space between the edges would fill up with new tissue or flesh and become unsightly. John told Dr. May he would be careful, but shortly he was back: Charlotte Cushman, he explained, had embraced him onstage with such force that the wound opened under her grasp. So Dr. May had to tell what he remembered as this "fashionably dressed, remarkably handsome young man" that there would always be a scar. John asked the doctor to say if questioned by anyone that the scar came from removal of a bullet.

Embarrassing. He was stage king and hero, warrior and chieftain, but asked to be described as wounded battler in some wholly imagined affair. He aspired to greater things than this. So he went about lower Maryland saying he was interested in land, or buying a horse. To some people he told the truth. One such was John Surratt, a twenty-year-old Confederate spy and blockade runner who carried news of Yankee troop movements in his boot heels or between the planks of his buggy or hidden in the pages of a book on John Brown. To contact such as Surratt was no great task in Maryland, or even in Washington, for much of the city prayed for a triumphal entrance of the rebels, cursed Lincoln and the abolitionists and the Northern troops crowding the sidewalks and encamped in every square. The saloons rang with denunciations of the Emancipation Proclamation, remembered Leonard Grover of the theater bearing his name. Once Lincoln came to Grover's alone save for Speaker of the House of Representatives Schuyler Colfax. When the play was over, Grover led the two to the President's carriage. They heard jeering laughter, not pleasant, Grover remembered, and found that the coachman, having accepted an offer of a drink, had taken more than that. He lay sprawled out on the sidewalk, clutching the reins. On the carriage box was a Union Army drummer boy who had lost an arm. There was no one else. Grover pulled the reins out of the coachman's fingers and jumped on the box to drive the President and Speaker Colfax home. Not a single person in the Washington crowd offered to help in any way.

"I have a proposition to submit to you," John told Surratt. His listener, tall, slim, intelligent, had found life as a spy "fascinating" and the Federal detectives "stupid." His older brother was in the Confederate Army, serving in the West. There was a twenty-two-year-old sister at home in the boardinghouse their mother ran. They had a tavern that doubled as a post office in Surrattsville, Maryland, named for the late head of the family, some thirteen miles south of Washington.

"Well, sir, what is your proposition?" Surratt asked.

John got up, looked under the bed of the room in which they were, into the wardrobe, through the doorway, and into the passageway. "We will have to be careful," he said. "Walls have ears." He drew his chair close to that of Surratt. He spoke in a whisper:

"Kidnap President Lincoln and carry him off to Richmond."

"Kidnap President Lincoln!"

The idea, Surratt remembered, struck him as "foolhardy"; he was "amazed, thunderstruck." But John was saying a captured Lincoln could be exchanged for who knew how many captured Confederates languishing in Northern prisons. To John his plan was eminently reasonable. He had promised his mother he would not join the Confederate Army. Here was the manner in which he could aid the Southern cause. That neither Edwin nor June nor Joe would dream of partaking was beside the point; what was happening in America was, after all, called the war of the brothers.

He needed time to consider this audacious scheme, Surratt said. For two days he turned it over in his mind. Kidnap the President. Capture Lincoln. Was it impossible? Often the President rode out alone to his Soldiers' Home cottage in a heavily wooded, remote area three miles from the Executive Mansion (present-day Upshur Street and Rock Creek Road, N.W.), using whatever army horse happened to be available. Once, mounted on a horse named Old Abe, he had his hat shot off. Perhaps it was a hunter, or someone signaling his family that he was near home, Lincoln told his old law partner made marshal of the District of Columbia, Ward Hill Lamon. Whoever it was, "he unceremoniously separated me from my eight-dollar plug hat." At the sound of the shot, the horse bolted for home. "I tell you," Lincoln said, "there is not time on record equal to that made by the two Old Abes."

Lamon was not amused. The memory of the danger in Baltimore on the way to Washington for the Inaugural remained in his mind. He had often reminded Lincoln of that, told him not to go about without a guard, sometimes slept outside his room festooned with weapons. Lincoln said Lamon was a monomaniac on the subject, and laughed about it. Finally on December 10, 1864, Lamon wrote him:

I regret that you do not appreciate what I have repeatedly said to you in regard to the proper police arrangements connected with your household and your own personal safety. Therefore he was submitting his resignation as marshal of the District of Columbia. *I will give you reasons which have impelled me to this course. Tonight, as you have done on several previous occasions, you went unattended to the theater. When I say unattended, I mean that you went alone with Charles Sumner and a foreign minister, neither of whom could defend himself against an assault from any able-bodied woman in this city. And you know, or ought to know, that your life is sought after, and will be taken unless you and your friends are cautious.*

Lincoln jollied his old friend out of resigning, and when Secretary of War Edwin Stanton assigned a cavalry detachment to accompany the President and Mrs. Lincoln on carriage rides, got rid of the soldiers, saying the jingling of sabers and spurs and the clatter of hooves made it almost impossible for him to conduct a conversation with his wife. Anyway, he added, the soldiers were such raw recruits that he felt himself more in danger from the possibility of one of their weapons going off than from any intentional assailant. He was no emperor or reigning monarch, he told people. He could not be surrounded by guards, self-imprisoned in some strongroom remote from life. And why would anyone want to get him out of the way, anyhow? If he was gone, Vice President Hannibal Hamlin of Maine would take his place, and Hamlin was so viewed in the South that his existence, Lincoln said, constituted a life-insurance policy more valuable than the whole of the prairie lands of Illinois. When late at night he walked over to the War Department through the White House grounds to see the latest army telegraph reports, his wife often told him to be careful, urging him to take a guard, or at least carry a heavy walking stick someone had given him. The trees planted by Thomas Jefferson had grown to enormous heights and shadowed out the thin gaslights, and anyone could walk in the grounds, anyone could hide in those shadows. "All imagination," Lincoln told his wife and her dressmaker. "What does anyone want to harm me for? Don't worry about me, Mother, as if I were a little child."

"Father, you should not go out alone. You know you are surrounded with danger." But he went alone.

So capturing him, Surratt reasoned, would not be impossible. And to do so could conceivably mean independence for the South. The plan was rash, surely, Surratt thought, but honorable. The President would be treated with all respect. Would a Northern soldier fail to make a prisoner of Jefferson Davis if the opportunity presented itself? There was a war on, and though he wore no uniform, Surratt thought of himself as a soldier of the South. His spying and blockade running was countenanced and financed by the highest officials of the Confederacy, up to and including Secretary of State Judah Benjamin. This action would serve his country. He told John he would go in with him.

Around the chief conspirator gathered others, attracted by his money, his charm, his inspiring presence, and the possibility of doing something for the Southern cause. Lewis Thornton Powell was a hulking and bull-like twenty-year-old born in Alabama whose family had moved to the rural area of Live Oak Station, Florida, along the railroad line between Jacksonville and Tallahassee. He joined the 2nd Florida Infantry at sixteen when the war began and fought in the Peninsula Campaign, at Chancellorsville, and at Antietam. Slightly wounded at Gettysburg, he was captured. He escaped and made his way South to join the irregulars serving with the Confederate raider Colonel John Mosby. After a while he gave up the war and went to Baltimore, where he came to the attention of the police for grabbing a maid in his lodging house by the throat, throwing her to the floor, and stamping on her. She had insulted him, he explained, when he asked her to make up his room.

John had met Powell once years earlier, outside a theater, and recognized the deserter from the steps of Barnum's Hotel in Baltimore. He bought Powell a suit of clothes, gave him money, bought him oysters, dazzled him. Powell saw the plan as a military operation, if one of a type different from those he had known for years, and addressed the plan's originator as "Captain" or "Cap." He saw himself as an honorable soldier, and he had been that, despite the brutishness that saw him carry the skull of a Yankee soldier he had killed for use as an ashtray. Powell had known nothing but war since leaving the home of his Baptist preacher father. A brother of his had died in Confederate service, and another was permanently crippled. Wherever he went he took new names—Payne, Paine, Wood. He would do whatever his new captain told him to do.

David Herold was a twenty-three-year-old sometime druggist's clerk who looked seventeen and acted no older. A trifling and frivolous boy whose late father had specified in his will that his son must have no part in any supervision of the father's estate, he had seven sisters who made him their pet. His main interest in life was hunting. "His most intimate acquaintances never heard him mention politics, his whole conversation being of his exploits with dog and gun." To Lewis Powell, or Payne, or Paine, or Wood, he was "a little blab," but from countless hunting expeditions he knew the areas south of Washington very well.

Samuel Arnold was a former schoolmate of John Booth who had not seen him in ten years until in Baltimore he got word his old friend wanted to renew their acquaintance. Arnold found the decade that had passed had produced a deep-thinking man of the world "with highly distinguishing marks of beauty, intelligence, and gentlemanly refinement along with a great flow of conversational power." Arnold became "perfectly infatuated" with the "social manners and bearing" of his schoolmate of former years. The money he was given also attracted him to the plan. He was a former Confederate soldier, as was Michael O'Laughlen, another former schoolmate who joined in. Edman Spangler, a stage carpenter at Ford's Theatre, who years earlier worked for Junius Brutus Booth in the remodeling of The Farm into Tudor Hall, was recruited.

George Atzerodt was a Prussian-born carriagemaker who doubled as boatman getting blockade runners and spies across the Potomac at Port Tobacco, Maryland. His role would be that of ferryman. There were others in the group. There were others who were asked to join and refused. One such was the New York actor Samuel Chester. Visiting Edwin, June, Rosalie, and their mother over Christmas 1864, John went to the elegantly named Houston Street House of Lords tavern with Chester. He spoke about being in on an important speculation. They finished their drinks and went out into Broadway, where at Fourth Street Chester said he would walk over to his home on Grove Street. "John, I bid you good night."

"Hold on—I want to tell you what this speculation is." Broadway was filled with people. Let them step into the quieter Fourth Street. There Chester heard the plan. Lincoln would be captured and taken to Richmond, carried to Richmond. Would Chester join in? Astonished, Chester said he could not think of participating in such a scheme. John said his party was bound together by a solemn oath to kill anyone who divulged the plot. "I carry a derringer loaded to shoot everyone who betrays us," he told Chester. The implied threat was unfair, Chester thought, and it hurt his feelings. "It is very wrong, John, because I have always looked up to you as a friend and have never done you any wrong."

"At any rate you won't betray me." After Christmas he left Edwin's and went back to Washington to stockpile revolvers, carbines, knives, ropes, and three horses, and to look closely at every route out of the city. On what was supposed to be a pleasure ride in southeastern Washington with John McCullough, the actor whose work in *King Lear* brought him an invitation to visit the Presidential box at Ford's Theatre, he got to talking about how if one was in a tight spot it would be easy to slip out of town along one of the byroads along the eastern branch of the Potomac. The idea seemed pointless to McCullough, who said that when he left Washington it would be in a railroad car. As it was, he had had enough of equestrian exercise. "I am all raw from riding this old horse. For God's sake, take me back to the hotel." Once McCullough came into his friend's room at the National Hotel without bothering to knock. The room's occupant was sitting behind a table holding a map, knife, and pistol. He was wearing gauntlets, spurs, and a slouch hat. As the door opened he grabbed the knife and rushed at the visitor. "John, what in the name of sense is the matter with you?" asked McCullough with a gasp. "Are you crazy?"

John stopped, put his hands over his eyes in the manner of someone rubbing away a dream, and asked how McCullough was. It was strange. It was also strange what John had quoted during the eastern branch horseback ride, and amusing what McCullough had countered with. John had quoted the Colley Cibber version of *Richard III*, McCullough told people in the Ford's Theatre green room: *The ambitious youth who fired the Ephesian dome/Outlives in fame the pious fool who reared it.* McCullough inquired the name of that ambitious youth, and John had to say, "Why—I—I've forgotten it."*

The usual meeting place for the conspirators grouped around their leader was the H Street, N.W., home of John Surratt's mother—three stories, attic, and basement. Mary Elizabeth Jenkins Surratt, forty-one, widowed two and a half years, had moved to Washington half a year previous from Surrattsville, Maryland, a hamlet of some forty persons centered on the tavern-post office she had leased out for five hundred dollars a year to a former Washington policeman. She was not well off, and rented out rooms at her

---

*The temple of Artemis, in Ephesus, Greece, numbered among the Seven Wonders of the World, was set on fire in 356 B.C. by one Erostratus, who said his motive for doing so was to transmit his name to future ages.

Washington place to make ends meet. The effect her son's new friend had upon her twenty-two-year-old daughter Anna and the young lady boarders was detailed in a letter John Surratt wrote a New York cousin with whom he corresponded: "I have just taken a peep in the parlour. Would you like to know what I saw there?

"Well, Ma was sitting on the sofa, nodding first to one chair, then to another, next the piano. Anna is sitting in a corner, dreaming, I expect, of J. W. Booth. Well, who is J. W. Booth? But hark! The door-bell rings and Mr. J. W. Booth is announced. And listen to the scamperings. Such brushing and fixing."

Anna bought a photograph of her brother's friend and put it in her room. She liked writing his name down on pieces of papers she left around. Her mother took to addressing him as "Pet." Their reaction to other new visitors was less favorable. Lewis Powell, improbably introduced as the Reverend Mr. Wood, a Baptist minister, Anna marked down as "a perfect fool" who "did not possess all his senses." She said of George Atzerodt that "such sticks" were not fit company for her. Her mother agreed, particularly after finding empty liquor bottles in the room where Atzerodt spent the night. She suggested to her son that he be kept from H Street. She did not refer to him by his name, for nobody in the boardinghouse could pronounce it. There he was known by the name of the town he lived in, Port Tobacco.

That winter, January and February and March of 1865, as Edwin in New York finished up the one hundred nights as Hamlet, John in Washington was acclaimed by the *National Intelligencer* as a flawless Romeo. "What perfect acting! We have never seen a Romeo bearing any near comparison with the acting of Booth." But he performed only rarely, turning down parts in favor of riding through lower Maryland along what all through the war was termed an underground route for Confederate smugglers, transporters of contraband, men going South to join the rebel army, letter-bearers from Southern agents in Canada, couriers bringing newspapers from Northern cities for the Richmond authorities to read within twenty-four hours of their publication. The area was entirely Southern in sentiment and filled with people who hated the Yankees and countenanced and abetted the travelers going along the underground route. Union patrols moved about the trails that passed for roads, and Union gunboats went up and down the rivers, but the area was so thinly settled and so filled with swamps and woods that it was an easy matter to avoid the North's soldiers and sailors. Here was the path along which Abraham Lincoln would be taken as prisoner and cargo.

Often the explorer came back to Washington exhausted and dirty. The actor Charles Warwick received a visit from him one day and found him splashed with mud to his boot tops and with mud on the bottom of his coat. The weather outside was wet and chilly. Warwick told him to take off his boots and dry his feet by the fire, and John did so and also accepted his friend's loan of a pipe filled with tobacco. His spurs were put to hang draping from the gas fixture. Warwick's room was tiny and narrow, with a plain bureau, a washstand, a couple of chairs, and a bed. It was in a Tenth Street boardinghouse just across from Ford's Theatre. A reproduction of Rosa Bonheur's *The Horse Fair* hung on a wall, along with J. F. Herring's *The Village Blacksmith*, *The Stable*, and *The Barnyard*. Apparently the owner of the boardinghouse, William Petersen, liked horses. John seemed done in, Warwick saw. He fell asleep on the bed smoking his host's pipe.

In New York in another house, Edwin's house, strange visions troubled the sleep of another Booth, the family's mother. She wrote John that the visions were about him, John told his fellow conspirator and former schoolmate Samuel Arnold. Her dreams were "fearful," she wrote. She wanted him in New York, and sent June down to Washington to urge him to come to her. Mrs. Booth had always been strangely aware of John's doings even when far from him, remembered the actress Anne Hartley Gilbert. Mrs. Gilbert knew it from John himself. "No matter how far apart they were, she seemed to know in some mysterious way when anything was wrong with him. If he were ill, or unfit to play, he would often receive a letter of sympathy, counsel and warning, written when she could not possibly have received any news of him."

When June arrived in Washington, John cautioned Sam Arnold not to tell him about the three horses he was maintaining—let him say they belonged, rather, to Sam. The brothers walked in a street, and John looked south across the Potomac to where, across the war-ravaged countryside, Grant's forces waited for warm weather so they could seek Lee's battered and starving scarecrows. Little was left of the once-grand Confederacy save a long half circle before Petersburg and Richmond, and little slice of North Carolina. "Virginia, Virginia," John said brokenly. He had many things on his mind, that February. He sat up with June until three-thirty in the morning on the fourteenth day of the month, writing an acrostic Valentine Day's greeting using June, June wrote Asia, as "a dictionary." It was for the young lady with whom he was in love and to whom he was engaged to be married.

John P. Hale of New Hampshire represented his state in the U.S. House of Representatives and the U.S. Senate. An abolitionist twenty years before there was an Emancipation Proclamation, he was before the war twice Presidential candidate of the Free Soil Party, which opposed the extension of slavery into the western areas of the country. He was hated in the South. Senator Henry S. Foote of Mississippi, one of the King Cotton fire-eaters who brought the war, Northerners said, snarled on the Senate floor before the fighting began that if Senator Hale ever came to Senator Foote's state, "he could not go ten miles into the interior before he will grace one of the tallest trees of the forest, with a rope around his neck, and with the approbation of every virtuous and patriotic citizen; and, if necessary, I should myself assist in the operation."

Before entering politics, Hale had been an excellent courtroom lawyer who knew how to sway a jury. He told the Senate that he thanked his Mississippi colleague for the kindly words, the "hospitable invitation," and in return would suggest that Foote come to New Hampshire, where the people would be very interested in listening to his views before engaging him in earnest debate so that the truth could be elicited. After that the Mississippian was known throughout the North as Hangman Foote. John C. Calhoun of South Carolina said that he would as soon argue "with a maniac from Bedlam" as Hale.

As a youth Hale's greatest pleasure, a schoolmate recorded, was "to spout before an awestruck assembly," and as a Bowdoin student with a "keen dramatic sense, he delighted in all forms of public speaking." He was best known in the North for the words he spoke when defending Bostonians who refused to return a fugitive slave to the slave's Southern master:

"John Debree claims that he owns Shadrach. Owns what? Owns a man! Suppose John Debree should claim an exclusive right to the sunshine, the moon, or the stars! Would you sanction the claim by your verdict? And yet the stars shall fall from heaven, the moon shall grow old and decay, the sun shall fail to give its light, the heavens shall be rolled together as a scroll, but the soul of the despised and hunted Shadrach shall live on with the life of God Himself!

"I wonder if John Debree will claim that he owns him then."

In early 1865 Hale was serving out his last days in the Senate, for he had been defeated in the November elections, partially as a result of a to-the-death feud he had waged with Secretary of the Navy Gideon Welles in his capacity as head of the Naval Affairs

Committee. The two detested one another. In Welles's diary Hale was characterized as "loudmouthed and insolent," a "Senatorial buffoon," and "old hack" who was "worthless and worse than worthless." He was in fact better at dramatic oratory than close legal reasoning, unhappy with technical treatises and research, while possessed of likable good fellowship and an excellent, sociable companion. Hale desired to go abroad and asked for a foreign ministership. Lincoln wished, he said, to "break his fall" from the loss of his Senate seat, and Secretary of State Seward told him he could have Spain. He would take up his new post in the spring.

Senator and Mrs. Hale had two daughters.

The younger of the two daughters was Lucy—Lucy Lambert, her mother's maiden name. She was twenty-four. By no means was she a beauty. Pressed for a description of her while once testifying under oath, the Ford's Theatre proprietor, John T. Ford, came up with one word: "stout." But she had something far beyond mere physical allure. The Harvard undergraduate and future U.S. Supreme Court justice Oliver Wendell Holmes met her on a Maine vacation while she was in boarding school in Hartford, Connecticut, and in April 1858 wrote that after parting from her he was "so cross" for three days that no one could come within "a mile" of him. Less than a week later he was writing to ask if he might address her by her first name—"Dear *Miss Hale* (need that formality be kept up any longer?)"—and saying how happy he was to learn that no young men in Connecticut could go riding with her, for school rules forbade it. "This affords me huge satisfaction." When the war came and she was graduated and went to live with her mother and father and six-years-older sister Elizabeth in Washington, Captain Holmes, U.S. Army, enthusiastically renewed their acquaintanceship.

He was not alone in the chase. President Lincoln had two principal secretaries, and one of them, John Hay, later secretary of state, wrote Lucy Hale of his thoughts after seeing her off on a trip: "I came back from the station wondering if there were anyone else in the world just like you; one of equal charm, equal power of gaining hearts, and equal disdain of the hearts you gain. The last glance of those mysterious blue-grey eyes fell upon a dozen or so of us and everybody but me thought the last glance was for him. I have known you too long. Since you were a school-girl—yes, even in those early days you were as puzzling in your apparent frankness and real reserve as you are today. You know how I love and admire you. I do not understand you, nor hope to, nor even wish to. You would lose to me something of your indefinable fascination if I knew exactly what you mean."

Then there was Robert Todd Lincoln, who had the White House conservatory send her flowers. And there was John Booth.

They met at their mutual residence, the National Hotel at Sixth Street and Pennsylvania Avenue, where she lived with her family. (Very few government officials, Secretary of State Seward being the outstanding exception, had private homes of any scope in Washington.) It would be impossible for her not to take notice of him, for he was a familiar figure at the National's weekly "hops," was not infrequently prevailed upon to give recitations in one of the hotel's tufted-sofa, potted-palmed, and mahogany-furnished parlors—and was, after all, John Booth.

There was the issue of her parents' reaction. Senator Hale had been in politics most of his life, had been friendly with Congressman Abraham Lincoln in the 1840s, remained friendly with him through the war. Now Lincoln's son was interested in Hale's daughter. And even on his own terms, Robert T. Lincoln was an impressive catch and would in fact go on to be a great success and a very rich man.

And this Booth was an actor. His family was composed of actors. And what were actors? It was said that when the players came to town housewives should hasten to take in their laundry from the line. What was the stage? Oliver Cromwell had said it was the province of the Devil and that actors were vagabonds doing Satan's work. No American Presbyterian who took religion seriously would think of entering a theater under any circumstances. Actors were sometimes accepted socially in the Cavalier South but never in the Puritan North. And the Hales were from New Hampshire. It was one thing for this actor to take Lucy and her sister Elizabeth to a play, or to sit chatting with them in a National Hotel parlor, and dance with them at a hop, but more than that Senator and Mrs. Hale did not wish to see. They felt John Booth was a splendid performer but wanted Robert Lincoln for a son-in-law.

But, as had been said, love will find a way. John told his brother June that he found in Lucy something worth more than all the money he could ever hope to make on the stage. She gave him a ring that he repeatedly kissed when he spoke of her to friends. Asia learned that she had said she would go to Spain with her family when her father took up his duties as minister there, but would return to marry John in a year, "with or without her father." Mrs. Booth wrote John from New York:

The secret you have told me is not exactly a secret, as Edwin was told by some one that you were paying great attention to a fine young lady in Washington. Now, my dear boy, I cannot advise you how to act. You have so often been dead in love and this may prove like the others, not of any lasting impression. You are aware that the woman you make your wife you must love and respect beyond all others, for marriage is an act that can not be recalled without misery if otherwise entered into—which you are well aware of.

To be united to a woman that you only think you love is not the thing. You are old enough and have seen so much of the world to know all this; only a young man in love does not stop to reflect and like a child with a new toy only craves possession of it. Think and reflect, and if the lady in question is all you desire, I see no cause why you should not try to secure her. Her father, I see, has his appointment.* Would he give his consent? You can but ask. First be well assured she is really and truly devoted to you; then obtain his consent.

You know in my partial eyes you are a fit match for any woman, no matter who she may be—but some fathers have higher notions. God grant, if it is to be so, it will prove a source of happiness to you both.

Now I am going to dinner by myself. Why are you not here to chat and keep me company? No, you are saying soft things to one that don't love you half as well as your old mother does. God bless you, my dear darling boy. It's natural it should be so, I know, so I won't complain. I cannot expect to have you always. God guard you forever and ever. Your loving mother.

If only he weren't an actor, Lucy said to him. She was a Victorian era daughter and, some said, a lifelong Daddy's girl. That John was an actor, she said, was the only thing she didn't like about him. Quick-witted, as he always was, he replied: If only she weren't an abolitionist. It was the only thing he didn't like about her. On Inauguration Day, March 4, 1865, she got him a ticket to stand on a stairway just above and behind where on the East Front of the Capitol the President for the second time took his oath of office. The President spoke his seven-paragraph speech. An actor who had spent his career offering great words, Richard III at Bosworth Field,

*Hale's designation as minister to Spain was officially announced the day before Mrs. Booth wrote.

Macbeth and Birnam Wood, Romeo, Othello, John listened to
what the journalist Noah Brooks years later said remained in the
memories of those who were there as something than which nothing could be more thrillingly recalled:

> Fondly do we hope—fervently do we pray—that this
> mighty scourge of war may speedily pass away. Yet, if
> God wills that it continue until all the wealth piled up by
> the bondsman's two hundred and fifty years of unre-
> quited toil be sunk, and until every drop of blood drawn
> with the lash shall be paid by another drawn with the
> sword, as was said three thousand years ago, so still must
> it be said, "The judgments of the Lord are true and righ-
> teous altogether."
> With malice towards none; with charity for all; with
> firmness in the right, as God gives us to see the right, let
> us strive on to finish the work we are in; to bind up the
> nation's wounds; to care for him who shall have borne
> the battle and for his widow, and his orphan—to do all
> which may achieve and cherish a just and lasting peace
> among ourselves, and with all nations.

Chief Justice of the United States Salmon P. Chase swore in
the President. He kissed the Bible. Artillery blasted off. The sun
came out from behind clouds that had poured rain previously and
made the streets muddy beyond precedent, but whose parting for
the rays made Lincoln tell Noah Brooks the next day that he was
just superstitious enough to consider this sudden light a happy
omen.

At the Inaugural Ball that night, Mrs. Lincoln, escorted according to protocol not by her husband but instead by Senator
Charles Sumner, was in white silk with overdress of rich lace, point
lace, and puffs of silk, with white fan and gloves, with wreath of
jasmines and violet encircling her head, and ornaments of pearl.
Her greatest terror was that her husband might discover what she
spent on herself, five thousand dollars once in a single several-
hours splurge, more than two months of his salary. The escort of
Miss Lucy Hale, it was seen, was the noted young actor Mr. J.
Wilkes Booth.

On the evening of March 15, 1865, John Surratt, Lewis Powell, and
two young ladies from the Surratt boardinghouse, Apollonia Dean
and Honora Fitzpatrick, attended a production of *Jane Shore* at
Ford's Theatre. They sat in a box overlooking stage left, which

John Booth had secured for them. Twice in the previous month President Lincoln occupied the same box to see John Sleeper Clarke, once with Lieutenant General Grant, up from the lines before Petersburg and Richmond. After the play the young ladies returned to the Surratt boardinghouse while the men went on to dinner and a meeting at the fashionable Gautier's Restaurant on Pennsylvania Avenue. Davy Herold was there, George Atzerodt, Sam Arnold, Michael O'Laughlen.

Their host ordered oysters for the group, champagne, cigars, cold meats, and cheeses. He outlined a definitive plan to kidnap the President. Time was short. Spring had arrived, and soon the Virginia roads would be dry and hard. Then the Yankee guns and wagons would be able to move and the Confederate lines would be in danger of being pierced. If that happened, the surrender of Richmond would follow.

The capture of the President, he said, would be accomplished in Ford's Theatre. They would seize him in the box from which Surratt and Powell had viewed *Jane Shore* that evening, lower him to the stage, and get him out the back door. They would handcuff him, chloroform him if necessary. The carpenter-stagehand Edman Spangler would douse the house lights so they could work in darkness.

The conspirators heard out their leader in silence, none interrupting, none indicating agreement or disagreement. Then John's ex-schoolmate Sam Arnold offered an opinion. The plan was utter madness, he said. Get the President down on the stage in front of an audience likely to contain a few hundred soldiers of the Union Army? Spirit him out the back past the actors? Then expect to pass through the city filled with troops, and police, and cavalry patrols, to a Potomac bridge—with nobody raising the alarm back at Ford's? "The height of madness," Arnold said.

It wasn't what John wanted to hear. Anyone who disagreed with the plan ought to be shot, he declared. "Two can play at that game," Arnold replied. The others got them calmed down—and the next day John apologized to Sam, saying it was the champagne speaking. The meeting went on, the theater idea shelved. They talked about some newly built barricades at the Potomac bridges. Could this mean the government had an inkling that a kidnapping was planned? They decided probably not. At five in the morning they broke up, their general agreement being that they should go ahead with a kidnapping, but not at a theater.

Two days later, March 17, their opportunity appeared to have arrived. They learned that the President was going to join an audience of wounded soldiers in viewing a matinee performance of *Still Waters Run Deep* at Campbell Hospital, one of dozens of such facilities in and around Washington. Located in a heavily wooded and thinly settled area, the hospital was reached by the Seventh Street Road, which led to the President's Soldiers' Home place. The road had presented itself to the conspirators in the past as a possible place to seize him. Now theater and place merged.

They rendezvoused in a tavern along the road at about two in the afternoon, all mounted. A carriage appeared carrying a single occupant. They surrounded it and looked in. It was not the President—they thought they recognized Chief Justice Chase. The carriage went on. They waited, Surratt and Arnold arguing that somehow the government was on to their plan, that the carriage was a decoy, and that at any minute cavalry would appear and arrest them all. John didn't think so. Perhaps Lincoln had gone by earlier and was at the Campbell Hospital. They could get him on his return trip. Leaving the others behind, John went up to the hospital and sought out the actor E. L. Davenport during intermission. "Hello, Ned," he said. "Who's in the house?"

Davenport mentioned some people. "Did the old man come?" John asked. Davenport said he had not. John turned to go. "You are in a great hurry," Davenport remarked.

"Yes, I'm trying a new horse and he is rather restive." He returned to the others and they went to the Surratt boardinghouse, John angrily slapping a riding whip against his leg as he entered. He went on to the National Hotel—to find Lincoln standing on the hotel balcony. His hospital outing had been changed in favor of presenting a captured Confederate battle flag to Governor Oliver Morton of Indiana. There was some difficulty in getting the flag correctly draped from the veranda over a replica of the American eagle, and Lincoln got a laugh by telling the crowd that the problem resulted from the eagle's objection to having the flag put over it. Down below stood Thomas Richardson, leaning against a lamppost. He had known John Booth for years. "Have you come to hear the great Lincoln speak?" Richardson asked. A woman wearing a thick blue veil came up—Richardson could not make out her features—and John said, "No, no; not now! I will see you shortly. Go away, now; go away! I will let you know! I will let you know!"

From the balcony Lincoln was speaking of a report that the desperate South was going to take black men into its army. "Don't you think Mr. Lincoln looks pale and haggard?" Richardson asked.

"Yes, he does." What a furious look John was wearing, Richardson thought. Actorlike, Richardson decided, he was showing how he could "transform his beautiful face into that of a demon." The day's activities had turned out farcical, ridiculous. That night Arnold and O'Laughlen left to get jobs in Baltimore, and soon Surratt also would be gone. Powell, Herold, and Atzerodt stayed in Washington, eating on John's money. The next night, March 18, he appeared as Pescara in *The Apostate* at Ford's Theatre. Louis Weichmann, one of Mrs. Surratt's boarders, never saw a man play with such intensity and passion. John's face as he put a woman to torture on the wheel in his capacity as the evil villain of the piece was hideous, malevolent, distorted, his eyes filled with a fierce glare, rolling in an ugly way, and, to Weichmann's thinking, ready to burst from their sockets. Four days later President Lincoln departed Washington to visit General Grant at his Virginia headquarters. It was the nearest approach to a vacation that Lincoln took in the war. John went to New York.

Edwin's great hundred-performance run of *Hamlet* ended on the day Lincoln left for Grant's headquarters. For all of that time audiences had risen and gone into the street, *Harper's* said, bearing with them forever "the golden thread of a fresh vision of beauty."

Adam Badeau was again staying at Edwin's, recovering from a bout of what was called camp fever incurred at Grant's headquarters in City Point. He renewed his acquaintance with his host's brother, whom he thought "excessively handsome. Even physically finer than Edwin." When Adam took his leave to rejoin Grant, John pleasantly wished him well. It seemed to Edwin in those days that his dead Mary was with him yet in spirit, and when he began a romance with Blanche Hanel of Philadelphia and reached an understanding about marriage with her, he said it was Mary who had sent Blanche to him. She was the only child of a prominent Philadelphia jeweler. The magazine publisher Alexander K. McClure thought her a "very beautiful and accomplished lady." They decided their wedding would be in September.

His great success as Hamlet and resulting designation as Prince of Players of the American stage did not change Edwin. In fact, he wrote Emma Cary, the widow of his friend Richard Cary, who had died in Union Army service, it meant that Edwin Booth was in a sense gone—that he was not present much of the time. "It's an awful thing to be somebody else all the while," he told Mrs. Cary. It made him feel more and more alone, more familiar with the unseen world than the real one "in which I find so little in sympathy with my soul." But perhaps Blanche could help once they were married. And he was glad that the war seemed about to conclude. "Yes, our news is indeed glorious. I am happy in it, and glory in it, although Southern-born. God grant the end, or rather the beginning, is now at hand. For when the war ceases, we shall only have begun to live—a nation never to be shaken again, ten times more glorious, a million times firmer than before."

He did not wish to argue about the conflict with John, did not want to hear his arguments about how the South was right, nor a bitter song he sang whose every verse ended with a prediction that soon Lincoln would be king of America. John went back to Washington to drink wine with the brothers John T. and Henry C. Ford, Harry to everybody, whose theater bore their name. In two weeks, he told them, something would happen that would astonish the world. "What are you going to do?" Harry Ford asked. "Kill Jeff Davis, take Richmond, or play Hamlet a hundred nights?" He visited Asia in Philadelphia.

She was pregnant, expecting her third child in August. If it was a boy, she had told him, it would be named for him—John Wilkes Booth Clarke. Earlier he had written her of winning a raffle. The prize was a complete set of clothes for an infant. Everybody laughed at the bachelor's trophy. "I was dreadfully shamefaced," he wrote, "but all at once, like a blessing, I recollected my expected nephew and was able to reply confidently, 'These are most acceptable. I am in expectation of the safe arrival of a little nephew or niece.' Quick as thought then the health and safety of mother and babe were wished, and I walked down the long room carrying my baby clothes which shall be sent to you express. Asia, I thank you for the coming child." He still could not get used to her actually being a mother, she wrote her Baltimore friend Jean Anderson, laughed outrageously at the idea, and said he couldn't believe it even as he played on the floor with her children.

Her marriage was not happy. Not for the first time her brother suggested divorce. When they parted he knelt by where she sat on a sofa and she stroked his black hair. "I hope you will keep well and get stronger, dear," he said. They kissed. "Oh, my boy, I shall never be happy till I see your face again," she said. Over her children's bed he had put a picture of himself, saying, "Remember me, babies, in your prayers."

In New York, he had spent an evening with Sam Chester, the actor he had failed to enroll in the abduction plot. They were again in the House of Lords on Houston Street in lower Broadway. They ate Welsh rabbit. He talked about Lucy Hale, and kissed the ring she had given him. He told Chester how she had gotten him a ticket to stand on the platform when Lincoln was sworn in a month earlier. "What a splendid chance I had to kill the President!" he said, slapping his hand on the table. Chester told him he must be a fool or crazy. "What good would it do to commit an act like that?"

John replied that if he did it his name would live in history. Chester said that he could gain glory and reputation in acting, and John told him that some people could not be reasoned with. He was like Edwin, John informed Chester, the Edwin who had once ordered him out of his house for expressing sentiments in favor of the Confederacy. A man at the next table seemed to be listening to their conversation, and John said, "If there is one thing I despise more than another it is a damned scoundrel that will listen to what others are saying!" They moved to another table, ate more Welsh rabbit, drank ale. He kept kissing the ring. When the bill came he refused to let Chester pay half. He went up to Newport, Rhode Island, and registered for an Aquidneck Hotel room as J. W. Booth & Lady.

Not Lucy, of course, not the daughter of a former U.S. congressman and senator and minister-designate to Spain checking into a hotel with a lover. All through their romance he had amused himself with other women, principally the nineteen-year-old, good-looking blonde Ella Turner, also known as Ella Starr, who resided in a Washington bordello run by her sister. The girls' mother owned it. She knew she would never have him for herself, and letters she wrote him showed the tone of their relationship: *My Darling Boy: Please call this evening as soon as you receive this note. I will not detain you for five minutes—for God's sake come. Yours truly, E.T. If you will not come write a note the reason why.* There were other women. *The saddest words of tongue or pen / are these few / it might have been. Eva. In John's room.* From one Etta: *I do as you desired and keep as secluded as a nun, which is not agreeable to me as you have found out ere this, but anything to oblige you darling.* And: *I know important business kept you away today. Will you please try & come tomorrow as soon after two as possible? You can dine privately with me. So do not mind your dinner. I trust you are feeling better today. Be very good until I see you. Anything that pleases you will be acceptable. God bless you, my precious friend. N. One sweet little kiss.*

■

Lincoln on his half holiday rode about the Virginia countryside on one of Grant's horses, so tall and ungainly, soldiers thought, that he gave the appearance of a praying mantis whose long legs were in danger of becoming entangled with those of his steed. He took carriage rides with his wife. They passed once by a graveyard along the James. "Mary," he said, "you are younger than I. You will survive me. When I am gone, lay my remains in some quiet place like this." The war had been very hard for her. Their son William Wallace Lincoln, very bright, far more promising than Tad, a scholarly little fellow who kept lists of dates and places and wrote poetry, had died in the White House at age twelve. She had endured constant, widespread, and unjust accusations that she was a rebel spy whose sympathies were with the Confederacy in whose service she had lost brothers and half brothers, including one, Alex, who had been the darling of her heart when they were young. She had always been ferociously jealous of her husband, and at a City Point review of the Army of the Potomac her half madness boiled to the surface as she sat in an ambulance-carriage with Grant's wife and his aide Colonel Adam Badeau, recovered from camp fever and back from Edwin's. He mentioned something about the President giving the wife of General Charles Griffin permission to visit the front lines in front of Richmond and Petersburg.

"What do you mean by that, sir?" Mrs. Lincoln demanded. "Do you know that I never allow the President to see any woman alone?" Adam tried to offer a reassuring grin. It had the opposite effect. "That's a very equivocal smile, sir!" Julia Grant tried to calm the President's lady, but Mrs. Lincoln demanded that the carriage be halted. "Let me out at once. I will ask the President if he saw that woman alone!" She reached past Mrs. Grant and clutched at the driver. The general's wife managed to quiet her. But the scene was so mortifying that Julia Grant and Adam Badeau agreed they must speak of it to nobody.

At another review her incipient insanity showed itself again. Traveling with Mrs. Grant, Adam, and Colonel Horace Porter in an ambulance, she saw General Edward Ord's wife, chic in feathered Robin Hood cap of a type popularized by the Empress Eugénie, riding near the President. "What does that woman mean by riding by the side of the President?" she raved. "Does she suppose that *he* wants *her* by the side of *him*?" The carriage was standing in a sea of mud, but she demanded to be allowed to get out. "There come Mrs. Lincoln and Mrs. Grant," said the unsuspecting Mrs.

Ord to the people she was with. "I think I had better join them."
She rode up and was greeted with a flood of horrifying insults
pouring out of the mouth of the President's lady. Badeau and
Colonel Porter were actually afraid that she would get out and
attack Mrs. Ord in front of the lined-up troops. Badeau began to
understand a puzzling remark the wife of Secretary of War Stanton
once made to him. He had happened to ask something about Mrs.
Lincoln, and Mrs. Stanton appeared to say that she did not speak
with Mrs. Lincoln. Badeau decided he had not heard correctly.
Surely the wife of the secretary of war must have social relations
with the wife of the President. "Understand me, sir," Mrs. Stanton
said. "I do not go to the White House. I do not visit Mrs. Lincoln."

The President bore his wife's rages martyrlike, soothing her
with soft words, an inexpressible sadness shining from the eyes of
a face that Colonel Theodore Lyman wrote his wife was the ugliest
he had ever seen. Lyman was not alone in his estimate of the
President's looks, and indeed Lincoln liked to tell about how once,
sitting in an Illinois railroad car, he was approached by a stranger
who said he had something in his possession that was Lincoln's
property. But, Lincoln asked, how could that be? The two had
never met. The other man explained that he had once been given
an award for being the ugliest person in creation, but now he had
met his master and could no longer in good conscience retain the
prize. He handed it over to Lincoln, a fine penknife.

On April 1 the forty miles of line north of Richmond and
south of Petersburg which Lee had held for nine months began to
crack. That was on a Saturday. The next morning Jefferson Davis
was handed a telegram while he sat at Sunday church services in
Richmond's St. Paul's. It was from Lee. Richmond must be evacu-
ated at once. The population began to run for it, wagons loaded
with valuables bouncing through the streets, people racing about
offering any amount of money for transportation out. In the evening's darkness the Confederate Army poured through. Ammuni-
tion magazines were exploded to save them from the Yankees,
gunboats were loaded with kegs of powder to be burned and sunk
in the James, the railroad trestle and bridge were readied for de-
struction when the last of the soldiers had gone. In the early morning hours of April 3, Monday, just before first light, the fuses in the
gunboats ignited the powder kegs and the boats vanished in a roar
of spray and noise that shattered windows two miles distant. The
immense tobacco warehouses, fired by government order, sent
flames hundreds of feet into the air, and cinders from those fires

came down to light new ones which would destroy a third of Richmond. Engineers of the departing Army of Northern Virginia lit piles of turpentine-drenched wood stacked on the bridges and they went up, long strings of flame spanning the James and reflected in the waters below.

The rebel army and government went on its way and behind it the capital of the Confederacy endured a fate no other American city ever knew. President Lincoln came and walked through the city with a dozen sailors armed with carbines, and his guard, William H. Crook, carrying a Colt revolver, to be seen by young Mary Beale, whom John Booth a few years earlier had taken from her crib to be placed on a silver serving platter—all actors were crazy, the child's nurse had declared—and to whom he had given a gold and blue enamel ring too large for her finger. Now it fitted. She looked at the President. There was something kind about his eyes, she thought.

Up from Newport and in Boston, his companion of the Aquidneck Hotel departed, John presented the man who had acted as his informal agent in some Commonwealth Avenue land purchases with a ring signifying his gratitude, and went to a shooting gallery, where he fired at targets over his shoulder and under his arm. He called on Edwin in the dressing room of the theater where he was performing. James Brown, Edwin's black valet whom John had known when he played Richmond, was with them. "Well, Jim," John said, "Richmond has fallen at last. What do you think of it?"

"Poor Richmond!" Brown said.

"Sorry, you rascal!" Edwin said, snorting. "You ought to be glad. It has been a great blessing to mankind that it has fallen." At once John had something to say, and the brothers began to dispute the war's issues.

"Good-bye, Ned," John finally said. "You and I could never agree on that question. I could never argue with you."

He went back to Washington, where Secretary of War Stanton was in a fury with Lincoln for the President's all but unguarded tour of the just-taken Confederate capital. "That fool!" Stanton raged. (Earlier he had wired the President, "Ought you to expose the Nation to the consequences of any disaster to yourself in the pursuit of a treacherous and dangerous enemy like the rebel army?")

On April 8, as Grant's men rushed westward after the fleeing Lee, President and Mrs. Lincoln sailed from City Point to Washington. With them were Senator and Secretary of the Interior-designate James Harlan of Iowa, reputedly the richest man in the Senate, and Mrs. Harlan. Robert Todd Lincoln had been paying marked attention to their daughter Mary, his interest in Lucy Hale—or hers in him—gone. Also along were Senator Charles Sumner of Massachusetts and his friend the French marquis Adolphe de Chambrun. To de Chambrun's thinking it was impossible to know the President and not feel the profoundness of his nature and enormous elevation of mind, and also the vast melancholy that overhung him. His powers of observation were extraordinary, the Frenchman felt, and extended in all directions. Once during the Virginia sojourn Lincoln had his carriage halted so he could look at an exceptionally tall and beautiful tree by the road. He extolled and defined its beauty, the trunk, the vigorous and harmoniously proportioned branches, and compared the tree's characteristics to others of different type. What mastery of descriptive language he had, de Chambrun wrote his wife in France, what absolute precision of mind.

Before the ship *River Queen* sailed for home, the President asked a military band to play "La Marseillaise" for the foreign visitor, and followed with a request for "Dixie." The tune was Federal property now, he said. "Besides, it is good to show the rebels that with us they will be free to hear it again." It was Sunday night. The travelers sat on deck and, as he so often did, the President recited aloud from Shakespeare. He spoke of the moral torment Macbeth felt after the murder of Duncan, and of how the murderer envied the victim's sleep:

> Duncan is in his grave.
> After Life's fitful fever he sleeps well;
> Treason has done its worst; not steel nor poison,
> Malice domestic, foreign levy, nothing
> Can touch him further.

He recited the lines a second time.

They passed George Washington's house and de Chambrun said that one day Mount Vernon and Lincoln's Springfield home would be equally honored. "Springfield!" Lincoln said. "How happy I shall be four years hence to return there in peace and tranquillity." At the Seventh Street wharf a carriage awaited. They rode toward the White House, and Mrs. Lincoln said the city was filled with enemies. "Enemies," the President said with an impatient gesture, "never again must we repeat that word."

NINE

WASHINGTON EXPLODED. Even as the President sailed North, Lee had surrendered at Appomattox. Bands played, parades wound their way through the streets, earth-shaking roars of artillery shattered the windows around Lafayette Square, people got drunk, flags waved, howitzers dragged from the Navy Yard fired as they moved along the avenues. The President was called upon by a great mass of people who greeted him with what his journalist friend Noah Brooks considered a display of absolute madness when he appeared at a window. The vast crowd looked like an agitated sea of hats, faces, arms. Tad waved a rebel flag. Lincoln told the people he did not wish to say much for fear of "dribbling" away the speech he planned for Tuesday evening, called for and led three tremendous cheers for the army and three for the navy, asked the band to render the captured "Dixie," and retired. To General William E. Doster it seemed as if he had put on new clothes and new grooming in his radiant happiness. "He seemed to me positively handsome."

In the evening all government buildings were illuminated, rockets and fireworks shot off into the sky, there were gorgeous transparencies everywhere showing words of praise and thanks— This Is the Lord's Doing; It is Marvelous in Our Eyes—U.S. Army, U.S. Navy, U. S. Grant—Glory to God Who to US GRANTED the Victory—speeches, songs, dancing. The once-great Confederate Army was down to weak shreds in North Carolina under General Joseph E. Johnston, preparing to surrender to William T. Sherman. Lee's men had stacked arms at Appomattox. Go home, obey the law, put in a crop, their ex-leader had told them. Farewell.

He walked through the city with Lewis Powell and Davy Herold, saw the crowds of triumphant Yankeedom, heard the cheers. At Fourteenth Street and Pennsylvania Avenue they ran into the song-writer Henry B. Phillips, who asked them to come for a drink. "Yes, anything to drive away the blues," John said.

"What is giving you the blues?" Phillips asked.

"This news is enough to give anyone the blues," John replied. He went on and met the actor Edwin A. Emerson and said, "Ned, did you hear what that old scoundrel did the other day?"

Emerson asked what he was talking about. "Why, that old scoundrel Lincoln," John said. He took a cane Emerson was holding, put it across his shoulders, and held each end in his hands. "He went into Jeff Davis's house in Richmond, sat down and threw his long legs over the arm of a chair and squirted tobacco juice all over the place." He was pulling down on the ends of the cane across his shoulders. It snapped. He handed the two pieces to their owner. "We are all slaves now," he told Harry Ford. How could Lee have given up? When he had accepted the sword put in his hands he had sworn he would never surrender it.

Yes, Ford said. But Lee was a brave general and a gentleman and must have known what he was doing. John mumbled that he himself was as good and as brave, and Ford said, "Well, you have not got three stars yet to show it." He went on Tuesday night with Powell and Herold to the White House grounds to hear Lincoln's promised speech. Washington was shrouded in mist. Across the Potomac at what had been the Arlington estate of Mrs. Robert E. Lee—now it had been seized for nonpayment of taxes and made into a giant Union Army cemetery—thousands of ex-slaves gathered to sing "The Year of Jubilee." The house was brilliantly illuminated, and colored lights blazed on the lawn.

The President stood on a balcony reading his prepared speech by the light of a candle held by Noah Brooks. Beneath him sat Tad Lincoln, catching the pages his father dropped as he finished with them. "Another, another," Tad kept saying. The theme of the speech was clemency for the South. Let the erring brethren come back into the Union with all privileges, Lincoln said. If 10 percent of the qualified voters of a state would take an oath of allegiance to the Federal government, let the state return, let her send congress-men and senators to Washington. Let the war be put behind the reunited union of states. As for the freed slaves and the possibility of giving them the vote, Lincoln said he thought it should be conferred upon those who could read and those who had served in the Union Army.

In the darkness John hissed, "That means nigger citizenship!" The word did not possess quite the pejorative connotation it would gain later. He had grown up with blacks, felt their transport to the New World was a blessing for them when contrasted with those left behind in Africa, had said he would do anything to elevate the race. Citizenship and voting, that was different. He began urging Lewis Powell to shoot the President as he stood on the balcony. John Brown had been hanged. Now Lincoln was doing Brown's work. One had been a criminal. What was the other? His voice was attracting attention, and Powell and Herold urged that they leave.

"Somebody ought to kill him," he had said as he snapped Ned Emerson's cane. "Now, by Christ, I'll put him through," he snarled at Powell and Herold when the President spoke of giving selected blacks the vote. "That is the last speech he will ever make," he muttered as they got him away.

Twenty-six years old, intelligent, well paid—he was good for twenty-five, thirty thousand a year, he told his fellow conspirators—engaged to a much-sought-after girl of the highest social standing and with a plentitude of other women on the string, the son of a great actor, charming, well beloved by his fellows, his dead father's favorite, his mother's pride and joy! How many men in the country—in the *world*—would have declined to change places with him?

Yet in those days after the fall of Richmond and the surrender at Appomattox, he took liquor as John Deery, the national billiards champion and a saloonkeeper, had never seen him do before. "He now sometimes drank at my bar as much as a quart of brandy in less than two hours." He went about Washington nights to see the thirty-five hundred celebratory candles flickering in the windows of the Post Office building, and the nearly six thousand at the Patent Office, and when he mentioned them in Grover's Theatre, heard the proprietors were planning their own big lighting display. In Pennsylvania Avenue he ran into a New York State schoolgirl visiting the city and spending much of her time with another girl who lived at the National Hotel with her parents. John had spoken to them of the importance of clear speech and had them read aloud while he carefully offered suggestions on their accents and expression. The girl told him she was headed for a shop to buy candies. Despite the elocution lessons, he misunderstood what she said.

"What do you want with more candles?" he asked. "The

windows are full of them now, and when they are lit I wish they would burn every house to the ground. I would rejoice at the sight." Something must be wrong with him, she thought. He had always been so winning, gentle, pleasant. "I guess I'm a little desperate this morning," he was saying, "and, do you know, I feel like mounting my horse and tearing up and down the streets, waving a rebel flag in each hand till I have driven the poor animal to death."

She started to say something and he interrupted her. "Don't you study Latin at school?"

She did. "Then tell me this: Is *tyrannis* spelled with two *n*'s or two *r*'s?"

She told him how she thought it was spelled. He went on, heard the horns and whistles, ringing bells, continual music, gun salutes, the cheers, the toasts to final victory, talked with Lucy at the hotel, gave Mrs. Surratt ten dollars to rent a buggy and wagon so, she said later, she could go to her Surrattsville place thirteen miles from the city to see about some money she was owed there. In the early morning hours of Friday he wrote:

Dearest Mother, I know you expect a letter from me. But indeed I have had nothing to write about. Everything is dull; that is, has been until last night. Everything was bright and splendid. More so in my eyes if it had been displayed in a nobler cause. But so goes the world. Might makes right. I only drop you these few lines to let you know I am well and to say I have not heard from you. Excuse brevity; I am in haste. Had one from Rose.* With best love to you all I am your affectionate son ever. John.

The letter was, of course, bland and perfunctory, quite different in tone from the one she had sent him two and a half weeks earlier. In that strange way she had of knowing him from afar, of knowing, as the actress Mrs. Anne Hartley put it, when he was in danger or in trouble, she had written of her sadness in parting from him when he left New York, of how she remained sad at his absence. Something hung in the air above him. She sensed it. *I have never doubted your love and devotion to me; in fact, I always gave you praise for being the fondest of all my boys, but since you leave me to grief I must doubt it. I am no Roman mother. I love my dear ones before country or anything else. Heaven guard you, is my constant prayer. Your loving mother.*

He slept. Not at the National Hotel. When the maid came in she found his bed made up. Perhaps he had been with Ella Turner in the bordello where she lived with her sister, 62 Ohio Avenue. He

---

**His sister Rosalie.*

returned to the hotel to be the last person entering the dining room for breakfast. Afterward he sat in a parlor and talked with Lucy, was shaved in a barber shop, and walked over to Ford's Theatre to pick up any mail they had for him. It was about noon, Good Friday, April 14, 1865. He was in a dark suit and light drab over-coat, wearing gloves and carrying a cane and with a black silk hat, slightly tipped, on his head. The theater manager, John T. Ford, off to occupied Richmond to be with an uncle he had not visited since the war began, had often in the past seen John Booth walking up to the theater. "As he passed, four out of five on the street would turn to look at him again, such was his personal magnetism." John T. Ford's brother Harry was standing in front of the building with some friends. "Here comes the handsomest man in Washington," Harry Ford remarked.

At that hour the United States flag was being raised on the flagpole at Fort Sumter, South Carolina, where four years to the day earlier it had been lowered following the rain of Confederate shells that began the war. The officer who had then surrendered the garrison, Robert Anderson, was there, and also the minister Henry Ward Beecher, who expressed thanks that the President of the United States had been spared to see the happy reuniting of the divided house, the end of the war of brothers.

The subject of the minister's consideration was at that moment in a White House gathering he had convened through Frederick W. Seward: *Acting Secretary of State: Please call a Cabinet meeting at eleven o'clock today. General Grant will be with us.* Frederick Seward, normally his father's assistant, held his temporary position because of Secretary William H. Seward's incapacitating accident of nine days earlier. The secretary had been out driving with ladies of his family. The door of the carriage kept opening. The coachman halted his team and got down from the box to see to it. As he stood on the pavement the horses began to move, picked up speed, and ran driverless through the street. Secretary Seward tried to grab the loose reins, caught his heel, and was pitched forward on his face into the street. When finally a passing cavalry officer halted the runaways and Miss Fanny Seward leaped out and ran back to where her father lay unconscious, she thought he was dead. He was not, although grievously injured, his right arm broken close to the shoulder, his jaw fractured, his face terribly bruised. He was taken home to lie with his arm in the air and his lower jaw and neck encased in heavy leather and steel fittings.

It was, of course, impossible for Seward to attend the Cabinet meeting, and so his son, acting in his stead, sat with Secretaries Stanton, McCullough, Welles, and Speed, and heard Postmaster General Dennison ask if the President would pursue the rebel leaders fled from Richmond, or simply hope they would depart the country. Lincoln replied he had no urge to take them prisoners and would wish them gone. "Frighten them out of the country, open the gates, let down the bars, scare them off—shoo!" He waved his hands as if driving chickens out of a garden. "Enough lives have been sacrificed," he said. "No one need expect me to take any part in hanging or killing these men, even the worst of them."

They spoke of reinstituting U.S. federal courts and custom-houses in the Southern states, harbor controls, the postal system. There was a general quality, Acting Secretary Seward felt, of kind-ness for the vanquished, a desire to restore peace and safety to the former enemy regions with as little harm as possible to feelings and property. Toward the end of the meeting the President spoke of a dream he had. It was a recurring dream, he said, and came to him before Fort Sumter, Bull Run, Antietam, Gettysburg, Stone River, Vicksburg. "I had this strange dream again last night, and we shall, judging from the past, have great news soon. I think it must be from Sherman." That was logical—all their thoughts were of him and of the force under Confederate General Joseph E. Johnston, which, though they could not know of it in Washington, was even at the moment preparing to surrender, with its commander writing Sher-man that to continue to fight would constitute murder, not battle.

In his dream, Lincoln said, he had a vague sense of floating away on some vast and distant expanse toward an unknown shore. As he had said, great events always followed. Someone said that this could not be upon this occasion, that the dream could not presage a great victory or defeat. For the war was over, or just about. Someone else said it was just a coincidence, the dream. Young Seward offered the opinion that at each of the times the President's dream occurred there existed possibilities of great change, and a resulting feeling of uncertainty led to the dim vision in sleep. "Perhaps," Lincoln said. "Perhaps that is the explana-tion."

The meeting ended. Seward reminded the President that the new British minister to the United States was waiting to be received for presentation of his credentials. Lincoln thought for a moment and said, "Tomorrow at two o'clock." "In the Blue Room, I sup-pose?" "Yes, in the Blue Room. Don't forget to send up the speeches beforehand. I would like to look them over."

Everyone left save for the Lieutenant General Commanding the Armies of the United States, who remained behind at the President's request. It was an awkward moment for Grant. The previous night Mrs. Lincoln had sent him a note asking if he would like to accompany the President and herself in a ride around Washington to view the illuminations. There was no mention of Mrs. Grant. The general declined, citing the press of urgent business. That morning Mrs. Lincoln had sent an invitation for the general, and Mrs. Grant, to join the Presidential couple in a visit to the theater. But Julia Grant still remembered her extremely unpleasant experiences with Mrs. Lincoln at City Point, and the manner in which Mrs. Lincoln had later accused her of being disrespectful by seating herself while the wife of the President was standing. She had also indicated that she expected Mrs. Grant to back out of her presence in the fashion of someone leaving a European royalty, and had nastily asked if it was Mrs. Grant's plan to succeed to her Executive Mansion position. Julia Grant discussed the theater invitation with Mrs. Stanton, to whom overtures for a theater party had also been extended, and was told that Mrs. Stanton would never sit in a box with Mrs. Lincoln unless Mrs. Grant was also present. That decided the matter for the general's wife. An outing under such terms and circumstances could hardly be happily anticipated. She told her husband to tell the President they were leaving Washington to visit their children at school in New Jersey. To stiffen his resolve she sent him a note reiterating her desire, which was delivered during the Cabinet meeting. He showed the note to Lincoln, who excused him from the theater expedition.

But that was not known at Ford's Theatre, where a White House messenger had reserved a box for the Lincolns and the Grants, and so an advertisement announcing the forthcoming attendance of the President and general and their wives was written and sent for insertion in Washington's afternoon papers, the *Republican* and the *Star*. Good Friday was always a slow night, and perhaps Grant's presence might bring in a few customers. Lincoln's wouldn't do much for the box office—it was too common an occurrence. In the past Grant had proved only mildly interested in going to plays—once Grover's had announced he was coming, put a huge UNCONDITIONAL SURRENDER across the front of the stage, adorned the boxes with elaborately inscribed names of his western victories, Donelson, Vicksburg, Chattanooga—and he had failed to show up, leaving President and Mrs. Lincoln alone with Secretary of State Seward to watch Edwin Booth play Richard III. Manager

Leonard Grover announced from the stage that the general had been called away but would return to see Edwin play Hamlet the following night. He did not. Sherman was the military's premier theatrical expert, an avid playgoer and self-appointed critic whose analysis of players sometimes could be heard by people seated rows away.

John Booth sat on the theater steps reading his mail, laughing out loud at one point. The day was very pleasant. Spring was early, and the lilacs were out. The actor Harry Hawk, who would be appearing that night, came by. "How do you do, Mr. Booth?" "How are you, Hawk?" He finished his mail and went inside to glance at a rehearsal and then stand in the alley behind the theater to chat with an actress and be taken note of by a black woman who lived in a little house fronting the alley. "I stood at my gate and looked right wishful at him." A few doors away was a little stable with a few stalls. He had rented it for his three horses when the kidnapping plan was going forth. When it fell through, he sold the horses. The lease on the stable remained in force.

The box reserved for the Presidential party, top stage left, was the one occupied by Lewis Powell and John Surratt and the two boarders from Mrs. Surratt's on the night the conspirators met at Gautier's Restaurant, March 15, one month less one day earlier. To accommodate the Lincolns and Grants, it was being enlarged and specially decorated. The enlargement was achieved by removing a partition separating it from the adjoining box, thus combining the two boxes into one large one. Carpenter Edman Spangler, the conspirator whom John had designated to douse the theater lights when he planned to kidnap the President at the theater, took down the wall with the aid of two other theater employees. For decorations Harry Ford had the men put two U.S. flags across the box balustrade and hang other flags at both sides of the double box. At the center pillar were the regimental colors of the Treasury Guard, white spread eagle and stars on a blue ground. Ford had borrowed it for the occasion. Attached to the colors was a framed portrait of George Washington. The box draperies were of buff satin hanging from the arches, along with curtains of Nottingham lace. The deep red figured paper was of a floral design.

Upstairs in a private apartment over the theater there was a rocking chair of black walnut with seat, arms, and back upholstered in red damask. It had been sitting around to be occupied by stagehands and lounging actors, and Harry Ford had noticed its top was becoming stained with hair oil or grease, and so had it put up in the apartment. He got it down and placed it in the box. There were side chairs and a small sofa.

"Your friends Lincoln and Grant are coming to the theater tonight, John," Harry Ford remarked. He knew his listener's views. "They've got General Lee here as a prisoner," Ford bantered on, "and he's coming too. We're going to put him in the opposite box." There was no smile in response to his spoofing. John left the theater.

At the White House the President informed his wife that the Grants would not be joining them that evening at the theater. Originally Mrs. Lincoln had invited Speaker of the House of Representatives Schuyler Colfax and then, believing the Grants would come, rescinded the offer, telling Colfax in a note that she would ask him for "some other evening soon." Now she reinvited him. But he had meanwhile decided to leave for a western trip and so could not accept.

Robert Todd Lincoln had arrived that morning from a brief stint as an officer on Grant's staff—he had spent the war years at Harvard—and was invited to come along. He replied that he had not slept in a decent bed for weeks, occupied as he had been with chasing Lee to Appomattox, and was exhausted and wanted to go to bed early. He gave his father the most recent photograph of Lee, which he had picked up in Virginia. Lincoln looked at the picture of the man to whom he and General Winfield Scott had offered the field command of the Union Army just before the war began and said, "It is a good face; it is the face of a noble, noble, brave man. I am glad the war is over at last." He told Mrs. Lincoln he would like to take a carriage ride later in the afternoon, and when she asked if he wanted any guests to accompany them, said, "No, I prefer to ride by ourselves today." His appearance and manner were remarkably changed from the sad picture he had presented all through the long years of war and terrible casualties. The weary look he always wore save for when telling funny stories, Secretary of the Treasury Hugh McCulloch had noted at the Cabinet meeting, had disappeared. His face was "bright and cheerful." McCulloch had never seen him "so cheerful and happy." Secretary of War Stanton said to Attorney General Speed as they went down the White House steps together after the meeting, "Didn't our chief look *grand* today?"

John Booth went to the livery stable of James Pumphrey on C Street behind the National Hotel and said he wished to rent a particular little bay mare. He would pick her up later in the afternoon. He went down Pennsylvania Avenue and stepped into the dining room at the Willard. He sat down and stared at Julia Grant as she dined. She did not care for the manner in which he regarded her. He went to Mrs. Surratt's boardinghouse and spoke with the proprietor, and shortly she left for her Maryland place in a rented buggy carrying two parcels she delivered to her tenant there, John Lloyd, an alcoholic former Washington policeman. General Grant got back from the Executive Mansion and told his wife that he had explained to the President that they were off to visit their children in New Jersey. They would leave on the four o'clock. Mrs. Grant said, "When I went in to my lunch today, a man with a wild look followed me into the dining room, took a seat nearly opposite to me at the table, stared at me continually, and seemed to be listening to my conversation." "Oh, I suppose he did so merely from curiosity," the general replied.

After lunch at the White House the President met briefly with Vice President Andrew Johnson, one of the many people, at least a dozen, with whom he spoke privately in the course of the day. One such was former senator and now minister-designate to Spain John P. Hale, who came to ask for a fellow New Hampshire man what Hale termed "an act of clemency and kindness." It had to do with a minor case of fraudulent representation in the sale of war supplies. Lincoln went along with Hale's request for a pardon. Senator John Creswell of Maryland came and talked about an old friend who had joined the Confederate Army and was now a prisoner. He asked if Lincoln could arrange for the man's freedom, and the President, besieged by many similar requests, said Creswell reminded him of some young people who held a party on an island. When the festivities were concluded, they discovered their boat had vanished. "They were in sore trouble, and thought over all manner of devices for getting over the water, but without avail. After a time one of the boys proposed that each fellow should pick up the girl he liked the best and wade over with her. The masterly proposition was carried out, until all that were left upon the island were a little short chap and a great, long, gothic-built lady. Now, Creswell, you are trying to leave me in the same predicament. You fellows will succeed in carrying off one after another until nobody but Jeff Davis and myself will be left on the island, and then I won't know what to do. How should I feel? How should I look lugging him over?

"I guess the way to avoid such an embarrassing situation is to let them all out at once."

The time for his carriage ride with Mrs. Lincoln was approaching, but first he walked over to the War Department to see if the telegraph had brought any news of a Johnston surrender to Sherman. The White House guard William H. Crook, who had been with him in Richmond, went along. They saw some loud drunks in the street, not an unusual sight at a time when the Union victory had seemed to impose upon many men an obligation to get tight. Liquor made this group unpleasant. "Do you know," Lincoln said, "I believe there are men who want to take my life? And I have no doubt they will do it."

Crook did not understand. They had, after all, walked entirely unmolested through the streets of the enemy's capital. "Why do you think so, Mr. President?"

"Other men have been assassinated."

"I hope you are mistaken, Mr. President."

"If it is to be done, it is impossible to prevent it."

He had said that before, many times. When on Inauguration Day, six weeks earlier, the secretary of war had spoken of keeping a better watch on the President's life, Lincoln told him, "Stanton, it is useless. If it is the will of Providence that I should die by the hand of an assassin, it must be so." He had recently had an odd dream. Not the one about vague driftings to an unknown shore that presaged great events. "It is strange," he had said to Mrs. Lincoln and Marshal of the District of Columbia Ward Hill Lamon a couple of weeks earlier, "how much there is in the Bible about dreams." He had always believed that in each dream, could we find it, there was meaning. He also believed, Lamon knew, that he was what the world calls a man of destiny, and as such was interested in visions, and strange and wonderful things, vagaries, far boundaries to what was seen by human eyes. He believed, Lamon knew, that the inevitable was right. He had never forgotten, and often spoke of, the double vision in the mirror he had seen back in Springfield the night he was elected President: one image clear, the other wan and faded. It meant, Mary Lincoln had said, that he would be elected to two terms and serve but one. "With that firm conviction, which no philosophy could shake," Lamon wrote, "Mr. Lincoln moved through a maze of mighty events, calmly waiting the inevitable hour of his fall by a murderous hand."

Yes, strange, the President said, how the Bible so often spoke of dreams. "There are, I think, some sixteen chapters in the Old Testament, and about four or five in the New in which dreams are mentioned. If we believe the Bible, we must accept the fact that in the old days God and His angels came to men in their sleep and made themselves known in dreams. Nowadays dreams are regarded as very foolish, and are seldom told, except by old women and young men and maidens in love.

"I had one the other night which has haunted me ever since. I am afraid that I am wrong to mention the subject at all; but somehow the thing has got possession of me, and, like Banquo's ghost, it will not down.

"About ten days ago, I retired very late. I had been up waiting for important dispatches from the front. I could not have been long in bed when I fell into a slumber, for I was weary. I soon began to dream. There seemed to be a death-like stillness about me. Then I heard subdued sobs, as if a number of people were weeping. I thought I left my bed and wandered downstairs. There the silence was broken by the same pitiful sobbing, but the mourners were invisible. I went from room to room; no living person was in sight, but the same mournful sounds of distress met me as I passed along. It was light in all the rooms; every object was familiar to me; but where were all the people who were grieving as if their hearts would break? I was puzzled and alarmed. What could be the meaning of all this? Determined to find the cause of a state of things so mysterious and shocking, I kept on until I arrived in the East Room, which I entered. There I met with a sickening surprise. Before me was a catafalque, on which rested a corpse wrapped in funeral vestments. Around it were stationed soldiers who were acting as guards; and there was a throng of people, some gazing mournfully upon the corpse, whose face was covered, others weeping pitifully. 'Who is dead in the White House?' I demanded of one of the soldiers. 'The President,' was his answer, 'he was killed by an assassin!' Then came a loud burst of grief from the crowd, which awoke me from my dream. I slept no more that night, and although it was only a dream, I have been strangely annoyed by it ever since."

"That is horrid!" Mrs. Lincoln said. "I wish you had not told it. I am glad I don't believe in dreams, or I should be in terror from this time forth."

"Well, it is only a dream, Mary. Let us say no more about it, and try to forget it."

But he spoke of it again to Lamon, quoting, " 'To sleep; perchance to dream! Aye, there's the rub.' " But "Don't you see how it will turn out?" Lincoln asked. "In this dream it was not me, but some other fellow, who was killed. It seems that this ghostly assassin tried his hand on someone else. As long as this imaginary

assassin continues to exercise himself on others I can stand it."
Then, seriously: "Well, let it go. I think the Lord in His own good
time will work this out all right."

With the guard Crook he entered the War Department,
learned there was no news yet of a Johnston surrender to Sherman,
asked Secretary Stanton if one of his aides, an officer so powerful
he could break fire pokers over his arm one after the other, might
accompany him to the theater that night, was told the officer had
work to do, and headed back for the White House. Crook would
be going off duty, and the President said, "Good-bye, Crook."

Always before the President had said "good night" and not
"good-bye." Crook was quite certain of that. "I remember distinctly the shock of surprise and the impression, at the time, that
he had never said it before."

In the carriage with his wife Lincoln said, "I have never felt so
happy in my life," and a certain unease took her. "Don't you
remember feeling so just before our little boy died?" she asked.

"We must be more cheerful in the future, Mary," he answered. "Between the war and the loss of our darling Willie we
have been very miserable. We have had a hard time of it since we
came to Washington." Now things would be different. They would
lay by some money and then go back to Illinois and he would open
a law office and do enough to give them a livelihood. And they
would travel—out to the West Coast, where perhaps Robert and
Tad might wish to settle, for there would be great opportunities for
the boys out there. Or perhaps when he got out of office they might
travel abroad, Europe, the Holy Land. Of all places on earth, he
longed most to see Jerusalem.

John Booth picked up his rented mare and went over to Grover's
and into the manager's office, where he wrote a long letter. He rode
up Pennsylvania Avenue and on the north side of Thirteenth Street
saw the actor John Mathews on the sidewalk. He had once tried
unsuccessfully to recruit Mathews for the kidnapping scheme.
Mathews wasn't interested. Now he was appearing at Ford's
Theatre—would be appearing that night. He had taken over the
room in the Petersen boardinghouse across the street from Ford's,
where John fell asleep smoking a pipe of Charles Warwick's, but
had vacated it a week before. "John," Mathews asked, "have you
seen the prisoners?" A long line of stragglers from Lee's army was
being marched through the street under guard. That was becoming
a common Washington sight. The marquis de Chambrun had

noted how people seemed to avoid looking at prisoners, "as though not wishing to hurt the feelings" of men now seen as pawns misled by the South's leaders. It was striking, he wrote his wife, how rapidly the people of the North had decided to forgive and forget. He also told his wife that he had been asked to go to the theater with the Lincolns but "with some hesitation" excused himself, "not liking, even at the risk of offending White House etiquette, to attend a theatrical performance on Good Friday."

"Yes," John said in response to Mathews's question about the prisoners, "I have." He put his hand to his forehead. "Great God!" he cried. "I no longer have a country!" He seemed extremely agitated and nervous to Mathews, who decided that he must have been drinking. He leaned over the horse's neck, took Mathews's hand, and gripped it so tightly that his fingernails dug in. "I wish to ask you a favor; will you do it for me?"

"Of course." Mathews had always liked him, found him "a most winning, captivating man." John was still holding his hand.

"I have a letter which I wish you to deliver to the publishers of the *National Intelligencer* tomorrow morning, unless I see you in the meantime. I may leave tonight, and it will not be much trouble for you to deliver the letter." It was very important, he said. He hesitated to trust it to the mails. Mathews decided it must have something to do with business matters, gold fluctuations or oil speculations or something of the kind, and agreed to do as asked. An open carriage passed up Pennsylvania Avenue. "John," Mathews said, "there goes General Grant. I understood he was coming to the theater tonight with the President." His listener turned hurriedly in the saddle with an anxious look, squeezed his hand, said, "Good-bye; perhaps I will see you again," and galloped after the carriage.

He went up past it, then reversed the mare to go back and to stare directly into the faces of the occupants. "That is the man who looked at me during luncheon," Julia Grant told her husband. The carriage went on its way to the depot from which the Grants would begin the trip to their children in New Jersey. The horseman who had gazed at them put his mount into his rented stable in the alley behind Ford's Theatre and had Ed Spangler feed and water her.

Inside the theater, the prop man James Maddox asked John if he'd like to get a drink at the Star Saloon next door. Maddox had always been fond of him. "He had such a very winning way that it made every person like him. He was a good-natured and jovial kind of man. The people about the house, as far as I know, all liked him." There was none of the gap often found between a starring player and the foot soldiers of a theater and a play. "No, thanks," John said. "I've a touch of pleurisy, and I don't think I'll drink anything." But he said he'd walk over with Maddox, "Peanut" John Burrough, a choreboy whose nickname came from his sales of that commodity to theatergoers, Spangler, and young W. J. Ferguson, a callboy whose duty it was to alert players that their cue to go onstage was coming up. Young Ferguson was hoping to be an actor, and now and then was given a small part. His stage debut had come a year earlier, when as an attendant escorting the body of Henry IV he got to ask John Booth as Richard III, "Towards Chertsey, my lord?" and to be told in return, "No, to Whitefriars, there to await my coming." He had always worshipped John, thinking him high-spirited, dashing, buoyant, amusing, and full of fun. Once a prompter forgot a cue signaling a flourish of trumpets, and John had picked up a wedge used for steadying scenery and heaved it at the prompter, carefully missing his head by a fraction of an inch, the toss unseen by the audience for the knights at arms blocking their view. The music drowned out Ferguson's loud laugh. He admired the star also for his ability with a foil. Once he saw him after rehearsal take on two opponents at once and disarm both in a moment, one of their swords flying up into the box the President would occupy for that night's play, in which Ferguson would get to say ten lines onstage.

In the saloon Maddox had a beer and Ferguson a sarsaparilla, and John said, "I think I'll reconsider and have a glass of ale." He paid the bill, the others his guests, and the group left, they to take an early dinner before the play and he to spend some time in the theater by himself. His brother would never have mixed with such as these. Edwin always left generous gifts for the stagehands and lighting people when he concluded an engagement, but to drink and gossip and chaff with them—impossible.

He went to the National Hotel, to be seen by a woman guest who had noticed that since Lee's surrender he had seemed more silent than usual, cooler, even cold. The woman had considered going to Ford's Theatre that evening with Mrs. Hale, the minister-designate's wife, Lucy's mother, but John Booth had advised the two not to do so, "that it was Good Friday, and that few people would be present, and the play would drag on that account." They decided to postpone attendance until the following night. He sat with Lucy in a parlor brilliantly lit in front, but dark in the rear, where they were. Lucy was in a huge red velvet armchair, her black silk outfit set off by the darkness and red background. He was beside and above her. It seemed to the woman that Lucy was as the charmed princess of *The Arabian Nights*, spellbound by a man whose qualities "made him a romantic maiden's ideal personified."

Then they dined, the woman, Mr. and Mrs. Hale, an English lady visiting Washington, Lucy and her unannounced fiancé. He took out his watch when they finished and said, "I must go." He bowed, walked to the door, came back, returned to the table, and took Lucy's hand. " 'Nymph, in thy orisons / Be all my sins remembered.' " He smiled and was gone. The others talked a while, and the woman kissed Lucy. "My dear, you look lovely tonight— sweeter and prettier than I ever saw you."

The President by then was back from his ride. As his carriage pulled up to the White House he saw Governor Richard J. Oglesby and General Isham Haynie walking away. "Come back, boys, come back!" he called, waving his arms at two fellow townsmen from Springfield. They turned and went inside with him and upstairs, where he read aloud from the ruminations of the humorist Petroleum V. Nasby on the probable results of the end of the war. He asked the two if they'd like to go to the theater with him, but they were off to a meeting of the Illinois senatorial and congressional delegations at Willard's. He continued reading to them, was informed dinner was served, and continued reading. Finally a servant explained to Governor Oglesby that as the President was going to the theater, he really had to get to the table.

He dined. Noah Brooks dropped in, suffering from a bad cold. The President told him he'd been thinking of sending for him to go to the theater, but Brooks went home to get to bed early and nurse his illness. The President signed a few papers, including the appointment of the territorial governor of Nebraska, and spoke briefly with a few people. The card of Senator William Stewart of Nevada was brought up with a note on it saying Stewart wished to introduce an acquaintance to him. Stewart got back: *I am engaged to go to the theater with Mrs. Lincoln. It is the kind of engagement I never break. Come with your friend tomorrow at ten, and I shall be glad to see you. A. Lincoln.* The card of Representative George Ashmun of Massachusetts was brought up, and Lincoln sent back a card of his own: *April 14, 1865. Allow Mr. Ashmun & friend to come in at 9 A.M. tomorrow. A. Lincoln.*

He went with his wife to his carriage. It was a little past eight o'clock. Former congressman Isaac Arnold of Illinois came walking up and asked to speak to him. "Excuse me now," the President said. "I am going to the theater. Come and see me in the morning." The carriage got rolling. Coachman Francis Burns and valet-messenger Charles Forbes were on the box. There were two cavalry outriders. The White House guard John F. Parker walked off to Ford's Theatre, a few minutes' stroll. Parker had held his job for eleven days, appointed from the Metropolitan Police to replace guard Thomas Pendel, who had been promoted to doorkeeper in place of the former holder of that post, fired by Mrs. Lincoln for lingering about after she had directed him to take notices to the newspapers of a forthcoming reception.

The carriage headed toward the home of Senator and Mrs. Ira Harris at Fifteenth and H streets. He was a former New York State Supreme Court justice elected to succeed William H. Seward when the latter became secretary of state. Seward's daughter Fanny felt that the senator's wife when met with the wife of Senator John Crittenden presented the appearance of "two very fat bundles of hair, feathers, lace and jewelry who grow dreadfully uninteresting." But Mrs. Lincoln was fond of Mrs. Harris. The President had gotten up during the Inaugural Ball six weeks earlier to give her his seat, and stood behind it while she sat with Mrs. Lincoln. She was not Senator Harris's first wife and had been the widow Mrs. Pauline Rathbone of Albany when he, a widower, married her. She had a son, Henry, who had been seventeen when his father died, leaving a large fortune earned in the manufacture of stoves.

The senator had a daughter, Clara. His marriage to the former Mrs. Rathbone made Clara Harris and Henry Rathbone stepsister and stepbrother. A different relationship came into being: They were engaged. He was twenty-eight and a major in the army. She was twenty-three and, like her mother, a friend of Mrs. Lincoln. Clara Harris had been at the White House to witness the President's nighttime speech on Tuesday, as had the marquis de Chambrun, and afterward sat chatting with the Presidential couple and the French visitor.

The carriage picked up Major Rathbone and Miss Harris and went to Ford's. The two couples entered. Mrs. Lincoln wore a black and white striped gown with black lace veiling on her hair and a black coal scuttle bonnet. Her coat was of black velvet edged with ermine. The President was in a black frock coat and silk hat. In his pockets were spectacles in a silver case, an Irish linen handkerchief with *A. Lincoln* worked in red, an ivory pocket knife trimmed in silver, a velvet eyeglass cleaner, a wallet of brown leather lined with purple silk containing, among other things, eight newspaper clippings favorable to him, and a Confederate States of America five-dollar bill with Jefferson Davis on its face.

The theater program boy, Joseph Hazelton, standing in the lobby, handed out four programs. Both Lincolns smiled at him. He had once been presented to the President at the White House through an army officer relative. "Joseph, I am glad to form your acquaintance," the President had said, and twice thereafter greeted him by name at Ford's. Earlier in the day young Hazelton had talked about his ambition to graduate from handing out programs to going on the stage with John Booth, whom he believed to be the best actor in the Booth family. "We have been good friends, Joseph, eh?" John had said when they finished their chat. "Try to think well of me. And this will buy a stick of candy." He handed over a ten-cent shinplaster—paper money. It was not his first gift. One day he had run into the boy at Tenth Street near Pennsylvania Avenue and taken note of his headgear. "Joseph, is that your best cap?"

"Yes, Mr. Booth."

"Well, Joseph, it pleases me not at all. I like not your cap. Come with me."

They went into a shop. "Kindly fit my young friend here with a cap more befitting his professional duties," he told the store-keeper. "One who makes known the players of great parts should be surmounted with a proper crown." He remarked to Joseph that Shakespeare was a great religious teacher but that people did not realize it because his lessons were cast in stage, dramatic, form.

The play whose program Joseph handed to the four members of the Presidential party, *Our American Cousin*, by Tom Taylor, was hardly of Shakespearean stature and still less of religious significance, but it might have qualified for possessing great parts, for it had made the careers of three players. Laura Keene had played in it some one thousand times since leaving Edwin in the lurch at Hawaii more than a decade earlier. Her precipitous departure from Honolulu was of a piece with her usual behavior, for she was capable of temper tantrums so dramatic that a notable one found her flinging goldfish around the room in her frenzy. She was an exacting theater technician, involving herself with scenery design, the duties of stage painters and carpenters, lighting mechanics. As manageress of her own theaters in several cities, she put on lavish productions. People who dealt with her knew she rigidly checked all expenditures, paying bills exactly on time but not a minute earlier. She was hard on her employees but had the reputation of sending them home well fed. She was universally referred to, behind her back, as The Duchess.

Our American Cousin had been playing in Chicago in June 1860 when Lincoln was first nominated for the Presidency, and many of the Republican delegates who saw it then had seen besides Miss Keene two other players whose names became famous for their roles in the play: Joseph Jefferson and E. A. Sothern. Like Edwin in Hawaii, both had their troubles with Laura Keene, as had a husband who gave her two daughters before vanishing. (The girls were forbidden to address their mother as anything but "Aunt Laura," and not everybody knew their real relationship to her.) Jefferson had ceased to be on speaking terms with her when off-stage. Sothern's penchant for elaborate practical jokes did not sit well with her. Both were gone from the play by April 14, 1865.

Our American Cousin, despite its long-lived popularity, was regarded as a silly farce dependent on grotesque characterizations and far-fetched assumptions. It had to do with a New England Yankee who becomes heir to an English fortune, and his relationships with the people he deals with when he goes to claim his prize: the harridan seeking to marry off her daughter to the American *nouveau riche*; the imbecilic British lord who mangles language and concepts and gets nothing straight; the grasping sharpster attempting to get hold of the money; and, of course, the sweet heroine who captures the Yankee's heart. Puns, misunderstandings, less than subtle insults, and one contretemps after another constituted the play.

The Lincolns, Miss Harris, and Major Rathbone mounted the staircase leading to the rear of the balcony, which curved around to the door of their box overlooking stage left. Ford's was on the site of a Baptist church whose cornerstone was laid in 1833. At about the time the war began it was converted to a theater by John T. Ford, who presented musicals in it—the Carlotta Patti Concert Troupe, George Christy's Minstrels. In early 1862 Ford halted productions to convert the building for theatrical showings of all types. He reopened it in March 1862 for a spring season before closing it for the summer. In the fall of 1862 the regular season opened with John Sleeper Clarke starring in *Paul Pry* and *Toodles*. A fire soon destroyed the building. John T. Ford constructed on the site a completely new theater, the last word in modernity with splendid acoustics, special fire hydrants, and first-rate arrangements for scenery movement. There were seats for twenty-four hundred people selling for twenty-five cents to a dollar, and boxes going for up to ten dollars, including the double-size one for which President Lincoln paid that sum. Police were stationed at the door to bar prostitutes from the premises.

The four people entered the box, not noticing that a small peephole had been drilled in the inner door with an awl, or that a rough cavity about three inches across had been cut into the plaster of the inside wall near the outside door opening on a short passage. Laura Keene was onstage as Mrs. Trenchard, the matriarch of an English family, trying to explain to the dimwitted Lord Dundreary the point of a joke. He kept saying he couldn't see it. "Well, anyone can see that!" she ad-libbed, gesturing toward the President and dropping a curtsy. The audience of some seventeen hundred broke into applause as the band, under William Withers, Jr., played "Hail to the Chief." With his hands on the box's rail, Lincoln bowed. He sat down in the rocking chair Harry Ford had placed just in front of the box's door, with Mrs. Lincoln in a chair at his right, Miss Harris beside her, and Major Rathbone in the small sofa at the far end of the box. It was eight-thirty, or a few minutes after.

John Booth was in the Herndon House hotel at Ninth and F streets, diagonally across from the Patent Office, in the room he had been renting for Lewis Powell, meeting with the room's occupant, the former drugstore clerk Davy Herold and the Port Tobacco boatman George Atzerodt. John wore a black suit, hip boots, and a dark slouch hat. The spurs on his heels he had inherited from his father. They were the ones Junius Brutus Booth had lent to Edwin for Edwin's first stage appearance as Tressel, the messenger in *Richard III*. He left the Herndon House for the alley behind Ford's Theatre, asked an actor to get Ed Spangler to hold his horse for him, was told Spangler was on scene-shifting duty, and got Peanut John Burrough to do it.

He entered the theater through the rear door, asked if he could cross the stage, and was told he could not, for the dairy scene was on. He went through an underground passage and reached the street. He went into the Star Saloon and ordered whiskey. Farther down the bar the President's coachman, Francis Burns, and his valet-messenger, Charles Forbes, were having a drink with guard John Parker.

John went up to the theater door, where ticket-taker John Buckingham was standing with his back turned but his arm blocking the entrance. He took hold of two fingers of Buckingham's hand and asked if Buckingham wanted a ticket from him. They had known one another for years and had taken tea together in Boston when John opened his first engagement as a star there, playing Richard III. Buckingham had then been impressed by the modest manner in which he said he was timid about playing a role made famous by his father, and competing with Edwin, and also because he knew Boston audiences could be coldly critical. But he had shown flashes of what Buckingham thought were positive genius that strikingly brought back memories of his father. Buckingham passed him through the door. In the course of the next half hour he came and went several times, once asking the doorkeeper for the time and once for a chew of tobacco.

He stood in front of the theater, and Captain William Williams of the city mounted police came by. They were acquaintances. Williams asked him to come for a drink but he declined, saying he had promised to look at Laura Keene in a particular scene. At a few minutes past ten Buckingham stepped next door to the Star Saloon to get a quick drink and saw him having one. Buckingham went back to the door, and a little later John came past him and went up the stairs to the balcony. He was humming a tune, Buckingham remembered.

He walked behind the dress circle seats, his all-black attire, almost like that of a stage villain, accenting an extreme paleness of his face noted by the actress Jennie Gourlay, below him looking up over the footlights, one of three members of her family appearing in the play. He continued his traverse of the rear of a theater of that Theater in which he had found his existence, Oak Chamber, Gothic Palace, Red Drawing Room, Prison, Rocky Pass, property room with masks, helmets, Yorick's skull, blunderbusses and swords, of Caesar slain by Brutus on the Ides of March after Calpurnia dreamed that the fountains of Rome ran red with her husband's blood, of Shylock crying for justice. His mother was in New York, Asia in Philadelphia awaiting the birth of a child, June playing in Cincinnati and Edwin in Boston. The April *Harper's* was on the stands with George William Curtis's analysis of Edwin's one hundred nights: *The tragedy of Hamlet is not only the vital curiosity about existence, the mastering love of life which almost subdues his soul with fear and doubt, and keeps it tense with eager questioning; but it is the conviction of a mind morbid with this continual strain that it is a most sacred duty to end another life, to plunge a guilty soul into the abyss.*

The play went on, the President once remarking to his wife, as he had earlier, on their ride, that he longed to see Jerusalem. She leaned against him, then whispered, "What will Miss Harris think of my hanging on to you so?" and he said, "She won't think anything about it." Not yet out of bed since his carriage accident, Secretary of State Seward had drifted into sleep as his daughter Fanny read aloud from *Legends of Charlemagne*. The doorbell rang, and a man told the servant who answered that he came to deliver some medicine sent by the secretary's doctor. Vice President Johnson was asleep in his suite in Kirkwood House at Eleventh Street and Pennsylvania Avenue. Another guest at the hotel, former governor Leonard Farwell of Wisconsin, had told him he was going to the theater that night; did the vice president wish to join him? Johnson declined. A card had that day been placed in the downstairs box for Johnson's rooms, Suite 65, after a hotel employee took it upstairs, knocked on the door, and received no response. The vice president's private secretary, William A. Browning, removed the card from the box later and wondered if it was for himself, for he had met its author in Nashville some time earlier. It read: *Don't wish to disturb you. Are you at home? J. Wilkes Booth.*

He walked to the door opening upon a short passageway leading to the Presidential box. Guard John Parker had taken a seat elsewhere and was watching the play. Valet-messenger Charles Forbes was sitting near the passageway door. There was a brief conversation, the delivery of an important message was spoken of, the cards of some government officials were displayed, and John Booth opened the door inward, closed it, and jammed the end of a length of wood, part of a dismantled music stand, into the cavity gouged in the wall, with the other end braced against the door so it could not be opened from the outside.

The door at the end of the short passageway leading to the box, with its recently drilled finger-size peephole, was ajar. Onstage the harridan with the marriageable daughter learned that the Yankee did not possess four hundred thousand dollars, as previously believed. He had given it to the sweet heroine.

"No heir to the fortune, Mr. Trenchard?"

"No."

"What!" shrieked the daughter. "No fortune!"

"Augusta," said the mother, "to your room!"

"Yes, Ma. The nasty beast!"

"I am aware, Mr. Trenchard," said the mother, "that you are not used to the manners of good society, and that, alone, will excuse the impertinence of which you have been guilty."

She swept indignantly offstage. Harry Hawk as Trenchard was alone in the brilliant footlights.

"Don't know the manners of good society, eh?" he drawled. "Wal, I guess I know enough to turn you inside out, you sockdologizing old man-trap." The laugh he got partially drowned the sound of the detonation that sent forward a bullet of nearly half an inch in diameter, fired from a distance of about two and a half feet, to enter below the left ear, go diagonally through the cerebrum for more than five inches, and shatter by shock waves the orbital plates of both eye sockets before halting in the anterior lobe of the right hemisphere of Abraham Lincoln's brain.

TEN

---

*B*LUISH SMOKE from the ten grains of black powder that sent the bullet forward filled the box. Save for when some Baltimoreans threw rocks at Buchanan, and when a maniac who believed himself the rightful king of England attempted with defective pistols to shoot Jackson, no President had ever been in danger from or menaced by anyone. Major Rathbone looked over and stood up.

President Lincoln slightly lifted his hands and dropped them. Rathbone stepped forward toward a shadowy figure emerging from the smoke who cried out, Rathbone thought, "Freedom!"

Rathbone saw a knife coming at him, threw up his arm, and took a slash in it extending from the elbow to the shoulder. He sagged back. The figure rushed to the front of the box. Miss Harris and Mrs. Lincoln had not moved from their seats. The President sat silent in his chair, eyes closed.

Rathbone gathered himself and lunged forward, grabbed at the figure, got a grip and lost it, but put his target off-balance so that a spur slashed the picture of George Washington at the front of the box and got caught in the Treasury Guards flag. Standing alone in the glare of the footlights, Harry Hawk saw a man catapult down some twelve feet out of the President's box to land awkwardly because of the flag dragging at the spur, and sink briefly to one knee before rising to wave a gleaming knife. Hawk turned and ran, stopped, turned. "My God, that's John Booth!" he gasped.

The audience took the detonation and sudden appearance onstage as part of the play. The actors and theater people knew better. The doorkeeper John Buckingham looked at the stage when

he heard the unexpected explosion, saw a man leap down into the
light, and recognized him when he stood up. Harry Ford was in the
box office. He looked through a window facing the stage, recognized who it was waving a knife, and decided that somebody must
have insulted John and that John was after whoever it was. Edwin
A. Emerson, backstage and waiting to go on, heard a popping
sound and was not alarmed, knowing that sets cannot always be
shifted noiselessly. Then he looked up from his script—he had
never played Lord Dundreary before and was checking his lines—
and was amazed to see the friend who had broken his cane a few
days earlier standing in the footlight glare. Also backstage, John
Mathews, who had in his frock coat pocket a letter to the *National
Intelligencer*, given him that afternoon for the next day's delivery,
heard what sounded like a shot and decided it was a new bit of stage
business directed against the idiotic Lord Dundreary. New stunts
at his expense were often added to the play. "That is done for the
purpose of frightening Dundreary," Mathews thought, and waited
for some reaction, a yelp from the dim nobleman, perhaps.

From the box Mrs. Lincoln, stunned by the sudden noise, for
she was always made nervous by such—her half sister, visiting the
White House, had seen how she started when someone dropped a
book—saw a man leap onto the stage, and confusedly thought to
herself that it was her husband, that he had stood up, lost his
balance, and tumbled over the balustrade. Then the man on the
stage, waving the dagger, shouted, *"Sic semper tyrannis!"* Thus always to tyrants. It was the motto of the commonwealth of Virginia
and the words Brutus was said to have uttered when he struck
down Caesar, although Shakespeare had not utilized them in his
play. "The South is avenged!" the man onstage cried.

Standing in the wings at stage right, waiting to go on with
young W. J. Ferguson, whose first spoken lines in a play had been
directed toward the Richard III of the man running across the stage,
Laura Keene was paralyzed by astonishment. She seemed in a daze,
Ferguson remembered. What on earth was John Booth doing onstage in *Our American Cousin?* He ran at the two, left hand extended
as if to ward them off, right hand holding the dagger. Ferguson
stepped back, and he went between them. The orchestra leader,
William Withers, Jr., had been arguing with Miss Keene about a
new song, "Honor to Our Soldiers," which had been scheduled to
be played between the first and second acts but which she had ruled
must be postponed. When Ferguson stepped back, Withers was
left standing in the runner's path. They had played at billiards the

night before. The knife ripped Withers's clothing as its holder rushed past.

The bright stage was empty, Harry Hawk having run off before turning and saying with a gasp that the man with the knife was John Booth. The audience waited for the play to go on.

From the Presidential box came a shout: "Stop that man!" It was Rathbone. Miss Harris immediately echoed him: "Stop that man! Won't somebody stop that man!" To the playgoers in their seats it was very odd. A man had leaped onto the stage brandishing a dagger, yelled, and run off. Now there were demands that he be stopped. Some spectators hesitantly stood up, and those behind them who thought it was all part of the play called, "Sit down!" and "Down in front!"

Laura Keene, in a handsome yellow satin dress, stepped from the wings onto the glaring stage and, looking up at the box, asked, "What is it? What is the matter?"

Miss Harris said, "The President is shot."

Then from next to her came what people remembered as unearthly sounds. They were screams and shrieks like those of a wild beast, horrible. It was Mary Lincoln. She was standing up and throwing her arms and hands about terribly. At once, instantly, surely, everybody knew what had happened and accepted it. There followed what seemed like a horrible carnival, a friend who was there told Walt Whitman, confusion mixing with terror, the sounds of chairs breaking, cries. To the actress Helen Trueman, who played the fortune-seeking harridan's daughter Augusta, what she saw and heard was the hell of hells. "Mrs. Lincoln's screams turned the house into an inferno of noise. There will never be anything like it on earth. The shouts, groans, curses, smashing of seats, screams of women, cries of terror, created a pandemonium."

People began jumping up onto the stage, breaking the music stands and instruments of the orchestra as they came. There was a fearful crush as spectators from the rear pushed forward, mashing others, knocking them down, and trampling them. "Order, order!" Laura Keene cried. "For God's sake, have presence of mind and keep your places!" But it was hopeless. She stepped forward and, assisted by young Ferguson, went over the footlights and toward a door leading to an alley on the south side of the theater. Past her surged a mob jumping over the footlights as the stage filled with screaming and shouting people. Jennie Gourlay came out from backstage and asked Edwin Emerson what was going on. They were in the middle of a crowd that, to Emerson's thinking, swirled hither and thither in hysterical aimlessness. He told her what had happened. She went down on the floor in a faint.

In front of the stage the young girl who a day earlier had been asked for the correct spelling of *tyrannis* was in danger of being severely injured by the people jammed about her who seemed to quiver with fear and excitement as they uttered hoarse shouts and yells. Her mother tried to help her up to the stage but was unable to do so in the crush. Finally a man picked her up and literally threw her upward over the footlights. She arose and looked up and saw Mrs. Lincoln and heard her terrible screams. The girl grew deathly sick. Emerson saw and took off his Lord Dundreary wig and fanned her with it.

In the dress circle, some forty feet from the entrance to the passageway to the President's box, Charles Leale had seen a man lifting aloft a dagger that, to Leale's thinking, gleamed like a diamond in the brilliant stage lights. Then he heard shouts that the President had been shot, followed by cries for a surgeon. Leale had been a doctor for six weeks, since his March graduation from Bellevue Hospital Medical College in New York. He was twenty-three years old and stationed at the Army General Hospital at Armory Square. He was in civilian clothes—wearing a uniform meant constantly being asked to show a pass by provost marshal police. He stood up, started vaulting over cane-seat chairs, and reached the door of the passageway leading to the upper stage-left box. People were banging on it and trying to force it open. Inside, the heavily bleeding Major Rathbone was trying to pry loose the piece of wood jammed into the wall cavity. From the stage and balconies rose wild yells: "Kill him! Shoot him! Burn the theater!"

Leale forced his way through the people outside the passageway. Rathbone got the wood removed. The door opened. Leale said to himself: "Be calm." He stepped inside. Rathbone was holding his severely wounded arm and asking for help. Leale put his hand under his chin, looked into his eyes, saw he was in no immediate danger, and went forward. Mary Lincoln and Clara Harris were standing by the high-backed rocking chair in which the President sat silently, eyes closed. Leale identified himself as a United States Army surgeon. "Oh, Doctor!" Mary Lincoln cried. "Is he dead? Can he recover? Will you take charge of him? Do what you can for him. Oh, my dear husband!"

The young doctor said soothingly that all that could possibly be done would be done. He asked one of the men crowding the passageway to get some brandy, and another to get some water. But the President appeared dead, Leale thought. He put his fingers on the right radial pulse and felt no movement of the artery. Remembering the brandished knife and having seen that Rathbone had been slashed, Leale began looking for a blade wound. It was difficult to do to with the President in a seated position, so he got some men to help him lie the President on the floor, he himself holding the limp head as they did so. He told a man to get the coat and shirt open to stomach level. He saw no wound. He reached forward and lifted the eyelids and at once saw evidence of brain injury. He ran his separated fingers through hair matted with blood and found an opening terrible in its size. From it he removed a clot of blood. From all over the theater came screams: "Kill the actors! Kill the goddamned rebels, kill the traitors!"

From an orchestra seat Dr. Charles Taft tried to get up on the stage while his wife, hysterical, screamed, "You shan't go! They'll kill you too! I know they will!" He got over the footlights, told some men he was a doctor, and had them lift him so he could grab the box's balustrade and clamber in, his cloak ripping off and falling on the stage as he did so. Laura Keene came into the box. She had raced out of the theater to an alley on the building's south side, up the stairs of an adjoining building connected to it, and through a door into the dress circle near the passageway. She was a social acquaintance of the Presidential couple—Mary Lincoln had several times had her to the White House. She got down on her knees by the President's head. Her sometime White House hostess had sunk into the box's sofa with her arms outstretched. Miss Harris sat by her, speechless. Major Rathbone stood, blood steadily flowing from his deep elbow-to-shoulder wound.

It seemed to Leale that the President had stopped breathing. He straddled him, opened the mouth, and put two extended fingers of his hand in as far back as possible, pressing the base of the paralyzed tongue down and outward to open the larynx for free passage of air. The President breathed shallowly. Leale had two men manipulate the arms to expand the thorax, pressed the diaphragm up to force air in and out, and slid his right hand under and beneath the ribs to stimulate the apex of the heart. A feeble beat and irregular breathing resulted. He leaned forward chest to chest and forcibly expelled air into the mouth and nostrils. He saw that for the moment the President could continue independent breathing. Still on his knees and straddling the President, Leale straightened up. The box was very dimly lit. In Leale's eyes the long body was heroic. The face was pale and in repose, the eyes closed, the countenance calm. He arranged the shirt and jacket as neatly as possible. "His wound is mortal; it is impossible for him to recover," he said.

Dr. Taft and Dr. Albert King stood by. Despite his youth and inexperience, medical protocol dictated that as the first to attend a patient, Leale was the physician in charge. He said that the President should be removed from the crowded, dark box. Somebody asked about transport to the White House, and Leale said that if it were attempted the jolting trip over the cobblestones would result in death before the destination was reached. Someone asked the nature of the wound and its seriousness, and Leale exactly repeated his earlier diagnosis and prognosis: "His wound is mortal; it is impossible for him to recover." What the President had related a few days earlier came into his wife's mind: *I fell into a slumber. . . . I thought I left my bed and wandered downstairs. . . . Before me was a catafalque. . . . "Who is dead in the White House?" I demanded.* "His dream was prophetic," Mary Lincoln gasped.

They must get him out of here to some nearby place, Leale said. He asked King and Taft to take hold of the President's shoulders. Some other men would support the torso, legs, and arms. They bent down. Laura Keene sat holding the President's head. Leale replaced her as they lifted the limp form. Leale saw people jammed into the area outside the box's door. "Guards, clear the passage! Guards, clear the passage!" he shouted. Soldiers lined up to keep people back.

The awkward procession went down the stairs with its burden and out into the street, an army captain with drawn saber leading. Several times Leale had the bearers halt so he could remove a clot of blood from the opening of the wound. Each time he did it the President's almost halted breathing seemed to improve. Across Tenth Street a man stood in front of a house holding a lighted candle and beckoning. They headed toward him slowly, stopping several times so Leale could remove a clot. All around them swirled the audience and people attracted by the commotion. Soldiers ran past them into Ford's, shouting at anybody inside to get out, they would shoot anyone who lingered, they would kill the rebels, burn the theater—"Clear out, clear out, you sons of bitches!" People ran out and away from the scene, horrified, terrified. One man ran with a purpose. It was former governor Leonard Farwell of Wisconsin. He raced to his hotel, the Kirkwood House, burst in, shouted at the desk clerk to guard the stairs, and bolted up to Suite 65.

"Governor Johnson!"

Farwell beat on the door, forgetting for the moment that Andrew Johnson was no longer military governor of Tennessee but
vice president. That was what had sent Farwell flying through the
streets. "Governor Johnson!" he screamed, pounding on the door.
"If you are in this room I must see you!"

Johnson got out of bed. He did not strike a light. "Farwell, is
that you?"

"Yes! Let me in!"

He opened the door. Farwell burst through, slammed the door
behind him, and fastened the latch. A moment later, when Farwell
had finished speaking, Johnson swayed and then staggered into his
arms. They held each other tightly.

On Tenth Street the slow procession made its way through the
swirling crowd under the spring moon. Once Taft replaced Leale in
holding the President's hand. He felt something oozing onto his
fingers, not blood. It was brain matter. The man with the candle led
them into the house across the street from Ford's Theatre and
toward a rear room. As they went through the narrow corridor
they were lost to the sight of Mary Lincoln behind them. "Where
is my husband? Where is my husband?" she shrieked. In the street
under the theater lights people gasped at the appearance presented
by Laura Keene. Her hair, her face, her yellow dress were smeared
with blood. She seemed a terrible apparition, horrible. Clara Harris
was in the same condition: "saturated literally with blood, my
hands and face."

They carried the president into the 9½-by-17-foot rear bedroom rented five days earlier by Private William Clark of Company D, 13th Massachusetts Infantry, assigned to duty in the Quartermaster's Department. On the wall he had hung photographs of
his three sisters alongside landlord William Petersen's reproductions of Rosa Bonheur's *The Horse Fair* and J. F. Herring's *The
Village Blacksmith*, *The Stable*, and *The Barnyard*. They put the
President into the bed where John Booth had fallen asleep smoking
Charles Warwick's pipe.

In Lafayette Square some half dozen blocks away, at a home whose
owner had that morning for the first time since his carriage accident
nine days earlier taken solid food, a servant answered a ringing
doorbell and admitted a strongly built young man who said he
brought a message for the secretary of state from Dr. T. S. Verdi,
his physician. He must deliver it personally. The servant said that
was impossible, for Mr. Seward was asleep. The young man moved

forward and clumped noisily up the stairs, the servant urging him to make less noise so as not to wake the secretary.

From his room the secretary's son Frederick heard the footsteps and discussion and opened the door. The young man told him he must deliver a message to Mr. Seward. Frederick told him the secretary could not be disturbed. Let the young man give him the message and it would be delivered in good time. The young man repeated that he must deliver it personally. To Frederick Seward he seemed dull, stupid. Once again he repeated that he must deliver the message personally. "Well," Frederick Seward finally said, "if you will not give me the message, go back and tell the doctor I refused to let you see Mr. Seward." The young man was silent, apparently uncertain of what to do. "I am his son," Frederick told the young man, "and the assistant secretary of state. Go back and tell the doctor that I refused to let you go into the sickroom because Mr. Seward was sleeping."

"Very well, sir, I will go," said the young man, who turned, took two or three steps, whirled, and showed a navy revolver pointed at Frederick's chest. He pulled the trigger. It misfired. He raised it and smashed it down on Frederick's head. Inside the secretary's room Fanny Seward heard a disturbance in the hall and thought that her brother and the servant and visitor were chasing a rat. Once one had been out there. She opened the door slightly. Then it burst in on her. She got a glimpse of Frederick covered with blood as the young man came in with a gun in one hand and a knife in the other and flung himself on her father. His knife came down seeking Secretary Seward's throat and caught his cheek, almost severing it from his face and instantly covering the brace and bandages protecting his fractured jaw completely red.

Fanny thought: "This must be a fearful dream." The knife was coming down again. She saw all the familiar things of the room, the bureau, a little stand, the *Legends of Charlemagne* she had been reading to her father when he fell asleep—and Lewis Powell raising his knife. "Then I knew it was not a dream." She began screaming.

There was a soldier-nurse assigned to Secretary Seward for the period of his recuperation. He leaped on Powell's back, took two backward stab wounds, hung on. Brought from his bed by his sister's screams, a second Seward son, Augustus, ran in. In the half light he saw two struggling men and thought his father had become delirious and that the nurse was trying to subdue him. Then he thought the nurse had gone out of his mind and was trying to murder his father. Augustus leaped forward, and Powell stabbed him. The secretary had rolled off the end of the bed. Powell broke loose and ran down the stairs. The servant who had opened the door to him had rushed into the street shouting "Murder!" A State Department messenger was coming in. Powell sank his knife into the man. Some impulse caused Powell to yell, "I'm mad! I'm mad!" Behind him were five bleeding people, Secretary Seward horribly disfigured, and Acting Secretary Frederick Seward in an unconscious state that would last for days.

Powell reached the street. His horse was there—but not Davy Herold, assigned to lead him out of Washington when Powell had proved unable to memorize the route. At the screams of the servant running out of the house, Herold put his spurs into his horse and ran for it. Powell mounted. At a walk he went off. The servant ran behind him shouting for help. After a time Powell whipped up the horse and vanished.

Three miles from Ford's Theatre, at the Washington City end of the Eleventh Street bridge spanning the Potomac, the Navy Yard Bridge, the Eastern Branch Bridge, Sergeant Silas T. Cobb of the 3rd Massachusetts Heavy Artillery and a couple of privates saw a horseman approaching. Throughout the war all bridges leading south had been closed at nightfall. Uncertain and soon-to-be-dropped regulations were still in effect but greatly relaxed. The previous day the President had ordered the end of restrictions on travel between Washington and the former Confederacy.

The horseman stopped in front of the soldiers. "Who are you, sir?" Sergeant Cobb asked. He took note of the rider's gentlemanly appearance and manner and that he had very white hands. He was probably a rich man's son on his way home after some Washington revelry, Cobb decided.

"My name is Booth."

Cobb asked where the man was coming from. "The city." He asked where he was headed. "I'm going home."

"And where is your home?"

"In Charles County, Maryland."

"What town?"

"I don't live in any town."

"Oh, you must live in some town."

"No, I live close to Beantown, but not *in* the town."

"Why are you out so late? Don't you know you're not allowed to pass after nine o'clock?"

"That's news to me. I had business in the city and thought if I waited I'd have the moon to ride home by."

Cobb told him he could pass. He walked the horse partway across, heading for the far end, then put her into a run and was gone.

ELEVEN

SECRETARY OF WAR Stanton's wife was in the children's nursery
when someone knocked on the door of the house. A moment
later she went upstairs to her husband. "Mr. Seward is murdered,"
she said.

"Humbug!" he snapped. "I left him only an hour ago." He
went downstairs and said to the man at the door, "What's this
story you're telling?" The man repeated what he had said to Mrs.
Stanton, and as he spoke people came running to say the President
had also been attacked. From distant streets voices could be heard
shouting. Those who had come to tell of what happened at Seward's met those who told of what had happened to Lincoln, and
a panic never known before or after gripped Washington. Immediate rumors spread: Lee's surrender had been a ruse and now the
rebel army, formed again, was on its way to put the capital of the
North to the sword; the entire Cabinet had been wiped out; it was
unsafe to stay at home and unsafe to be in the streets; tomorrow
the city would lie in ruins. Running men were taken for the Confederate infantry, riders for the Confederate cavalry.

Stanton went to Seward's, confirmed the attack on his colleague, and heard that the President had been shot. With Secretary
of the Navy Welles he hailed a "night-hawk," a late-hours cab. Its
driver said he was too terrified to handle the horse, so Chief Justice
David K. Cartter of the District of Columbia shoved him aside and
jumped up on the box. He took the two Cabinet ministers through
the surging crowd. They came to the house where Lincoln was.
Both secretaries peered down into their chief's face.

It came into Welles's mind—Father Gideon, Lincoln used to

163

call him—that the features were so calm and striking that never before had the President seemed more impressive. Stanton looked down and listened to the labored breathing rise and then almost die away before it rose again. Like an Aeolian harp, he thought. Stanton had heard that breathing before. It was when he held his sick child in his arms. The child had died. He collected himself and became in that moment the functioning government of the United States. There was no one else.

Convinced that he faced a gigantic rebel plot, that the war was on again in a new and terrible form, he sent orders to the dozens of forts and military posts in and around Washington to turn out every man. Soon bugles and the long roll of drums sounded from every direction, and beneath a moon flashing in and out from behind scudding clouds, cavalry patrols plunged through the streets. There was something terrifying about the sounds the soldiers made, the hooves clattering on the cobblestones, the clanking sabers, the shouted orders. Few people went to bed that night, and many sat gathered together not wanting to be alone, like frightened children. The shadows of trees in the moonlight became suddenly menacing, ghostlike, and the low rumbling sound of people talking everywhere in the streets, subdued, no laughter, was background for the horrible rumors fed by the distant rolling of the drums calling to arms the men of the fortifications off to the south of the city.

In the middle room of the Petersen house Justice Cartter, told to do so by Stanton, began taking evidence from people who had been in Ford's Theatre. In the front parlor Mrs. Lincoln sat on a horsehair sofa with Miss Harris. Major Rathbone crumpled over in a faint before them. It had been his blood that so frightfully daubed his fiancée and Laura Keene, not that of the President, although no one seemed to realize that. "Oh, my husband's blood, my dear husband's blood!" Mrs. Lincoln kept screaming when she looked at Miss Harris. Actually the President bled very minimally, and whenever the doctors were told Mrs. Lincoln was coming down the corridor to the rear bedroom to see him, they slipped a napkin under his head so she would see nothing—a dozen napkins in all during the long night. When Rathbone fainted, Miss Harris took out her handkerchief and stuffed it into his wound, and he was seen to and taken home. Mrs. Lincoln's almost continual screams could be heard throughout the house: "Oh, why didn't he kill me? Why didn't he kill me? Kill me! Kill me! Kill me too!" She went in to where her husband lay diagonally on the bed—he was too tall for it, and when Dr. Leale had asked if the foot could be removed it proved too difficult to accomplish. "Do live!" Mary Lincoln cried to her husband. "Do speak to me!"

She bent down to kiss him and call him by endearing names. "Live but for one moment to speak to me once, to speak to our children. Send for Tad—he will speak to Tad, he loves him so!" But Tad was back in the White House, crying to doorkeeper Thomas Pendel, "Oh, Tom Pen! Tom Pen! They have killed Papa dead. They've killed Papa dead!" He had been at Grover's with his tutor to see *Aladdin, Or the Magic Lamp*, starring the actress Effie Germon in the title role, when a messenger came in to tell the tutor that the President had met with an accident and that he must take Tad back to the White House immediately. When they had left, the assistant manager went onstage to tell the audience they must disperse, the President had been shot, and then wired the manager, who was in New York, of what had happened at Washington's other leading playhouse. THANK GOD IT WASN'T OURS.

It was not the only telegram sent from the capital. In the center room of the first floor of the Petersen house, sitting across from Judge Cartter as he interviewed witnesses, Secretary Stanton sent out message after message alerting all troops. He wired General Grant, at a late dinner between trains in Philadelphia, to return to Washington at once. Facing him at a small table in the center of the room, Cartter quickly found out just who had shot the President. Harry Hawk, who had run from the man leaping on the stage to say with a gasp, "My God, that's John Booth!" told what he knew. Laura Keene, covered with Rathbone's blood, carefully said that she did not know who had shot the President but that she did know who had jumped from the box. There was never any doubt about what had occurred. After all, the deed had hardly been done in the dark, but in the brightest of lights, stage lights, in front of a crowd of theatergoers, a large number of whom recognized who it was, and in the presence of at least a dozen people who had drunk with, talked with, been with the individual in question that very day. From the steps of the Petersen house an officer asked if there was anyone present who knew stenography, and former corporal James Tanner, who had lost both feet in the war and then studied at a business college, volunteered his services. "In 15 minutes," he remembered, he had enough testimony written down to hang the man who shot Lincoln "as high as Haman." Telegrams naming who it was went out at Stanton's dictation to all points.

Robert Todd Lincoln drove up with Senator Charles Sumner.

Sumner had been sitting at home with two other senators, sharing a bottle of wine. A servant burst in on them. "Mr. Lincoln is assassinated in the theater. Mr. Seward is murdered in his bed. There's murder in the streets."

Sumner said, "Young man, be moderate in your statements. Tell us what has happened."

"I have told you what has happened."

They made for the White House. Everything seemed in order there. Inside, Thomas Pendel—Tom Pen to Tad Lincoln—had earlier heard from an army sergeant, "Have you heard the news? They have tried to cut the throat of Secretary Seward." Pendel assumed he was referring to the secretary's carriage accident. "Oh, Sergeant, I guess you must be mistaken!" The man left and was back in a few minutes. "I tell you that it is a fact; they tried to cut Secretary Seward's throat."

Then Sumner appeared to ask if the President had returned from the theater. He had not. Then came people saying he had been shot. Pendel hurried to Robert Todd Lincoln's room. (He had been studying Spanish, he told people later, with Presidential secretary John Hay and "a college friend." He never revealed the name of the "college friend." There were those who thought they knew who it was whom Hay had long known, and Robert pursued during his Harvard days and after, and who had a particular interest in studying Spanish.)

Pendel said, "There has something happened to the President. You had better go down to the theater and see what it is." Young Lincoln left with Sumner. Then Tad came in. Pendel put his arms around the boy as he kept repeating over and over, "Oh, they've killed Papa dead." Pendel took him to the President's room in the southwest corner of the White House and turned down the bed. Tad undressed and got in and Pendel covered him up and lay down with his arms around him, talking until Tad fell asleep.

In the first-floor rear bedroom at the Petersen house on Tenth Street, Robert looked down at his father. Senator Sumner took the President's hand and spoke to him. The doctor said, "It's no use, Mr. Sumner. He can't hear you."

"No," Sumner said. "He isn't dead. Look at his face. He is breathing."

"It will never be anything more than this."

As with Stanton thinking of an Aeolian harp, it seemed to Sumner there was something musical about that breathing. Almost like a melody.

By then the news of what had happened had spread through Washington. When it reached the National Hotel, the woman who had dined that evening with Mr. and Mrs. John P. Hale and their daughter and her secret fiancé was asleep. She awoke to what she remembered as an indefinable sound. "Doors were slamming all over, and a murmur of voices was heard." At first she thought that someone was ill. But the sounds continued. She wondered if there was a fire, got out of bed, and opened the windows to hear the continual noise of horses running by, but no fire bells or alarms. She threw on a wrapper and went into the main salon, learned that the President had been attacked, and sat with others in horror and terror. Then soldiers came demanding to search John Booth's room—he was the man who shot the President, they said. Despite the intense seriousness of the moment, people took what the soldiers said as a joke. "We all laughed at the absurdity of such a thing," remembered Walter Burton, the night clerk. He was a friend of the man the soldiers named, had walked home from the Capitol to the hotel on Inauguration Day with him, often sat up nights behind the hotel desk with him, drinking a little liquor the barkeep left when he closed up and smoking cigars John offered. Good cigars also, Burton remembered, two for a quarter.

As time passed Burton ceased to smile at what the soldiers had said, and grew angry on his friend's behalf. "All night long I watched the door, confidently expecting to see Booth come walking in to give the lie to this foul story." In the salon the woman awakened by the slamming doors and murmuring voices said when she heard the story, "Oh, no, that is impossible!" But it was repeated and confirmed over and over. There could be no doubt. Lucy Hale came in. People grouped about her. There was a scream, and Lucy fell prone on the floor. She was carried to her room.

In the Petersen house the labored breathing grew louder, the stertorous sound, like incessant moaning, reaching clearly to the front room where Mrs. Lincoln was. She was possessed by what all who saw her termed indescribable agitation, crying, "Why didn't he kill me?" over and over again and saying with a moan, "My husband's blood!" when she looked at the bedaubed Clara Harris. Robert Todd Lincoln knelt before her, holding her hands. He sent a man to the home of Senator James Dixon of Connecticut to ask Mrs. Dixon to come. She was in bed but heard what was said to the servant who answered the door, "A message from Captain Robert Lincoln for Mrs. Dixon," and thought at once of her army son as her heart stood still. She flung open a window, learned what was

wanted, and hurried to Mary Lincoln. At intervals she would help
her walk to her husband's bedside. At dawn, with the light full
upon him, the President's wife could see how the area around his
right eye behind which the bullet had lodged was discolored, dark.
He uttered a loud, gasping moan. She fainted, but Mrs. Dixon
caught her and helped her to an open window. It was raining
heavily outside. She was taken back to the front room.

The doctors had not a hope of doing anything. The enormous
derringer bullet, almost half an inch across, had driven a disc of
bone almost an inch in diameter three inches into the brain. Then
the bullet had split and a fragment of it had gone on to a depth of
seven and a half inches from the point of entrance. A Nelaton
probe tracing the path confirmed what Leale had said twice in the
Ford's Theatre box. The doctors put mustard plasters and hot
water bottles on the President.

After being on his feet for some seven hours, Gideon Welles
took a seat at the foot of the bed. Robert Lincoln came in and stood
with his head leaning on Charles Sumner's shoulder. Elizabeth
Dixon brought in Mary Lincoln. The sound of the President's
breathing was subsiding, and only a gentle rise and fall of the chest
showed he yet lived. She bent and kissed him. "Oh, my God, and
have I given my husband to die?" she cried.

Outside, dismal rain came down on the streets and tethered
horses and the houses where scarcely an adult had done other than
sit up all night, afraid to show a light for fear of becoming a target
for invading armies, some nodding off into sleep to awake wondering if it was all a nightmare. To the marquis de Chambrun the
soldiers everywhere seemed intensely dangerous, many of them
weeping and all appearing ready to fire at anyone making a false
move. At first it seemed to de Chambrun that people refused to
believe that the President had actually been shot and was dying,
that such a thing was beyond the bounds of possibility. Then they
came to believe it. How cruel it was. He had endured the war for
four years, and had known but five days since its effective end at
Appomattox.

The tiny bedroom, almost of a size with the log cabin in which
Abraham Lincoln had been born fifty-six years earlier, grew almost
entirely silent, with the President seemingly not breathing for minutes on end as those who had served him looked at their watches
to mark the moment of his passing. In the next room former
corporal Tanner's note-taking of testimony had long become re-
dundant; Judge Cartter knew all that was needed. In the front room
Mary Lincoln moaned. The rain beat down. There was at times not

the slightest movement to be felt in the President's pulse, but young Dr. Leale, who had not been off his feet since the moment he rose to leap over chairs and go to the door of the theater box, held the dying man's hand in his own for a purpose: He knew the President was beyond reach because of the evidence of blood pressure on his brain as indicated by paralysis, dilated pupils, protruding and bloodshot eyes, but gripped the hand so that should for a moment recognition and reason return, just at the last, as was sometimes said to occur, his patient would know that he was not alone—"that he was in touch with humanity and had a friend."

At 7:22 A.M. the heart ceased to beat. The clergyman of the church the Lincolns attended began to pray. Stanton had come in from the center room and was weeping. "Thy will be done, Amen," the Reverend Phineas Gurley ended. "Amen," the others echoed. Stanton raised his hands. "Now he belongs to the ages." Coins were put over the eyes, and the white bedsheet drawn up over the face. Leale went out into the rain bareheaded. He had left his hat on the seat at Ford's Theatre. Would this assassination, he wondered, finally destroy the long-suffering country which had gone through so much war? How could the United States ever really be made a united nation, the aim of the great conflict, when such a thing could happen?

Mrs. Lincoln came out. She looked across the street at the theater. "Oh, that dreadful house!" she cried. "Oh, that dreadful house!" Bells were tolling all over Washington, and in the steady rain the great decorations everywhere were coming down in favor of emblems of mourning. Good Friday was traditionally a day of solemnity to be followed by the joyousness of Easter; but this year, Washington realized, all was reversed. Good Friday had been filled with happiness and thanksgiving for the ending of the war, but Easter would be mournful. It did not escape people's thinking that, as with Jesus Christ, Abraham Lincoln suffered his death wound on Good Friday, and that like Moses it would not be given to him to lead his people into the Promised Land: peace. Those concepts, and that he was so suddenly dead, and so shockingly so, made him at once almost a holy figure. In the moment of his passing he was at once realized for what he was and taken for what he had done, and anyone who dared to say a word against him was in danger of being beaten to death or lynched on the spot, as the police discovered when, with drawn revolvers, they forced mobs back from those who had spoken against the dead man—now universally and at once Our Martyred Leader.

Across the country in every city or town reached by telegraph service, the news came in with the morning newspaper: The President had been shot and could not recover. It was the greatest shock the American people had ever received. For those who knew the man who shot Lincoln, the shock was beyond description. John Ellsler, who the previous year had sought oil with him in the Pennsylvania fields, found as he sat at his breakfast table in Columbus, Ohio, that after he looked at his newspaper he was unable to move or speak. Then it seemed to him that he felt as if he was on fire. He sat feeling all love, all friendship, vanish from his universe.

Working as a member of the company at Ellsler's Columbus theater, Clara Morris—"He was so young, so bright, so gay," she said of John Booth; she had seen him kiss a street urchin and joked with him about her Grecian costume in *The Marble Heart*—learned of the assassination without learning the name of the assassin. She and her roommate bought black cotton and were tacking it on a window when a man came by and told them who had killed Lincoln. The roommate, Hattie, had in her mouth tacks that she almost swallowed when she laughed. Clara laughed also, and then told the man this was a poor subject for jest. The two actresses finished their work and went inside. There was a knock on the door. Hattie answered as Clara worked on a costume. She heard Hattie stammer, "Why—why—what?" and turned quickly. Ellsler came in slowly. He was a dark-complexioned man, but his face was frighteningly livid, his lips as white as his cheeks. "His eyes were dreadful, they were so glassy and seemed so unseeing."

Clara knew his devotion to his children. All she could imagine was that his look must be produced by disaster to one or more of them. "What is it?" she asked. "Oh, what has happened to them?" She gave him a chair.

He sank down and very faintly said, "You—haven't—heard—anything?"

Hattie stammered, "A man—he lied though—said that Wilkes Booth—but he did lie—didn't he?"

"No. No! He did not lie—it's true!"

They burst into tears. Ellsler stood, stared into space, and said in the same far, faint voice, "So great, so good, a man destroyed, and by the hand of that unhappy boy! My God! My God!" He walked out as if in a trance. At the closed theater Mrs. Ellsler, whom Clara Morris had never seen shed tears for sickness, sorrow, or trouble of her own, cried.

Across the country the lighted transparencies hailing victory, and Japanese lanterns set aglow within by candle, the flags, signs, pictures, and mottoes, the illuminations and bunting came down as, so suddenly, the black emblems of mourning went up. In Philadelphia young John Drew of the Drew-Barrymore theatrical family went running to tell his mother of the President's assassination. "Are you sure?" she asked. She sat wordlessly and then took out a letter Lincoln had sent to thank her for seats at a production. She gazed at it silently for a time and asked without raising her eyes, "Who did such a monstrously wicked thing?" He told her.

"No!" He had often been a guest in her home. "No! It is unthinkable!" Edwin came into her mind. "The brother of one so kind . . . Will our profession ever atone?"

Also in Philadelphia, John Sleeper Clarke was shaving when he heard a scream from his wife, Asia. He ran to her. Five months pregnant, she was in bed with a newspaper in front of her. She pointed to the headline. He could not halt her cries. Even as he tried, the bell rang and a U.S. marshal came to arrest him. She screamed again and again. She thought of her father, who held all life sacred, who would kill nothing, and that were he alive he would cry, "The name we would have enwreathed with laurels is dishonored by a son." This to Junius Brutus Booth would be, she thought, as was David's son to David: " 'His well-beloved—his bright boy Absalom!' " *O my son Absalom, my son, my son Absalom! Would God I died for thee, O Absalom, my son, my son!*

Her husband was not the only person arrested by Secretary of War Stanton's orders. Soon taken into custody were the men who had rented horses to the assassin, the inmates of Ella Turner's sister's bordello, the actors and employees at Ford's Theatre, George Atzerodt, Mrs. Surratt and her sister and daughter—John Surratt was in Elmira, New York—and Lewis Powell, who wandered about after attacking Seward and the others and eventually found his way to the Surratt boardinghouse to be seized by police there. Junius Brutus Booth, Jr., was appearing at Pike's Opera House in Cincinnati. When he came down in the morning Emil Benlier, the hotel clerk of the Burnet House, saw he was about to take a walk, and told him it would be best for him not to go out into the streets.

June did not understand. He asked why he should not go out. "Haven't you heard the news?" the clerk asked. June had heard nothing—he had just come down from his room. Benlier said no more. June went to a friend standing nearby and demanded to know if the clerk was crazy. The friend said he was not. June returned to the desk, and Benlier told him. He suggested that June return to his room, and it was well that he did so, for moments later a mob of five hundred came into the hotel. "They would have hanged him in a minute if they could have laid their hands on him," Benlier wrote. Smuggled out of the hotel, he was arrested and imprisoned.

In New York the Thomas Bailey Aldriches went to Edwin's home. The owner was appearing in Boston. As they went through the streets they saw black trappings going up in place of the gay decorations of victory, and heard the steady hammering of nails which resounded in every city and village of the North and West. Newsboys were shouting the headlines of their papers, including the assassin's name. "O God," Mary Ann Booth moaned to them, "if this be true, let him shoot himself, let him not live to be hung! Spare him, spare us, spare the name that dreadful disgrace!" The postman rang the bell and handed in a letter written hardly more than twenty-four hours before, at 2:00 A.M. on Friday morning: *Dearest Mother: Everything is dull. I only drop you these few lines to let you know I am well. With best love to you all I am your affectionate son ever. John.*

All his life Edwin Booth had trouble sleeping, and his sleep was always uneasy, and when he was awakened by somebody he became momentarily violent, liable to throw things. His valet James Brown came into his room. They were in the home of Orlando Tomkins on Franklin Square. Tomkins was an apothecary. His family ran the Boston Theatre. Not ten days earlier, Orlando Tomkins had been presented with a gold ring in appreciation for his work in looking into the purchase of some lots on Commonwealth Avenue: The ring was inscribed *JWB to OT.* The family had always liked the donor of that ring. When he stayed with them, Mrs. Tomkins remembered, her little son used to go into his room and have "famous pillow fights" with him.

James Brown woke Edwin, who angrily demanded to know what this meant. The servant said, "Oh, Massa Edwin, you never could guess what has happened! Something dreadful! The President has been shot, and, oh, Massa Edwin, I am afraid Massa John has done it!" He handed over a newspaper.

Edwin read of the dagger flourished in the bright stage lights and the cry "*Sic semper tyrannis!*" shouted to the theater audience—and knew. It was true. Others had said: Impossible. The actor John McCullough had cried, "I won't believe it. I can't believe it." John Ellsler had said at first, "I could not, would not, believe it." Not Edwin. "My mind accepted the fact at once," he told Joseph Jefferson. "It was just as if I had been struck on the head by a hammer."

TWELVE

HE LAY in agony with his face turned to the wall in an upstairs bedroom of the home of Dr. Samuel A. Mudd near Bryantown in Lower Maryland twenty-five miles southeast of Washington. His left leg was broken—a straight fracture of the tibia two inches above the ankle. It had snapped when he landed on the stage of Ford's Theatre, his balance undone by the spur caught in the Treasury Guards flag adorning the President's box.

He had come running out of the theater's rear entrance to where Peanut John Burrough sat on a stone bench holding the reins of the livery stable mare. Peanut John stood up, to be knocked down by the butt of the knife that had slashed Major Rathbone's arm and cut orchestra leader William Withers's clothes. The mare danced about, but he got a foot into a stirrup and was aboard. He pointed her up the alley, dug in the spurs, clattered over the cobblestones to Ninth Street and from there in a rush to the Capitol and the ungraded hill leading down to the Navy Yard and the bridge. Sergeant Cobb let him pass, as he would also Davy Herold, fleeing Lewis Powell's carnage at the Seward house. The two riders met at Soper's Hill some eight miles down from Washington City.

They rode through the remote and unpeopled countryside with no telegraph and no railroad and where half a dozen houses and a tavern-post office store marked the only towns, and came down the Brandywine Pike to the house owned by Mrs. Surratt in the tiny settlement named for her late husband. It was rented out to John Lloyd. They had sequestered guns and equipment there when planning the kidnap of the President earlier in the spring, and that afternoon Mrs. Surratt had delivered a package to her tenant to be held for picking up.

It was midnight. Drinking by himself and intoxicated, as he often was, Lloyd was awake. Davy Herold dismounted and went inside. "Make haste and get those things!" he told Lloyd. Herold took a carbine but his companion did not, for to carry it would have been almost impossible for him. He had difficulty even sitting his horse for the pain of the shattered leg. Herold handed up a bottle. That helped, but not enough. He needed the services of a physician. They detoured from the direct road down to the Potomac and Virginia, and headed for the home of Dr. Mudd.

It was sixteen miles over primitive, rough roads from Surrattsville, every jolt agonizing. Once the mare fell. At four in the morning Herold dismounted and knocked on Mudd's door. The doctor was an 1856 graduate of a Baltimore medical school, the son of a locally prominent family which had owned a hundred slaves working extensive tobacco plantations. Mudd was violently anti-North, a position not at all unique in the area. (In Prince Georges County, where Surrattsville was, one single voter cast a Lincoln ballot in the 1861 election.)

Herold told the doctor that his companion had taken a fall from his horse and injured his leg. They got him down onto a sofa in the parlor for an examination to be conducted by candlelight.

Doctor and patient had met before. Five months earlier the actor J. Wilkes Booth, saying he was interested in buying land, spent a night in Mudd's house. In December they had with several of the kidnap conspirators spent an evening in the National Hotel in Washington drinking wine and smoking cigars. It was Mudd who had introduced the conspiracy leader to John Surratt, whom he knew from Surratt's Washington-to-Richmond blockade running and message-carrying. But—Mudd said later—he did not recognize his patient as J. Wilkes Booth. His wife backed up the story. She did not take the injured late-hour stranger for anyone she had ever seen before, she said, and averred that she never really got a good look at him, for his face was covered by a shawl and some whiskers that she saw were false when they slipped.

Mudd examined the patient, cutting off his boot to do so. A splint would help. Rest was called for, keeping all weight off the leg. He wrapped the injury in cotton and splinted it with pieces of a bandbox pasted together. The patient complained of severe pain in his back, severe enough to make it difficult for him to breathe properly. Mudd felt it came from riding, and likely that was true, for going thirty miles with a leg that could not support pressure in the stirrup could well injure the back.

He was put to bed upstairs. Herold dozed in a chair. At about seven breakfast was served to the doctor and his wife and Davy Herold, who talked cheerfully of his hunting experiences in the neighborhood and who did not, the Mudds said, appear to have a care in the world. He had been "frolicking around for five or six months," Herold remarked, and Mrs. Mudd replied that all play and no work makes Jack a bad boy. "Your father ought to make you go to work." "My father is dead and I am ahead of the old lady," Herold replied. He looked about seventeen or eighteen to the doctor and seemed never to have needed a shave. By the time they rose from the table, Abraham Lincoln was dead and would soon be returning to the White House in a hearse led by an officer on foot carrying an unsheathed saber and flanked by ten privates marching with arms reversed below the dripping gray Saturday morning skies.

All who saw the small procession took off their hats at once and stood with pale faces and, often, streaming eyes under the great profusion of flags now draped in black and half-masted where but the day before they had exuberantly floated for the victory the North had sought for so long. Many years later General William Doster remembered the piercing wail the crowd at Fifteenth Street and Pennsylvania Avenue emitted when Lincoln went by. Never before or since, he wrote, had he heard such a sound. They were blacks who keened, and they seemed to know, he remembered, old then, that what was lost was not to be replaced; as indeed it was not, not for them nor for the rebels either. Only Lincoln could have healed the great wounds the country had suffered in the war, as the decades to follow showed.

He arrived at the White House where his wife, his widow now, had been taken from room to room, refusing at one after another to enter, for something within reminded her too forcibly of him. "Oh, no, not there," she kept saying. "Oh, I couldn't go in there." Finally Mrs. Dixon and Mary Jane Welles, the secretary of the navy's wife, got her to bed, where at an hour before noon her summoned dressmaker-confidante, Elizabeth Keckley, came to find her emitting unearthly shrieks in a terrible convulsion of grief. Only Tad could calm her, saying, "Don't cry so, Mama! Don't cry or you will break my heart. Papa was good and he has gone to Heaven. He is happy there. He is with God and Brother Willie. Don't cry, Mama." With great effort she would calm herself for a time.

Twenty-five miles away, Dr. Mudd's patient slept on. Herold

took lunch with the doctor and his wife and then said that he and his companion must be on their way. Where might a carriage be hired? Mudd said he was going over to Bryantown, four miles away, to pick up his mail and see some patients; let the visitor accompany him and perhaps a vehicle might be found. Mrs. Mudd asked if she might go up and see the injured man, and her husband said, "Yes, certainly you can." A tray sent up for lunch had been brought back untouched, so the guest had not eaten all day. Nothing at all had been heard from him save a request, conveyed by Herold, that he be lent a razor, some shaving soap, and water. Perhaps a shave would make him feel better, Harold had explained. To Mrs. Mudd's thinking a tray with cake, some oranges, and a glass of wine might be in order. She went in and asked how he was feeling.

"My back hurts me dreadfully," he said. "I must have hurt it when the horse fell and I broke my leg." He asked if there was any brandy in the house. She said there was not, but they had some good whiskey she would be happy to bring. He declined. He lay with his face turned to the wall throughout the conversation. "I guess you think I have very little hospitality," she said. "You have been sick all day and I have not been up to see you." He did not reply. She went downstairs. Herold returned to say that he and her husband had tried to borrow the carriage of the doctor's father, but that he needed it to go to church the following day, Easter, the services for which ministers all over the country were rewriting previously prepared sermons to say that even as One had been put on the Cross on Good Friday to die for Man, so Lincoln had been given to suffer his death wound on that day for America, that here was the Christ of the people of the New World and of modern times. Herold did not mention to Mrs. Mudd that he had learned in Bryantown that the entire area was swarming with Union cavalry seeking the man who killed Lincoln.

They would go their way by horseback, Herold said. With two crude crutches put together by one of Mudd's employees out of a piece of planking, the patient descended the stairs, his mustache now gone and his false beard, Mrs. Mudd said, becoming dislodged as he painfully hobbled down. "So much of his face as could be seen presented a picture of agony." She told Herold it would be best for him to stay. "If he suffers much we won't go far," Herold said. "I will take him to my lady-love's not far from here." He helped him onto the livery stable mare.

They left, and after a time the soldiers came and found the

boot Mudd had cut off the injured leg and saw that inside it was inscribed the name of its New York maker and that of the customer: *J. Wilkes*, the name he had used in his early stage days. Then it was clear exactly who the assassin was, for in the excitement and wild rumors it had been said in Bryantown, and even in Richmond, that it was Edwin Booth who had killed Lincoln and then leaped down onto the Ford's Theatre stage. When John T. Ford, in the former Confederate capital to visit an uncle not seen since the war began, heard the news, he laughed. "Edwin Booth is in Boston," he said. It did not occur to him that another Booth might be involved.

In Boston there were no such misunderstandings. A letter for Edwin was delivered to Orlando Tomkins's Franklin Square home: *A fearful calamity is upon us. The President of the United States has fallen by the hand of an assassin, and I am shocked to say suspicion points to one nearly related to you as the perpetrator of this horrid deed. God grant that it may not prove so! Out of respect to the anguish which will fill the public mind as soon as the appalling fact shall be fully revealed, I have concluded to close the Boston Theatre until further notice. Please signify to me your cooperation in this matter. In great sorrow, and in haste, I remain, yours very truly, Henry C. Jarrett.*

He replied: *With deepest sorrow and great agitation, I thank you for relieving me of my engagement with yourself and the public. The news of the morning has made me wretched, indeed, not only because of a brother's crime, but because a most justly honored and patriotic ruler has fallen, in an hour of national joy, by the hand of an assassin. The memory of the thousands who have fallen in the field in our country's defense cannot be forgotten by me, even in this, the most distressing day of my life. While mourning, in common with all other loyal hearts, the death of the President, I am oppressed by a private woe not to be expressed in words. But whatever calamity may befall me and mine, my country, one and indivisible, has my warmest devotion.* His career was over, he knew that, he said. He would never step on a stage again. Only death, most welcome, would free him, he said, of what he was now—of this. And the sooner the better.

Meanwhile, there was his mother to think of. He wired her that he would take the midnight train from Boston to New York. A brave Orlando Tomkins accompanied him, afraid to send any telegrams confirming their progress from way stations for fear of what might happen if anyone discovered the identity of the man he was with. In the morning they were at the Seventeenth Street home, Edwin in a long cloak and soft hat pulled down, a figure in Lillian Woodman Aldrich's eyes as spectral as if the grave had given up its dead. A small group of friends had gathered to receive him, all weeping. He was stonelike, the only one not to cry, maintaining what Mrs. Aldrich described as an almost frozen silence. To William Bispham he seemed a man stricken to the ground and in actual danger of losing his mind. "Nothing but the love poured out for him by his friends saved him from madness. His sanity hung in the balance."

All agreed he must not be left alone for a minute, and when he went to sleep that night it was in a room whose second bed held Thomas Bailey Aldrich. On the wall hung a life-size portrait of John, the glimmer of the gas streetlights outside making the picture seem almost alive, a living presence, like a poor misguided ghost, Aldrich thought. They had neither the heart nor the courage to have it removed.

The subject of the painting had left Dr. Mudd's to approach the vast fifteen-mile-long Zekiah Swamp, an uninhabited damp wasteland of bogs, stagnant ponds, snakes, sluices of water, decaying vegetation, and dense growths of dogwood, gum, and beech. He and Davy Herold blundered about heading south, lost their way in the darkness, and came upon a native of the region to whom they offered ten dollars if he would lead them to the residence of Samuel Cox, a local grandee and well-known Confederate sympathizer.

It was past midnight when their guide brought them to Cox's house, some five miles from the Potomac. The moon was out, and in its light Cox was shown India ink initials JWB on the back of one of his caller's hands, and told he stood in the presence of the man who hardly twenty-four hours earlier had fired the shot that killed Abraham Lincoln. Cox was flabbergasted. He had heard of the President's death, and now the man who caused it was asking, in the name of his mother, for his mother's sake, that he be given help. Cox thought of his neck and his family, of the danger in which he would place them both if he took the fugitives in to his house, where black servants would at once know of their presence. He temporized. Let them spend the night outside and he would see what could be done. They went off to huddle in a ditch where at dawn Cox found them. He directed them to a little pine forest a mile from his home and said he would send help soon. His emissary would whistle in a particular fashion so they would know him as a friend.

They lay on the patch of clearing in the forest. Easter Sunday was cold and dreary, unlike Washington to the north, where a warm spring and rains had brought the city's fragrant lilacs into early bloom. Ever after there were those who never again knew that aroma without being at once reminded of those days of draped flags, tolling bells, muffled drums, solemn trumpets, thudding minute guns, of tears and sobs for the departed one who to Walt Whitman seemed to have been as the captain of a ship that had weathered a terrible storm but came into port with the captain dead on the deck.

In the morning, Easter morning, when women all over the country forewent seasonal finery for mourning black and when church choirs sang no hymns of life reborn, of Life conquering Death, but offered instead dirges—Black Easter, it was called—Samuel Cox's emissary came to the pine forest. He was the farmer-fisherman Thomas A. Jones, Cox's foster brother. "Tom," Cox had told him, "I had visitors this morning."

Jones asked who, and why the visitors had come. Cox replied that they wanted to get over the Potomac into Virginia. Then he asked if Jones knew that President Lincoln had been assassinated. Jones did. He heard it from some Yankee soldiers the previous evening.

Cox asked, "Tom, can't you put those men across?"

"Sam, I will see what I can do." Jones had spent the war putting men and supplies across the Potomac, ducking Yankee gunboats and land patrols so that letters and newspapers and spies could reach Richmond. He went to the pine forest and whistled the notes Cox had demonstrated for him. Davy Herold came out of the clearing with his carbine cocked. To Jones he looked hardly more than a boy. "I come from Cox," Jones said. "He told me I would find you here."

Herold led him thirty yards into the undergrowth to John Wilkes Booth—so he would be remembered in the history books, never as John Booth or Johnny Booth, as he had been known all the twenty-six years of his life—and Jones saw a man lying on the ground with his head supported on his hand and with pistols and a knife nearby. There was a blanket partially covering him, a donation from Cox, and he was exceedingly pale and looked to be in pain but, Jones remembered, "I have seldom, if ever, seen a more strikingly handsome man."

He greeted Jones in a pleasant voice and impressed his visitor as courteous and polite. It was clear his leg was intensely painful, swollen and discolored. His main concern was for newspapers so he might see what was being said of what he had done. "Very desirous to know what the world thought of his deed," Jones remembered. Jones told him he would come each day with food and newspapers, but that for the moment the fugitives must stay hidden where they were to avoid the hue and cry of the area and the Yankee searchers. When it was not suicidal to do so they would attempt the river. Jones pointed out a spring thirty or forty yards away and told Herold to be cautious when drawing water from it, for there was a footpath nearby that people sometimes used.

In Washington workmen began preparing the East Room for the President's funeral, but the sounds of construction of a wooden platform to hold the coffin utterly unnerved Mary Lincoln as she lay upstairs refusing all sympathy calls save those of Secretary Stanton and Senator Sumner. Each time a hammer came down on a nail she was reminded of a pistol shot, and the son of the secretary of the navy and Mrs. Welles, Edgar, wrote an urgent request that the work go forth more quietly. As silently as possible, workmen draped the room in black, the mirrors and paintings, the chandeliers and columns. A few blocks away another mourning woman also lay in her bed. In the bordello run by her sister, Ella Turner had put her lover's picture under her pillow and covered her face with chloroform-soaked material. Revived, she told the doctors she did not thank them for saving her life.

Away from the White House and the bordello, the world sought the assassin. He was said to have been spotted in Pottsville and three other Pennsylvania towns, in Brooklyn and in Chicago, where the police arrested a McVickers Theatre actor who resembled him. Rumors spread that he was still in Washington—in secret passages below Ford's, in the streets disguised as a black woman, in an abandoned house. A man on crutches was seen entering a house on Pennsylvania Avenue between Eleventh and Twelfth streets, and at once police and soldiers came to search every residence on the block. The sight of two Confederate officers being escorted through the streets raised a cry of "Booth!" and a mob instantly materialized ready to tear them to pieces, as had almost been done to a man who unwisely had said something in praise of Jefferson Davis, or throw a rope around their necks, as was done to a shopkeeper near Ford's who ventured to say the actors there were not to blame for the President's death. The two officers were hurried into the office of the provost marshal, and an army general and the minister-designate to Spain, John P. Hale, went out to offer assurances that neither of the men was the President's slayer. The crowd did not disperse, and the Confederates were taken out the back door to the safety of the Old Capitol prison, where they joined hundreds of people locked up there on suspicion of helping the fugitives. It could not have been easy for Hale to speak so in public, for the world was learning whose fiancée his daughter had been. LUCY HALE'S GRIEF, a *New York Tribune* story was headlined. *The unhappy lady—the daughter of a New England senator—to whom Booth was affianced, is plunged in profoundest grief; but with womanly fidelity is slow to believe him guilty of this appalling crime, and asks, with touching pathos, for evidence of his innocence.* Her father used every bit of influence he could call on to keep her name out of the papers, and had friends write letters to editors averring there was no truth at all to the stories, that she had hardly known the assassin and had no personal relationship of any kind with him.

For Edwin Booth it was of course impossible to say such a thing. He sat in his New York home in his frozen silence. Word came that he was to be imprisoned, like his brother June and Asia's husband, but friends begged authorities not to do it, and so he was put under a kind of house arrest, to receive letter after letter telling him he would soon be killed, his residence burned. *You are advised to leave this city and this country forthwith. Your life will be the penalty if you tarry 48 hours longer. Revolvers are already loaded with which to shoot you down. You are a traitor to this government (or have been until your brother's bloody deed.)*

Herein you have due warning. Lose no time in arranging for your departure. We hate the name of Booth. Leave quick or remember
                                                    Outraged Humanity.

As with his mother to the Aldriches, he repeated that his only hope was that John would not live to be hanged. As for himself, he wrote Colonel Adam Badeau at Grant's headquarters in Washington, "Oh, how little did I dream, my boy, when on Friday night I was as Sir Edward Mortimer exclaiming, 'Where is my honor now? Mountains of shame are piled upon me!' that I was not acting but uttering the fearful truth." U.S. marshals came and searched his trunks and read his letters looking for incriminating evidence. He sent off a paid notice to the newspapers:

My Fellow Citizens:
      It has pleased God to lay at the door of my afflicted family the lifeblood of our great, good and martyred President. Prostrated to the very earth by this dreadful event, I am yet but too sensible that other mourners fill the land. To them, to you, one and all, go forth our deep, unutterable sympathy; our abhorrence and detestation for this most foul and atrocious of crimes.

For my mother and sisters, for my remaining brothers and my own poor self there is nothing to be said except that we are thus placed without any agency of our own. For our present position we are not responsible. For the future—alas; I shall struggle on in my retirement bearing a heavy heart, an oppressed memory and a wounded name—dreadful burdens—to my too welcome grave.

The man who killed Lincoln was to spend six days and five nights alone with Davy Herold in the old tobacco bed covered with broom-sedge in a little clearing in the dense thicket of young pines, the weather always chilly and misty, the swollen and discolored flesh mortifying around his broken leg bone, fever coming and going. They could not light a fire for fear its smoke might invite attention from the searchers swarming about them, soldiers at fifty-foot intervals beating Zekiah Swamp. Once a mounted patrol came by and the livery stable horses nickered. Had the cavalry horses heard and replied, troops would have been upon them in a moment. Herold took the two deep into the swamp, swam them into a bog, and clinging to an overhead branch, shot them. The bodies sank, but when soldiers came to ask Samuel Cox if he had seen two mounted strangers, his thoughts were on the possibility that buzzards might come and show where the carcasses were. He stood on a knoll near his house looking off to the swamp and said of the soldiers to his son, "If those men enter below the spot where the bodies of the horses are, I shall hang for it." Buzzards did not appear, and the horses were never seen again.

On Tuesday after delivering bread, butter, ham, a flask of coffee, and newspapers hidden in his overcoat pocket as he ostentatiously carried a bucket of corn for his hogs running at large in the woods, Thomas Jones went to Port Tobacco. It was the traditional day for the transaction of public business there. He found the town alive with troops, and in the barroom of the Brawner Hotel was introduced to Captain William Williams of the Washington mounted police, who moments before Abraham Lincoln was shot had asked his acquaintance John Booth, standing in front of Ford's Theatre, to come for a drink. Now Williams asked Jones to join him in one. There was something about Jones that attracted the policeman's attention. Just before they lifted their glasses to their lips, Williams said, "I will give one hundred thousand dollars to anyone who will give me the information that will lead to Booth's capture." It was only part of the sum that the U.S. government and various states and cities were offering.

"That is a large sum of money and ought to get him if money can do it," Jones said, and drank. He had what Williams called a come-to-the-Lord-and-be-saved expression. But beyond the sanctimonious look, Williams and some other detectives with him thought they saw something. There was no movement or change in Jones's face, but Williams's suspicions were aroused, and in time Jones would be arrested and plied with liquor to get him to talk. It would not work, and by then the fugitives were gone from Jones's care.

Yet inside, Jones felt shaky, and when he saw bills posted everywhere ordering all citizens to join in the hunt for the assassin, "and that to furnish bread and water to him meant death, I felt shakier than ever." It did not occur to him to turn his charge in. Samuel Cox had put him in his care. He was depended upon. What he considered a poor devil hiding in a thicket needed him. He was never to regret losing out on the vast sums of money that might have been his. The war had cost him everything, and all he had accumulated in twenty years of toil had been swept away, he said, a quarter of a century on, when he and Williams met again, but had he turned in the fugitives, his money would have been accursed. The South was down and out, and Tom Jones with it, "But, thank God, there was something I still possessed—something I still could call my own, and its name was Honor."

On Wednesday, just as he had dreamed, Abraham Lincoln lay in his coffin in the East Room among weeping people. His catafalque dressed with black silk and with domed white-lined canopy was so tall that the room's central chandelier had to be removed. Two other lighting fixtures were swathed in black, as were the windows and mirrors and chairs. General Grant in white gloves and sash was at one end of the coffin and President Johnson with his arms crossed over his breast at the other. There were masses of flowers, a cross of lilies at the dead man's head, an anchor of roses at his feet. At sunrise artillery pieces all over Washington began to boom at one-minute intervals. No places of business opened. At noon the city's church bells began to toll. When the services were over the body was borne on a hearse strung with black tassels and flounces and drawn by six white horses to the Capitol, the bells of Washington and Georgetown and Alexandria tolling as minute guns from all the batteries in all the fortresses ringing the country's capital thudded in the distance. The 22nd U.S. Colored Infantry led other troops, societies, groups, associations with draped banners, bands playing dirges, muffled drums beating. Light artillery pieces rumbled by, officers with their staffs, and then the funeral car with the silver-trimmed casket riding eight or ten feet above the level of the street.

He lay in state. From inside the top of the Capitol his friend Noah Brooks looked down from the great dome at the casket far below covered with lilies, roses, magnolias, wreaths of lilac, and saw two endless lines of mourners creeping in dark lines across the pavement of the rotunda to form parentheses around the raised coffin and then joining to go to the door and vanish. The lines never stopped. For the death of Lincoln a sorrow was felt that the passing of Caesar, Charlemagne, Napoleon never knew.

For his assassin there was not a single word of anything but universal and bitter condemnation. The slayings of Julius Caesar, William the Silent, and Henry of Navarre had found their defenders. No such ever appeared for that of Abraham Lincoln. From every Sunday pulpit of Black Easter ministers denounced the man who killed him as "an accursed devil . . . fiend . . . miserable, wretched assassin . . . demon in human form . . . debased assassin." (One Massachusetts clergyman who failed to mention the events of Friday night was given fifteen minutes by his congregation to get out of town.) They had said of the South, Love thy neighbor, the people of the North told one another, and had made to welcome home the prodigal son. But see what had been the North's reward. It was a sign that the South was lost to Christianity, that its Confederacy would forever bear an inextinguishable stigma sending it to posterity eternally infamous.

Lincoln had perished for his country's sin, slavery, ministers told churchgoers, slain by a second Judas. Like Christ, he had been a long time dying from his Good Friday mortal wound, the one on a cross, the other on a bed in the Petersen house, each in the end a dying god. He had died so that his country's new birth might occur; he was after Washington the second Founder of his country. Who had killed him was beyond execration. America "revolted with horror," wrote The Times of London correspondent to his paper, and the man who slew Lincoln was "the vilest assassin known to history." He would own an "immortality of infamy."

People the world over, high and low, understood all as soon as the news reached them. Expressions of sympathy and horror began to pour in from every country and every level, the Duke of Brunswick, the Septentrion Masonic Lodge of Ghent, the Turners Society of the Grand Duchy of Baden, the Society of Primary Instruction of Chile, the Corps Legislatif of France, the New South

Wales Branch of the Irish National League of Sydney, the Odd
Fellows of Bermuda, the Office of the Board of Works of the White
Chapel District of London, Count Bismarck and the Prussian
House of Deputies, His Highness Aali Pacha of Turkey, a "public
meeting of the trading and working classes of Brighton at the Town
Hall," Queen Victoria and the Empress Eugénie: "Vile assassin
. . . horrid crime . . . cowardly, cruel atrocity . . . odious act,
appalling tragedy . . . cruel death." To the Massachusetts legislature
Governor John A. Andrew tellingly quoted Shakespeare:

> Besides, this Duncan
> Hath borne his faculties so meek, hath
> Been so clear in his great office, that his virtues
> Will plead like angels, trumpet-tongued, against
> The deep damnation of his taking-off.

It was not only the North and the rest of the world beyond
American borders that in one voice damned the man who shot
Lincoln. It was the South also. "The heaviest blow which has ever
fallen upon the people of the South has descended," said the *Richmond Whig*. This assassination, the paper said, was an appalling,
deplorable calamity, a terrible blow. In a Charlotte, North Carolina, church, Jefferson Davis heard from the minister that what had
been done was "folly and wickedness, a blot on American civiliza-
tion, infamy." To his daughter he said, "This terrible deed was
done by a crazy man who, no doubt, thought he was the savior of
the South, though really her worst enemy. This is the bitterest blow
that could have been dealt to the Southern cause." Robert E. Lee
first refused to hear details of what had happened but finally said
a crime unexampled had been committed.

In Charleston, South Carolina, former governor William
Aiken, before the war the South's largest slaveholder, said of the
assassin: "Our expression of disgust for the dastardly wretch can
scarcely be uttered. Can it be believed that in the nineteenth century a human being could be found to have in his bosom so
diabolical an idea? The heart sickens." When General Sherman,
accepting General Johnston's surrender, told him the news, which
had not yet reached the remote North Carolina section where they
met, "the perspiration," Sherman wrote, "came out in large drops
on his forehead" and he denounced the assassination as "the greatest possible calamity to the South, a disgrace to the age." From
their prisoner-of-war camp sixteen Confederate generals wrote
Grant that the greatest misfortune that could befall the Southern

people, or any individual Southerner, would be the idea that anything could be felt for the assassination other than unqualified
abhorrence and indignation. "Our heart stands almost still as we
take our pen in hand to speak of the tragedy," said the *Intelligencer*
of that Baltimore where the assassin had spent his youth. "We have
no words at command with which to express anything that we feel.
Our heart is too full to say more. All of us feel as if we were passing
through a horrid dream." The *Baltimore Sun:* He was diabolical,
wicked.

Word spread that four hundred Confederate prisoners held at
Sherman's headquarters camp were slaughtered to the last man
when their captors learned of the assassination. Nothing could stop
the soldiers from falling upon them, the marquis de Chambrun
wrote his wife. (The report was untrue, although Sherman had in
fact been frightened of what his men might do.) In remote Southern
outposts the Union troops receiving the news wept uniformly. The
officer George Haven Putnam, whose later career would be in his
family's publishing house, never before or after saw a mass of men
so sobbingly overwhelmed with one emotion as the grouped soldiers who heard their adjutant brokenly tell them: "Lincoln is
dead."

In the little clearing amid the pines, where each day Thomas
Jones came with food and tidings, the fugitives lay on wet earth and
read the newspapers. Jones and the simple Davy Herold, and his
aching leg and rising fever, and the dripping skies and slight vista
of the tiny patch of open ground constituted the assassin's universe. He had seen himself to be in the family tradition of generations when he did as he did: His grandfather, Richard Booth, had
run away from home to attempt to join the American colonialists
rising against the tyrant George III; his father had been named for
that Junius Brutus who fought Rome's despotic Tarquins; and he
himself had been named for the John Wilkes whose fame was based
on opposition to the Crown. He had seen himself dispensing justice
to an absolute autocrat who was brother to the Russian czars and
committed offenses for less than which Charles I lost his head. Here
was Caesar. Deservedly Caesar had been slain.

He must write of what he had done. He had with him a little
appointment book for the previous year, 1864, three and a half by
six inches, with brown leather binding and red leather lining and
front and back leather pockets with flaps marked for tickets and
postage stamps, and a loop for a pencil. At the top of the first page
he had written, in another life as a romantic actor, *Ti Amo*, which

correctly should have been *Te Amo*, for *I Love You*, perhaps meant for one of the four actresses whose photographs were there, including Effie Germon, who had played Aladdin in the play that Tad Lincoln departed to learn of his father's death wound; perhaps for Ella Turner, who tried to kill herself in her sister's bordello; perhaps for a young woman in Tudor Hall, his rented-out childhood home, who had taken his photograph from a mantel of the house and kissed it heartbrokenly after troops came thrusting swords into garments packed away by the home's owners; perhaps for one of two women in New York, one on West 25th Street, the other on Clark Street, and whom the police had learned were close to him; and perhaps for Lucy Hale, the fifth woman whose photograph was in the little appointment book. In the pine clearing, alone save for Herold, sought by thousands of soldiers, by tugs, steamers, gunboats patrolling the Potomac he must cross, he wrote under the space for April 14:

> Friday the Ides. Until today nothing was ever thought of sacrificing to our country's wrongs. For six months we had worked to capture. But our cause being almost lost, something decisive and great must be done. I struck boldly and not as the papers say. I walked with a firm step through a thousand of his friends, was stopped, but pushed on. A colonel was by his side. I shouted "Sic semper." In jumping broke my leg. I passed all his pickets. Rode sixty miles that night, with the bone of my leg tearing at every jump.
>
> I can never repent it, though we hated to kill. Our country owed all her troubles to him, and God simply made me the instrument of His punishment. I care not what becomes of me. I have no desire to outlive my country. The night before the deed, I wrote a long article and left it for one of the editors of the *National Intelligencer*, in which I fully set forth our reasons for our proceedings. He or the gov't—

He interrupted his writing. Perhaps the pain of his leg, or the fever, overcame him. Perhaps Jones came. He could not know that his letter to the *National Intelligencer* would never see light there. "Great God!" the actor John Mathews had cried when it fell out of his coat pocket. "There is the letter John gave me in the afternoon." Mathews had fled Ford's Theatre for his room with shouts of "burn," "hang," "lynch" ringing in his ears. He opened the letter. He read that its author had devoted his money, time, and energies to arranging the President's kidnapping—"capture" was the word used—but had been unable to get it done. Twenty or thirty thousand dollars had been expended, but all attempts failed.

"The moment has arrived," Mathews read, "when my plans must be changed. The world may censure me for what I am about to do; but I am sure that posterity will justify me.

"Men who love their country better than gold or life: J. W. Booth"—and Davy Herold and Lewis Powell and George Atzerodt. The terrified and bewildered Mathews asked himself, alone in his room, what to do now. "I thought to myself, 'What should I do with this letter?' It could only convict him, and that has been done already, because the people in the house have recognized him. If this paper be found on me I will be compromised—no doubt lynched on the spot. If I take it to the newspaper office it will be known and I will be associated with the letter, and suspicions will grow out of it that can never be explained away, and I will be ruined." Mathews threw the letter into his fireplace and burned it to cinders.

He had written in his letter, and in his little appointment book, solely of a political slaying, but this did not at all suggest itself to Colonel Adam Badeau. To Badeau what he had done had to do with things far more complex, and more personal to the slayer. It had to do with the fact that John Wilkes Booth was an actor, of a family of actors; it had to do with his family and the family troubles that characterized Shakespeare's plays in which he and his family had appeared, what weighed down Romeo, Hamlet, Lear: love, hatred, death, bastardy, murder, great passions. Involved also was the limelight actors seek as they read their lines and take their cues. "It was all so theatrical in plan and performance," Adam wrote. "The conspiracy, the dagger, the selection of a theater, the cry 'Sic semper tyrannis'—all was exactly what a madman brought up in a theater might have been expected to conceive; a man, stock of this peculiar family, the son of Junius Brutus Booth, used all his life to acting tragedy."

The same thought came to the Englishman Charles Wyndham, back home beginning the work that would eventually make him one of his country's leading impresarios. At first he refused to credit the reports from America that the actor J. W. Booth had killed Lincoln. "This seemed impossible." Then he wondered if perhaps the manner of the doing was in itself confirmation of the assassin's identity. His friend, Wyndham reasoned, must have thought he was doing something heroic, like a stage knight-errant.

He was mad, yes, Wyndham decided—but so theatric was his way
of doing the terrible work that it showed "the madman had not
overborne the actor." In fact the whole of his part in history was
like a play. As private in the Richmond Grays, Lincoln's slayer had
seen what could be called the first fatality of the Civil War, John
Brown swinging at the end of a rope. With his derringer he had
killed what might be called the war's final victim. The first act and
the last.

Madman, Badeau had said. Madman, Wyndham had said.
"The madman!" thought the actress Charlotte Cushman in Rome
when she learned the news from the American minister Rufus
King. At first King heard only that Lincoln and Secretary Seward
had been attacked, with no other details, and that was bad enough
for Miss Cushman, who was a close friend of the Seward family
and always stayed at the secretary's home when playing Washington. "In our country, in these modern times," she said incredu-
lously to Minister King. "It is too theatrical a thing to be done by
an American!" Then came the news of who had shot Lincoln. "I
cannot keep from weeping," she wrote her daughter-in-law, who
had been one of the late Mary Devlin Booth's closest friends. "The
horror makes my blood run so cold as to bring the tears to my eyes
and cheeks." It was Miss Cushman who had a couple of years
earlier opened up the surgical incision on the assassin's neck when
they embraced onstage. "I am unable to think or to feel or to do
anything else but sit and clasp my hands in dread and fear," she
wrote. "My heart feels as though it were cramped up in a vice."

Madman. The madman. But where was any evidence of madness before the evening of April 14, 1865? Here was a young man
eminently successful in his profession, extremely likable, engaged
to a prominent and appealing woman, on the best terms with his
mother and his sisters and—save for political discussions with
Edwin—with his brothers, a man possessing many friends, many of
whom he had known from boyhood—including Sam Arnold, a
letter from whom concerning the failed March kidnap attempt,
found in the National Hotel room, put the authorities on Arnold's
trail, along with that of another longtime friend and kidnap conspirator, Michael O'Laughlen. John Booth had been rated as kindly
and sociable and generous by all who knew him best, and was
universally admired and liked by the members of his profession.
Where was any sign of madness?

That Edwin was a deeply disturbed personality no one questioned. That their father had been insane seemed apparent. Rosalie

was silent and withdrawn. The youngest member of the family, Joseph, had suffered, he said himself, from what he termed "melancholy insanity" from childhood on, and he was seized by an attack of it when on Secretary Stanton's order he was arrested. He had been in England and then Australia for three years since suddenly vanishing in 1862. "No news yet of Joe," his brother John had then written a family friend. "Have hunted every place I can think of. I can't tell what to do, poor Mother will take it so hard." After a time Joe established communication and had gone from Australia to California to sail to New York. He had learned of the assassination when his ship docked at Panama. He was told that a man named Booth had killed the President, but "I did not think anything of that. I knew there was a hundred Booths." Then he learned who the Booth was. "My own brother." Joe felt his reason leave him. "I was insane in Panama," he told the detectives who arrested him. "That news made me insane."

It would not have surprised the oldest brother, June, that the youngest had become mentally ill. When Joe disappeared in 1862, June wrote Edwin that he felt Joe was "not sound in mind." He did not mean positive madness, June went on, "but a crack that way, which Father in his highest had and which I fear runs more or less through the male portion of our family myself included." He was so concerned with his own possible insanity, June wrote, that it was his practice never to do anything on impulse, but to think everything through. So June was on record as saying, in 1862, that he felt all men of his family were liable to be unbalanced. But no one had ever said that directly about John.

Yet to Asia in Philadelphia, her husband in jail, her life shattered forever for what her most beloved brother had done, it seemed that John must have been mad. It must have been Lincoln's trip into Richmond that set him off, she reasoned, thinking it was ungenerous for the President to stride into the enemy's capital and to parade there over his prone victims. (And in fact General Grant had never gone into the city, saying to his wife when she asked if he would do so, "I would not distress these people. They are feeling their defeat bitterly, and you would not add to it by my witnessing their despair, would you?") And the visit to the theater, Asia thought: To go at such a time, with Washington ringing with the clang of joy and triumph—it must have seemed to John that the President had no pity for the South, but was jubilantly celebrating its defeat and its desolated homes. Such was what must have detonated her brother's reason, she decided. She lay in her home guarded by police, under perpetual surveillance. The government ordered her to Washington, and when she said an approaching confinement made it impossible for her to travel, she was told to produce a medical assertion that this was so. Only with the greatest difficulty could she find a doctor who would come to her house and certify her condition. She was followed by a detective from room to room. All mail was opened before it was handed to her.

Among the letters were ones from Edwin. "Think no more of him as your brother," he wrote. "He is dead to us now, as he soon must be to all the world, but imagine the boy you loved to be in that better part of his spirit in another world." And: "I have had a heart-broken letter from the poor little girl to whom he promised so much happiness." Lucy Hale had written that if necessary she would marry her fiancé at the foot of the scaffold. Few friends came to Asia, and those who did sorrowed with her covertly, if at all. She did not cry and seldom spoke.

There was one letter that for a moment lit her darkened world. The eighteen-year-old girl who had played Aladdin for Tad Lincoln at Grover's on Good Friday and whose picture the fugitive had in his appointment book was a comedienne-singer, ingénue, and soubrette. She was to marry four times; it was said that she kept the stage door Johnnies busy wherever she appeared. Asia received:

> Dear Madam:
>   Although a perfect stranger to you, I take the liberty of offering my sympathy and aid in your great sorrow. If my mother or myself can be of the slightest use to you in any way in this world we should be only too happy. I should have offered before, but illness prevented. May God help and bless you is the constant prayer of
>
>   Effie Germon.

There were some things, Asia wrote, that should be treasured like precious gold.

In the forest clearing he lay beneath the dripping skies and mist, and read Thomas Jones's newspapers. The entire theatrical profession was under attack, and ministers said that henceforth the stage would be odious in America, that his act proved what many had always said, that the theater was the rival sinful of the church holy. "Would that Mr. Lincoln had fallen elsewhere than at the very gates of Hell—in the theater," said a Detroit pastor. "How awful and severe the rebuke which God has administered to the nation for pampering such demoralizing places of resort. The blood of Abraham Lincoln can never be effaced from the stage." A Jacksonville, Illinois, clergyman said that the President in a theater "had been out of God's jurisdiction and forfeited the divine protection."

Men were shot for slowness in criticizing what John Wilkes Booth had done, beaten, dragged through the streets by a rope around the neck, strung up on trees or lampposts. In Richmond little Mary Beale, whom once a young actor had brought from her nursery to be put on a silver serving platter, and to whom he had given a ring, had it taken from her finger by her parents and buried in the garden. Not of an age completely to understand, she went with her two long blond braids hanging down and looked at the grave of her ring there among the dandelions and violets, a forbidden pleasure now. The *Philadelphia Press* remarked that it sympathized with Edwin but that henceforth he would never be able to go before the public bearing the name he did. Perhaps one day he might change it to something else and resume his career.

In Washington plans were made for Abraham Lincoln to go 1,662 miles home to Springfield, in a black-draped train of eight coaches, six for mourners, one for the guard of honor, and one for his coffin on a raised pedestal with that of his son Willie resting by. The engine was swathed in black. Preceding it would travel at a steady twenty miles an hour a pilot engine, and all along the route guns would pulse and bells toll and the sides of the tracks be thickly lined with people, entire towns turning out at midnight or in the small hours of the morning, bands playing dirges, draped flags held up, raised signs: We Mourn Our Loss. The Darkest Hour in History. Oh, The Pity of It, Iago—The Pity of It. He Lives in the Heart of His People. Rest In Peace Noble Soul. Gone to Glory. Of the thirty million people of the North, seven million would see his slow train pass, and one and a half million file by as he lay in state in a dozen cities.

As the bells tolled and muffled drums rolled, the assassin of the second father of the country was feverishly sought. From Headquarters Middle Military Division, Washington, Major General Winfield Scott Hancock published an appeal: *To the Colored People of the District of Columbia and of Maryland, of Alexandria and the Border Counties of Virginia: Your President has been murdered! Think of this, and remember how long and how anxiously this good man labored to break your chains and to make you happy. I now appeal to you to aid in discovering and arresting his murderer. He is believed to be lurking somewhere within the limits of the District of Columbia or the States of*

Maryland or Virginia. Go forth, then, and watch, and listen, and inquire, and search, and pray, by day and by night, until you have succeeded in dragging this monstrous and bloody criminal from his hiding place. You will hunt down this cowardly assassin of your best friend as you would the murderer of your own father.

All his life he had heard Shakespeare quoted, and quoted Shakespeare himself. If in the Ford's Theatre box he had seen himself as Brutus doing thus always to tyrants, in the dismal thicket he might have thought of Richard III:

> The lights burn blue. It is now dead midnight!
> Cold, flareful drops stand on my trembling flesh.
> What do I fear? Myself? There is none else by:
> Is there a murderer here? No!—Yes!—I am.
> My conscience hath a thousand several tongues,
> And every tongue brings in a several tale,
> And every tale condemns me for a villain!
> Perjury, perjury in the highest degree:
> Murder, stern murder in the direst degree:
> All several sins, all used in each degree,
> Throng to the bar, crying all, Guilty! Guilty!

THIRTEEN

HE HAD BEEN with Davy Herold for six days and five nights in the clearing in the sighing pines; and Thomas Jones came and said the moment had come to cross the Potomac. In the tiny settlement of Allen's Fresh, a few houses in the wilderness, Jones had heard a cavalry officer tell his men the fugitives had been spotted to the south, in St. Marys County. The soldiers saddled up and headed out.

That meant, Jones reasoned, that at least for a little while the immediate area would be free of those and the other bluecoats who had made it their business to visit every house in lower Maryland, including his, several times in the past days. He loitered about for a time after the cavalry left so as not to attract attention by a hurried departure, and then slowly rode his gray mare out of Allen's Fresh. Evening was coming. It had been misty all day, with dense clouds and an intensely damp atmosphere. Gray fog from the swamp just below the little cluster of houses covered his road. He went to the thicket where the fugitives were.

"Friends," Jones said, "this is your only chance. My boat is close by. I will get you some supper at my house, and send you off if I can." He had planned for this moment, having his former slave Henry Woodland go out each morning to fish for the shad running in the river, establishing thus the boat's legitimacy and saving it from the possibility of being stove in by the soldiers, as happened to other boats.

Jones and Herold got the assassin up on the gray mare with the greatest difficulty. He could not suppress a moan of anguish when he put his swollen and inflamed leg over the saddle. They set out in the darkness for Jones's house. It was some two and a half miles distant over cart track and trails part of the way, but unavoidably over a public road for one stretch. Jones went on ahead, halting frequently to see if all seemed safe and then whistling for Herold to lead the horse to him. The croaking of a frog or far barking of a dog, and the wings of a night bird overhead, made Jones's heart beat quicker and his breath come faster. When he whistled his come-ahead it sounded to him as loud as a trumpet, and the tramping of the slowly advancing mare like the approach of a troop. Jones was about forty-five, somber, a nonsmoker and nondrinker, uneducated, a widower with several children, born to what in the South was called the overseer class. He was all that stood between John Wilkes Booth and the full power of the U.S. government. He knew what awaited him if things went wrong.

There were two widely separated houses to be passed on the public road. The houses had people inside who might glance out, dogs that might bark. They crept past them unnoticed. Jones felt he could breathe now. They came to the grounds of his home and stopped under an old pear tree. The Potomac was another mile on through uninhabited wooded land marked by deep gullies and ravines.

"Now I will go in and get something for you to eat, and you eat it here while I get something for myself," Jones whispered.

From the horseman in the darkness he heard back, "Oh, can't I go in the house just a moment and get a little of your warm coffee?" The request was so pathetic that Jones felt his throat choke up. "It cut me to the heart that this poor creature, whose head had not been under a roof, who had not tasted warm food, felt the glow of a fire, or seen a cheerful light for nearly a week, there in the dark, wet night at my threshold, made this piteous request to be allowed to enter a human habitation."

But it would be impossible to comply. "Oh, my friend," Jones said, "it would not be safe. I have Negroes in the house, and if they see you, you are lost and so am I." He went to his former slave Henry Woodland. "Did you bring that boat back to Dent's Meadow where I told you?" he asked. The meadow was a secluded clearing on the high Potomac bluffs, with below it a tiny valley through which flowed a spring feeding into the river. Woodland told him the boat was there, as it had been for each of the past few nights. Jones asked how many shad Woodland had caught that day. About seventy. They chatted some more. Jones managed to get some food out to the men under the pear tree, ate himself in his kitchen, and went outside.

They slowly made their way through the rough and hilly terrain to the Potomac, two walking, one riding. It would be impossible to get the horse down the great high bluff bordering the shore, and so Jones and Herold carried the crippled man, each movement torture for him. There was a swell on the river. It was about 10:30 P.M., Friday, April 21—one week since the derringer bullet entered Abraham Lincoln's head.

Jones got his boat from its berthing place in the spring where Henry Woodland had left it. The boat was about twelve feet long, flat-bottomed, dark lead in color. Jones had bought it a year earlier for eighteen dollars. They got the assassin into the stern, where he would use an oar to steer while Davy Herold rowed.

Jones got out an oilcloth coat and shielded a candle and on a compass brought from Washington along with the little appointment book showed the course the travelers must follow. Before them was the vast river, shimmering, lonely, frightening, two miles across at that point, the far shore almost invisible even in daylight, ships of the Union Navy's Potomac Flotilla patrolling it and Chesapeake Bay and adjacent waters with, offshore, the North Atlantic Blockading Squadron also watching should the assassin try to get away by sea. Wax drops from the candle dripped onto the compass. They must make for Machodoc Creek on the Virginia side, Jones said, and there find Mrs. Elizabeth Quesenberry. Like himself, she had been active during the war in helping Confederate agents. She would help them, he thought, Jones said, if the fugitives indicated they came from him.

Jones said good-bye and started to shove the boat off. From the stern came, "Wait a minute, old fellow." Jones was offered money. He said he would take eighteen dollars—the price of the boat. More was proffered. Jones said that what he had done was not for money. The sum he had mentioned was handed over. Then, in a choked voice, "God bless you, my dear friend, for all you have done for me. Good-bye, old fellow." For a moment Jones could hear the oars moving in the water, and then the sound died away. He climbed up the bluff and got his mare and went to his home. Shortly he joined the hundreds of others locked up in Washington's Old Capitol prison on suspicion or whim. He revealed nothing to his questioners and eventually was freed. He believed that the assassination of Lincoln was the worst blow the South had ever been struck. He never regretted what he had done for John Wilkes Booth.

■

In the darkness out on the great river they quickly lost their bearings. The winds and tides pushed them about. Any splash or apparent light could be a Yankee gunboat. They paddled around, confused by the numerous broad inlets opening into the river, hopelessly lost. Dawn was coming. They put into shore—still on the Maryland side of the Potomac, nine miles west of Dent's Meadow instead of eight miles south, at Machodoc Creek.

They paddled inland on a spring and hid on its shore as best they could. When the skies lightened, Herold recognized their location. He had been there on hunting trips. He left his companion and went to a local landowner who knew him, and knew also that this trifling boy who used to hunt his land, whom Thomas Jones noted in six days had never said "anything of the slightest importance," was now the escaping accomplice of the assassin of Abraham Lincoln. Reward posters naming him were everywhere. The man offered some food for Herold to bear away, but refused to permit the object of the greatest manhunt in history to be brought into his home. So they spent the day, Saturday, waiting for darkness to come so they might attempt the great river. Lincoln's funeral train was on its way West.

Into the appointment book went:

> After being hunted like a dog through swamps, woods and last night being chased by gun-boats till I was forced to return wet, cold and starving, with every man's hand against me, I am here in despair. And why? For doing what Brutus was honored for—what made Tell a hero.* And yet I, for striking down a greater tyrant than they ever knew, am looked upon as a common cutthroat. My act was purer than either of theirs. One hoped to be great himself, the other had not only his country's but his own wrongs to avenge.
>
> I hoped for no gains. I knew no private wrong. I struck for my country and for that alone. A country groaned beneath this tyranny and prayed for this end, and yet now behold the cold hand they extend to me. God cannot pardon me if I have done wrong. Yet I cannot see any wrong except in serving a degenerate people. The little, the very little, I left behind to clear my name, the government will not allow to be printed. So ends all. For

*After sending an arrow through an apple placed on his son's head by order of the Austrian governor Gessler, the Swiss patriot used a second arrow to kill the despot. Schiller's tragedy and Rossini's opera were popular treatments of the matter.

my country I have given up all that makes life sweet and
holy, brought misery upon my family, and am sure there
is no pardon for me in the heavens since man condemns
me so. God, try and forgive me and bless my mother.
To-night I will once more try the river, with the intention
to cross; though I have a greater desire and almost a mind
to return to Washington, and in a measure clear my
name, which I feel I can do.

I do not repent the blow I struck. I may before my
God, but not to man. I think I have done well, though I
am abandoned, with the curse of Cain upon me, when, if
the world knew my heart, that one blow would have me
great, although I did desire no greatness. To-night I try
once more to escape these bloodhounds. Who, who can
read his fate? God's will be done.

After sunset they went out again on the water and this time
found their way to an inlet a mile from their destination. When it
became light Herold went to Mrs. Elizabeth Quesenberry, the
woman recommended by Thomas Jones, told her he was an escaped Confederate prisoner of war, had a brother with a broken
leg, and needed a carriage. She refused him anything, then changed
her mind as he walked away and said she would send some food to
where the boat was. Her choice for its deliverer was a Confederate
agent who had been in on the abduction scheme. Now his only
concern was to get rid as quickly as possible of two men association
with whom could certainly put a rope around his neck. Thomas
Harbin passed them off to William Bryant, a local farmer, with the
suggestion that they get Bryant to take them to the home of Dr.
Richard Stuart, eight miles away. Herold offered Bryant ten dollars.
The farmer got out his horses.

Dr. Stuart was accounted the richest man in Virginia's King
George County and was a relative of Robert E. Lee, two of whose
daughters had stayed with him for part of the war. His wife had
served as a bridesmaid at Lee's marriage to Mary Custis. He had
spent some unpleasant time in Union custody for assisting rebel
spies and agents. Now there appeared at his home two men whom
to help would bring more than unpleasantness. He said his house
was filled with friends and relatives returning from the war and that
there was no room for additional guests. They said that if Dr.
Stuart knew their circumstances he would understand the urgency
of their need for shelter. "I don't want to know anything about
you," he kept saying.

He repeated that it was impossible that they stay. They asked him as a physician to attend to the injured man's broken leg; he refused, saying he was not a surgeon. They asked if he could arrange them transportation to Fredericksburg. Impossible. Could they at least have something to eat? He said they might—in the kitchen.

So they took what was offered them there, like tramps, or persons of a class quite different from that of a rich doctor. As they made do, Stuart came in and dropped an elephantine hint, using their transporter, William Bryant, as his weapon: "The old man is waiting for you; he is anxious to be off; it is cold and he is not well and wants to go home." So they had to finish quickly and go, be off, be gone. They could try the nearby cabin of a black tenant farmer, Stuart said. Perhaps William Lucas would take them in.

They went with Bryant, who took them to Lucas's, dumped them there, and departed. It was past midnight. Lucas had been asleep when the barking of his dogs awakened him. He found two men, one crippled, on the doorstep of his modest home. He heard, "We want to stay here tonight."

Lucas saw what color the men were. "You cannot do it," he said. "I am a colored man and have no right to take care of white people. I have only one room in the house and my wife is sick."

"We have been knocking about all night, and don't intend to any longer; we are going to stay." The crippled man was pushing his way into the cabin. "Gentlemen, you have treated me very badly," Lucas said. The man on crutches pulled out a knife. "Old man, how do you like that?" he asked.

"I do not like that at all," Lucas answered. "I was always afraid of a knife."

"We were sent here, old man, we understand you have good teams," the lame man said. Lucas replied that he needed his horses for planting corn. "Well, Dave," the lame man said to his companion, "we will not go on any further, but stay here, and make this old man get us his horses in the morning." The black man got his wife up and they spent the night on the cabin porch while the visitors, or appropriators, occupied their home for the night. In the morning Lucas was told his horses were needed to transport the men to the ferry at Port Conway on the Rappahannock River. "I thought you would be done impressing teams since the fall of Richmond," Lucas said. He took the two for Confederate soldiers. "Repeat that again," the crippled man said. Lucas was silent. His son Charlie, who lived nearby, appeared, to be told he would be

given twenty dollars for transportation to Port Conway, his father's horses and wagon being the means by which it would be
done. A note on paper from the appointment book was written out
for delivery to Dr. Richard Stuart:

> Forgive me, but I have some little pride. I hate to
> blame you for want of hospitality, you know your own
> affairs. I was sick, tired, with a broken leg, and in need of
> medical advice. I would not have turned a dog from my
> door in such a condition. However, you were kind
> enough to give us something to eat, for which I not only
> thank you, but, on account of the reluctant manner in
> which it was bestowed, I feel bound to pay for it.
>
> It is not the substance, but the manner in which
> kindness is extended, that makes one happy in the accept-
> ance thereof. "The sauce to meat is ceremony; meeting
> were bare without it."*
>
> Be kind enough to accept the enclosed five dollars
> (though hard to spare) for what we have received.
>
>   Yours respectfully,
>   Stranger.

But five dollars was too much to throw away for the satisfaction of insulting this ice-hearted doctor. He hadn't that much
money on him in the first place, had never dreamed that more than
a week into his flight from Ford's Theatre he would hardly be out
of Maryland and still angling to get across the Rappahannock. He
rewrote the entire letter, substituting "two and a half" for "five,"
inserted that amount, and sealed the letter for delivery by one of
the Lucas family.

Charlie Lucas drove the fugitives to Port Conway, some ten
miles distant. The war and marauding Yankee gunboats had combined almost to empty the little town in which James Madison had
been born in 1751. Port Conway's population consisted of one
aged man and the recently married Mr. and Mrs. Williams Rollins.
Rollins fished and farmed, and during the war made a little money
helping Confederate agents going North or coming South. It was
midmorning when Charlie Lucas dropped off his passengers on the
little ferry wharf. Rollins was there, preparing to go out and check
his nets for running shad.

They asked if he would take them the few hundred yards
across to Port Royal, where the hand-poled ferry was lying at dock.

*From Macbeth.

He replied that he had to see to his nets, but would from his boat let the ferryman know there were passengers waiting. In an hour or so, by noon, the tide would make the river high enough for the ferry. It would be too low until then.

They sat and waited. Three ex-Confederate soldiers heading home rode up, local boys, Private William Jett, eighteen, Private Absalom Bainbridge, also eighteen, and Lieutenant Mortimer Ruggles, twenty-one. Herold engaged Willie Jett in conversation, saying that he and his crippled companion were brothers by the name of Boyd, that they were veterans of A. P. Hill's Corps of the Army of Northern Virginia—the unit with which Lewis Powell had served—and that they wanted to get South to join in any further fighting against the Yankees that might be going on down there. The story sounded improbable to Jett. Finally Herold told him the truth: "We are the assassinators of the President."

Something in Jett's reaction must have communicated itself to the lame man sitting on a wagon on the ferry slip, for he took his crutch and limped over and said, "I suppose you have been told who I am?"

Jett confirmed that he had.

"Yes, I am John Wilkes Booth, the slayer of Abraham Lincoln, and I am worth just $175,000 to the man who captures me." That was the sum recent newspapers had been quoting; additional cities and states were adding their contributions to the Federal government's reward. He showed the JWB on his hand. The young ex-soldiers looked at him and found his coolness impressive. His suit, Absalom Bainbridge saw, appeared seamed and raveled as from contact with thorny underbrush. He was wearing a black slouch hat. Unshaven, he was pulling on what was coming back of the mustache shaved off at Dr. Mudd's on Saturday afternoon, the day after he shot Lincoln.

The ferry came, poled over by the black man who ran it for its owner. He took them across the quarter mile of water, the crippled man sitting on Ruggles's horse. They landed on the slip at Port Royal and went up into the town to the home of a man who lived with his two spinster sisters. Jett asked one of the women if she could offer shelter to a soldier wounded in the war. She consented and then changed her mind, saying her brother was away and that it would be improper for two women to entertain gentlemen in the house. She suggested the travelers go on the farm of Richard Garrett, three miles south on the way to Bowling Green.

He knew the Garrett family, Jett said after they left the

women's place. They headed for their home, five men making do with three horses, Ruggles and Bainbridge mounted on one, Herold sitting behind Jett, and John Wilkes Booth alone. They arrived at a farmhouse standing in the midst of Caroline County pines, with orchard, yard, outbuildings. There was a long driveway leading to it from the road. At the entrance Herold said that he needed new shoes, and so would go on to Bowling Green a few miles south, returning after he made his purchase. "I'll be with you soon, John. Keep in good spirits."

"Have no fear about me," was the reply. "I am among friends now." He raised his hat to Bainbridge, who indicated he would remain on the road with Herold and leave the introduction to the Garretts to Jett and Ruggles. "Come and see me again," the fugitive said politely. To Bainbridge such calmness and savoir-faire was almost unearthly. The area, after all, was filled with Yankee patrols, and with deserters from both sides; there was no effective government, no law. And here was the most sought-after man in history, with a fortune on his head. "Booth impressed me at that moment as the most reckless man I had ever met. In my own country, amid scenes with which I had been familiar since childhood, I did not feel that I was perfectly safe. If he felt any premonitions of danger, as I certainly felt that in his position he should, he gave no signs of them. He seemed as light-hearted and careless as a schoolboy just released from his studies."

The three men—Jett, Ruggles, and the fugitive—went down the driveway. Richard Garrett was on the porch of his home. "Mr. Garrett," Jett said, "I suppose you hardly remember me."

"No, sir, I believe not." Jett identified himself as the son of a longtime friend of Mr. Garrett's from Westmoreland County and then introduced Mr. John W. Boyd, a soldier wounded at the siege of Richmond. "Can you take care of him for a day or two until his wound will permit him to travel?"

Garrett said he could. He invited the three men into the house. Ruggles and Jett said they were headed for Bowling Green and must be on their way after helping their wounded companion onto the house's veranda. He sat down there and one of the sons of the house, young Richard, brought him a glass of water. Jett and Ruggles left. Richard asked the visitor if his wound pained him.

"Yes, it has not properly been cared for and riding has jarred it so that it gives me great pain." He did not seem inclined to talk, and when Mr. Garrett brought him a pillow he leaned back and sat dozing in a chair.

In Washington at that hour, midafternoon of April 24, Lieutenant Edward Doherty of the 16th New York Cavalry was sitting with a fellow officer of his regiment on a park bench opposite the White House when a messenger came up and handed him an order sent to the commanding officer of the 16th. It told him to have an officer and twenty-six enlisted men with three days' rations and forage report at once to Colonel Lafayette C. Baker. It was signed by General Christopher C. Augur, commanding the forces in and around Washington. Appended to it was an order by the 16th's commander telling Lieutenant Doherty to comply.

Doherty went to his barracks, had "boots and saddles" sounded, and in less than half an hour was with Colonel Baker, the head of the War Department's Detective Bureau. From reports sent by a vast force of searchers, reported sightings, interrogations, and perhaps intuition, Baker had decided that John Wilkes Booth and David Herold were heading for Fredericksburg and were in that area now. He wished Lieutenant Doherty to take his men there. Two civilian detectives, both ex-officers of the District of Columbia Cavalry, former Lieutenant Colonel Everton Conger and former Lieutenant Luther Byron Baker, Colonel Baker's nephew, would go along. The command would travel by water down Aquia Creek to Belle Plain on the government tug *John S. Ide*, a propeller-driven steamer of 186 tons. It was waiting at the Sixth Street Wharf.

The cavalrymen and two detectives clattered to the steamer. To Doherty his command of two sergeants, seven corporals, and seventeen privates was not impressive, composed as it was, he felt, of the deadbeats from several companies of the regiment—"Those who have all sorts of excuses for remaining in camp while others are out, men who are either sick or pretending to be." One of his soldiers certainly did not fit that description. Sergeant Boston Corbett was a fearless battler whose single-handed fight against more than two dozen of the famous Colonel John S. Mosby's raiders earned Mosby's personally proffered compliments when at last Corbett was overcome. He had been sent to the notorious Confederate prison camp at Andersonville, Georgia, survived while others died in multitudes, and been exchanged and returned to duty.

Corbett's name was not always what it had become. He was born Thomas P. Corbett in England in 1832, came to Troy, New York, when he was seven, and grew up to be a hatmaker. He married. His wife died in childbirth, as did the infant girl she delivered. He turned to drink. While working at his trade in Boston he experienced a rush of religious passion of the most intense type, gave up liquor, and, after the fashion of Jesus renaming His disciples, renamed himself after the city of his spiritual rebirth. He became a great shouter for street evangelists, standing on a soapbox nights and praising the Lord, and falling to his knees by day whenever a fellow hatter took the Lord's name in vain. In the summer of 1858, shouting God's glory in the streets, he was approached by two prostitutes suggesting he could do better to avail himself of their offerings.

When he went home after the encounter, Boston Corbett decided to make sure that no possible impure thoughts could ever come to contaminate his mind. With a scissors he cut open his scrotum and snipped off his testes. Then he went to a prayer meeting. Swollen up and in pain, he was eventually taken to Massachusetts General Hospital, where he spent a month recovering. The Mad Hatter.

When the war came he enlisted in a New York outfit where he became known to his fellow soldiers as The Glory-to-God-Man. When the regimental commander was once angrily rebuking the troops for some real or imagined dereliction of duty, Corbett interrupted to say, "Colonel, it's wrong to swear and use God's name in an oath. Don't you know you are breaking God's law?" Outraged, Colonel Daniel Butterfield, who in time rose to be chief of staff of the Army of the Potomac, ordered him thrown into the guardhouse. There Corbett spent his time shouting out religious hymns. Ordered to keep quiet, he refused. Told to apologize to Butterfield, he replied that while he had only offended the colonel, the colonel had offended God. Defeated, Butterfield had him freed. He went on to serve with distinction. He said he always prayed for a rebel soldier's soul before shooting. He continued to preach to his fellows, saving souls, praising the Lord.

After seven hours on the *John S. Ide*, the cavalrymen of the 16th New York and the two detectives went ashore at Belle Plain, sixty miles from Washington, to spend all night and into the dawn knocking on doors to ask whether anybody had seen two men, one lame, heading South. No one had. Sometimes Conger and Baker went on alone and represented themselves as ex-Confederate soldiers looking for two friends, one crippled. Nobody had anything of interest to offer.

The command drifted southeast and learned that the previous evening the north side of the Rappahannock had been pretty well swept by cavalry making for Fredericksburg. They decided to cross the river and go down the south side. They made for the ferry that could get them over. They came to Port Conway. The shad fisherman William Rollins was on the little wharf. Baker showed photographs of the men they sought, given to him by his uncle, Colonel Baker of the War Department's Detective Bureau. Had Mr. Rollins by any chance seen the two men pictured? Yes. He had.

When young Richard Garrett that morning looked at his family's sleeping guest he saw that two enormous revolvers, thirteen inches long, were hanging on a belt slung across the sleeper's bedpost. With them was a knife, and on the mantel of the room an expensive set of field glasses with several adjustments. How white Mr. Boyd's brow was, Richard thought. White as marble. And his hand thrown above his head was as white and soft as a child's. Mr. Boyd was different from other soldiers who had stopped with the family, Richard reflected. The others had skin roughened and tanned from exposure.

The guest arose and went downstairs and out onto the lawn, where all morning he lay under an apple tree. The weather had turned warm and sunny. Apple blossoms drifted down on him and he seemed to enjoy it, never brushing them off. The children of the house grouped around him, and he showed them his compass spattered by the wax of Thomas Jones's dripping candle and laughed at the puzzlement on their faces when he made the magnetized needle move by holding the point of a pocket knife above it. He gave them a humorously done nonsense story about a man who decided to commit suicide by jumping off the U.S. Capitol but changed his mind in midair and by flapping his hands and pedaling his feet got back up to safety. Two of the older Garrett sons were just back from Lee's surrender at Appomattox, and they proposed he join them in shooting at a fencetop target with an ancient pistol. He fired five rounds. The target remained untouched. He examined the weapon. None of the bullets had left the chamber. They all laughed together.

At about noon, before lunch was served, he asked young Richard to get down a large map that hung on a wall. The boy spread the map out on the floor and, leaning heavily on a chair, his crutches placed against the wall, Mr. Boyd knelt by the map and studied it, marking a route from Norfolk and then to Charleston and Savannah. Richard asked where he was planning to go. To Mexico, he replied. That seemed strange to Richard, for the previous evening he had talked about going South to keep up the fight against the Yankees. He was tracing a line through the Gulf of Mexico to Galveston.

At lunch the subject of the President's assassination came up, Mr. Garrett saying he didn't believe the story. "It is some idle report started by stragglers." But one of the sons fresh from Appomattox, Jack, said he had talked with a neighbor who had seen a Richmond paper. The story was true. And the man who had done it had a one-hundred-thousand-dollar price on his head. He was an actor, Booth. Not Edwin. A brother. "That man had better not come this way, for I would like to make one hundred thousand dollars just now."

"Would you do such a thing? Betray him?" the guest asked.

"He had better not tempt me, for I haven't a dollar in the world."

One of the ladies of the household wondered aloud why the assassin had done what he did. It must have been for money, she felt. The guest asked whom she thought had put up the cash. She could not offer a logical answer. He said, "No. It is my opinion he was not paid a cent, but did it for notoriety's sake." Lunch ended.

Mr. Rollins at the ferry slip had seen these men? When? Just about twenty-four hours before. They had crossed over the river in company with three local boys back from the Confederate Army. Heading where? Mrs. Bettie Rollins thought she could guess. "Jett has a lady-love over at Bowling Green, and I reckon he went there." The lady-love, Izora Gouldman, sixteen, was a daughter of the Bowling Green family which owned the town hotel.

It was fifteen miles to the southwest. First the command had to get over the Rappahannock. The man who ran the ferry went to work, but his craft could transport only a few horses and men at a time, so it would be almost sunset before the soldiers and two detectives could hope to be ashore on the southern side at Port Royal. They had been on the go with no rest save for on-the-run meals since getting off the *John S. Ide* the previous evening.

At the Garrett farm, Bainbridge and Ruggles came up from Bowling Green to drop off Davy Herold, who was introduced as Mr. Boyd's cousin David Harris. Bainbridge and Ruggles headed on toward Port Royal, three miles north, but before they reached it ran into an ex-soldier who had served with Bainbridge in the war. He was coming from Port Royal. "The town is full of Yankees in search of Booth," he told them. Bainbridge and Ruggles wheeled their horses and galloped to Garrett's. The house guest was back to lying on the ground in the waning sunlight. He arose and hobbled over to them. "Well, boys, what's in the wind now?"

They told him what they had learned, and Bainbridge pointed to a thick stretch of forest by the house and said, "Get over there at once, and hide yourself. In those wooded ravines you will never be found." "Yes," Ruggles said, "get over there as quickly as you can, and lose no time about starting."

"I'll do as you say, boys, right off. Ride on! Good-bye! It will never do for you to be found in my company." He hurried as best he could to the house, urgently and in agitated fashion asked one of the Garrett boys to rush upstairs for his pistols, and with Herold made for the woods. Bainbridge and Ruggles left, Ruggles to retain the impression of an individual who at all times showed impressive calm and courage while facing great peril. Ruggles had seen no braggadocio in the hunted man. He had seemed disappointed by the world's reaction to what he had done at Ford's Theatre, and when Herold spoke of the deed as they rode the previous day, he had said it was nothing to brag on. He had mentioned going to Mexico, for he said he saw the South had no refuge for him. When Ruggles asked if Europe was not a possibility, he was told European monarchs did not like assassins—they set examples.

In the forest the fugitives waited. Down the road came the Yankee cavalry, pounding past the Garrett driveway as they made for Bowling Green. When they were gone, Mr. Boyd and Mr. Harris returned to the house. Their reception there was chilly. The family found their behavior suspicious: two very heavily armed men, one with two great revolvers and a knife and the other shouldering a gun—Herold was carrying the carbine picked up at Mrs. Surratt's tavern—who dash madly to hide in the woods? Something was not right. An explanation was demanded, and Herold said, "I will tell you the truth, over there in Maryland the other night we got on a spree and had a row with some soldiers and as we ran away we shot at them and I suppose must have hurt somebody." Mr. Boyd's contribution was that he had been afraid the Yankees were going to make him take an enforced oath of loyalty to the Union, as was being done all over the South.

The stories didn't go down. The Federals weren't going to send a couple of dozen cavalrymen galloping in the wake of two fellows who had been on a spree, and still less to force a cripple to take the loyalty oath. The Garretts had children in the house, women—including Mrs. Garrett's spinster sister, Lucinda Holloway, a schoolteacher. They didn't want any trouble coming to their place. The men would have to leave. Jack Garrett bluntly said they were no longer welcome. They asked about renting the family's horses and a wagon to get them to Fredericksburg and a railroad. Jack wouldn't have it. But there was a black man nearby, Ned Freeman, who could be applied to. They gave him ten dollars, and he went off to find Freeman wasn't home.

Darkness had come. It was difficult for Jack Garrett simply to throw them out. He compromised, saying as they would be leaving early in the morning—no doubt Freeman would come and accommodate them—they could sleep, not in the house, but in the tobacco barn. They bedded down there. Jack and his brother William and their father were still uneasy. Perhaps these strangers would decide to steal their horses in the middle of the night. Jack and William locked the barn door from the outside and for additional safety decided that they'd bunk for the night in the nearby corncrib. Everyone, then, was settled in, either at the house or in the corncrib or the tobacco barn, and silence enveloped the Garrett farm as the last hours of the night of April 25 came and passed.

The atmosphere was quite different in the room at the Star Hotel in Bowling Green where Willie Jett had been asleep, for he was looking up into the hard faces of Detective Baker and Detective Conger, who held a lit candle in one hand and a revolver in the other.

"What do you want?" Jett asked.

"We want you. We know you. We know you took Booth across the river."

"You are mistaken in your man."

"You lie!" Conger put his revolver against Jett's head. "We are going to have Booth. You can tell us where he is or prepare to die." Outside in the hall and down in front of the hotel and behind it, cavalrymen of the 16th New York were standing guard. Mrs. Gouldman, the wife of the proprietor and mother of Jett's young lady friend Izora, was told by Lieutenant Doherty that should any opposition be offered his men would burn her establishment and take all connected with it to Washington as prisoners.

Soldiers with drawn revolvers crowded in on Jett. A Gouldman son, wounded in the war, lay motionless in his bed across the room. Jett asked if he could speak to Conger privately. It was arranged. The men they sought, Jett told the detective, were at Garrett's farm to the north. He was put on a horse with reins attached to those of two soldiers, in the center of a group of cavalrymen instructed to shoot him immediately if he tried to escape. It was past midnight. The command headed back through the dust and sand of the road they had just traversed. There was no moon, and no stars could be seen.

At about two in the morning they got to the Garrett driveway. Orders were given in a whisper: The troops were to file in as quietly as possible and take up positions in a circle around the house and outbuildings. Baker went up on the porch and thundered on the door. A window opened cautiously. Baker reached in and grabbed the arm of Mr. Garrett. "Open the door. Be quick about it."

The order was complied with. The farmer saw his yard was filled with men carrying unsheathed swords and unholstered revolvers. The door he opened was forcefully shoved, and men crowded in. "Don't go in, there are women undressed there," Garrett cried. "Damn the women," Baker said with a snarl. "What if they are undressed? We shall go in if they haven't a rag." Soldiers searched the house and found only family members.

"Where are the men who have been staying with you?" Baker demanded. Garrett began to say that after the men had run off to the woods he had no longer wanted them to remain in his house—

"I don't want any long story," Baker interrupted. "I just want to know where those men have gone." Garrett suffered from a slight speech impediment, which intensified when he was agitated. Now his powers of expression degenerated into protracted stuttering. "Bring a rope, hang the damned old rebel, and we will find the men afterwards," someone yelled. Detective Conger said, "Bring a rope and I'll put him up to the top of those locust trees."

One was brought and knotted around Garrett's throat, and in his nightclothes he was dragged into the yard. Awakened in the corncrib by the commotion, Jack Garrett came out and was taken in hand and brought up. "Don't hurt Father," he begged.

The detectives demanded to know where the two men were. Jack said, "We were becoming suspicious of them, and Father told them they could not stay with us—"

"Where are they now?" Baker interrupted.

"In the barn, locked up for fear they would steal the horses." His brother William, still in the corncrib, had the key. Soldiers got him up and out and told him to unlock the door, go into the tobacco barn, and get the fugitives to surrender. He protested, "They are armed to the teeth and they'll shoot me down." Baker stuck a revolver in his face. They went to the tobacco barn, some fifty yards from the house, and soldiers surrounded it. Young

Garrett unlocked the door and went in. Outside there was heard the sound of a conversation held in low tones. Then, more loudly, "You have betrayed me, sir; leave the barn or I will shoot you."

From outside Baker shouted for the men inside to turn over their arms to young Garrett. "If you don't, we shall burn the barn, and have a bonfire and shooting match!" At the door Garrett cried, "Let me out! He's going to shoot me!"

Baker shouted, "You can't come out unless you bring the arms!"

"He won't give them to me! Let me out quick!" Baker opened the door, and Garrett bounded out. He pointed to the candle Baker held. "Put that out or he will shoot you by its light," he whispered in a frightened voice. That would not be difficult, for tobacco barns required circulating the air so that leafs could be cured, and there were wide gaps between each board of the walls. Baker placed the candle on the ground and stepped away from it.

From inside a voice called, "Oh, Captain! There is a man in here who wishes to surrender." The words were delivered in a tone that carried to the frightened members of the Garrett family gathered on their porch, and in what Baker felt was a "full, clear, ringing voice—a voice that smacked of the stage."

At the door Davy Herold was whimpering, "Let me out." He was told he could emerge if he brought his weapons with him. The voice from inside called, "He has no arms. The arms are mine, and I shall keep them and may have to use them on you gentlemen."

Herold could be heard weeping. "Let me see your hands," Lieutenant Doherty said, and the door opened and two hands were thrust forward. Doherty grabbed them and yanked Herold out, and he was immediately bound and then tied to a tree. From inside the barn came, "Tell me who you are and what you want of me. It may be that I am being taken by my friends."

"It makes no difference who we are," Baker shouted back. "We know you and we want you. We have fifty well-armed men stationed around this barn. You cannot escape." The detective was exaggerating the numbers of his force, but his point was correct. The men of the 16th had all their weapons on full cock. There was, they knew, more than one hundred thousand dollars waiting for them.

From inside came: "Captain, this is a hard case, I swear." He was balancing himself on a crutch while holding a revolver in one hand and the carbine in another as he stood partially surrounded by furniture and other goods brought for safekeeping during the war by Port Conway and Port Royal homeowners menaced by the Yankee gunboats. "I am lame," he called out into the darkness of the barn, his voice carrying to the darkness outside, lit only by the single candle burning on the ground where Baker had left it. "Give a lame man a chance."

Perhaps he had suspected, perhaps he must have known, that it would one day come to this, for the final lines he had written in his appointment book were:

I have too great a soul to die like a criminal. Oh! may He spare me that, and let me die bravely. I bless the entire world. I have never hated nor wronged any one. This last was not a wrong unless God deems it so, and it is with Him to damn or bless me. I do not wish to shed a drop of blood, but I must fight the course. 'Tis all that's left me.

The last words were Macbeth's. Now like Macbeth, like Lear shouting defiance, like Richard III before his foemen, he stood alone and called, "Draw up your men twenty yards from here, and I will fight your whole command."

Fight the whole command. One actor, crippled, against twenty-six enlisted men, an officer, and two ex-officers of the greatest army in the world, with revolvers, carbines, swords, horses. To Baker the concept, the tone of the voice, the words themselves, the style, seemed to be studied, theatrical, utterly theatrical. He must want to come out and fight until he dies, Baker thought. "We are not here to fight, we are here to take you!" Baker shouted.

From inside came a request for time to consider. Baker shouted he would hold off any action for two minutes, no more. From inside there was one more request echoing out into the dark: "Captain, I believe you to be a brave and honorable man. I have had half a dozen chances to shoot you. I have a bead drawn on you now, but I do not wish to kill you. Withdraw your men from the door and I'll go out."

"Your time is up," Baker called. "If you don't come out we shall fire the barn."

"Well, then, my brave boys, you may prepare a stretcher for me." A pause. "One more stain on the glorious old banner." The clear and ringing-toned words carried clearly to the Garretts huddled on their porch, sung out, Detective Conger thought, in a singular, stagelike voice. Conger came from the back of the barn and asked Baker if he was ready. Baker was. Conger thrust a handful of dry corn fodder through a crack in a barn wall and scratched a match.

At once the fire caught. The interior of the barn started to brighten. In a moment it was quite light. Soldiers pressed up to the walls and through the wide gaps looked in and saw a man on two crutches with a revolver and carbine. He dropped one crutch and made as if to fling a table on the flames, but saw it would do no good. He stood still as the flames went upward toward the barn roof, widening as they rose. They rolled, like a billow, Baker thought, across the roof to the opposite side and the floor below. Conger was surprised by the appearance of the man he was looking at—all the photographs showed a mustache. This man had no mustache, and bore a striking resemblance, the detective thought, to Edwin Booth. For a moment it came into Conger's mind that some mistake had been made.

Baker cautiously inched open the door to see drawn up to full height a man with his hat off, with wavy dark hair tossed back from a high white forehead, with his lips firmly compressed. The appearance was that of a lion hunted to his lair. "Booth was standing under and within an arc of fire," Baker wrote. "Not the brilliant lighting of the theater. The roaring of the flames was not like the swelling music of the orchestra." But there was an audience, the soldiers peering in, and, where the proscenium arch of a theater would be, the top of the barn now a rising conflagration, making the Garrett house windows flare with the reflection and lighting up the cleared land of the homestead in the midst of great forests. Young Richard looked at Mr. Boyd standing in great waves of fire. "He was as beautiful as the statue of a Greek god, and as calm." Baker: "Booth, as an actor, had been said to have the form of an Apollo. Now it was the picture of an Apollo in a frame of fire."

He threw away his remaining crutch, dropped the carbine, and sprang toward the door, holding his revolver. Watching through the side of the barn, Sergeant Boston Corbett heard a Voice. It was, he said, that of God Almighty, and It directed him to shoot. He did so. The bullet took his target in the side of the neck and went through on a slightly downward path, piercing three vertebrae and cutting the spinal cord.

He pitched forward, completely and permanently paralyzed below the neck, an immediate quadriplegic. The detectives and soldiers rushed into the flaming barn. He was lying on his face. "He must have shot himself," Conger said.

"No," Baker said. "I had my eye upon him every moment." And it would have been impossible for him to inflict a downward wound in the back of the neck with his thirteen-inch revolver unless he turned it upside down and pulled the trigger with his thumb, which he did not.

They dragged him out to under an apple tree. He was conscious but in terrible pain. "Tell Mother—tell Mother—" he said, and fainted. The heat from the flames was so intense that they carried him to the porch of the house and put him on a straw mattress produced by Mrs. Garrett. A cloth was dampened with brandy and placed against his lips. He opened his eyes. "Oh, kill me, kill me," he said.

"No, Booth," Baker said. "We don't want you to die. You were shot against orders."

The unbearable pain dropped him into unconsciousness again, and then he came to, his breast heaving and tongue protruding. Baker thought he was asking if there was blood in his mouth, looked, and told him there was none. He seemed to wish to say something, and Baker put his ear to his mouth and heard, "Tell Mother I died for my country. I did what I thought was best."

They were all soldiers who had been through the war. They knew what the result of such a wound must inevitably be. Conger left for Washington to tell Colonel Baker and Secretary Stanton and through them the world that the search for the man who killed Lincoln was over, taking with him the weapons, the candle-splattered compass, a knife, a pipe, and the appointment book with the first draft of the letter to the cold Dr. Stuart along with the five-dollar bill that was too much to give the man, and the pictures of five women: the actresses Fanny Brown, Helen Western, Alice Grey, and Effie Germon; and, of course, Lucy Hale.

In horrible agony, he asked to be turned on his face. He asked to be turned back over. The schoolteacher Lucinda Holloway, Mrs. Garrett's sister, dampened a cloth with water and wiped his face and smoothed his hair back. The burning barn collapsed upon itself. Dawn was coming, its light replacing that of the dying fire. He asked Baker to raise his paralyzed hands so he could see them. Baker did so. They were utterly limp. He said with a gasp, "Useless." Gasping, he said it again: "Useless, useless."

FOURTEEN

HER HUSBAND in jail because of what her brother had done, her home invaded by detectives, entering the last stages of a pregnancy whose result if a boy she had but twelve days earlier expected to name John Wilkes Booth Clarke, Asia was dangerously ill. Her mother in New York decided she must go to her.

The sculptor Launt Thompson, who had shared with Thomas Bailey Aldrich the duty of not leaving Edwin alone, offered to escort Mrs. Booth to a Philadelphia train leaving from Jersey City. They took a horse cab for the Hudson River, and as they drove through the Manhattan streets from Edwin's house, Thompson heard newsboys yelling. He understood what they were calling out. He drew the curtains of the carriage and closed the window so the mother might not hear, and all during the trip endeavored to smother by loud and incessant talk what the boys were shouting.

They reached the ferry, and he hurried Mrs. Booth's shrouded figure to a secluded corner of the deck and left her for a moment to buy a paper. In the train he handed it to her. "You will need now all your courage," Thompson said. "The paper in your hand will tell what, unhappily, we must all wish to hear." On the moving train, surrounded by strangers talking about the news, she read of what had happened at the Garrett farm.

In Philadelphia, awaiting her mother's arrival while lying on a couch, Asia received an old employee of the Walnut Street Theatre. He stood steadying himself by a center table. His face was very pale and working nervously. He did not raise his eyes.

"Is it over?" she asked.

"Yes, madam."

"Taken?"

"Yes."

"Dead?"

"Yes, madam."

She lay with her face to the wall. Her heart beat like a piece of strong machinery, it seemed so powerful and loud to her. She silently offered thanks to God. Behind her she heard the man begin to sob, and then the sound of the street closing behind him.

By then the body of Mrs. Booth's son and Asia's brother was lying on the monitor *Montauk* anchored in the Potomac. Borrowing a darning needle from the Garrett women, Lieutenant Doherty had sewn it into the saddle blanket from his horse, and then Detective Baker and a corporal departed with it on the wagon for whose hire the dead man had advanced Jack Garrett ten dollars to be offered to the wagon's owner, Ned Freeman, for transportation South. The ten dollars were handed over to Baker. He made his own arrangements with Freeman, but to go North, not South. All day long, as the exhausted men and horses of the 16th New York Cavalry rested at the Garretts', and as Abraham Lincoln's train moved slowly West, the ramshackle wagon labored the thirty dusty miles to the Potomac and the *John S. Ide*. Once it broke down, and when Ned Freeman knelt to fix it, blood from the silent cargo dripped on him. Blood from this murderer would never wash off, Freeman said. Once some ex-Confederate soldiers coming the other way asked what was on the wagon—"a dead Yank?"

They reached the *John S. Ide* and headed North to Washington, the blue blanket gray from the dust and the big *U.S.* letters on it dark with blood. The face of the body was clean, for Mrs. Garrett had washed it and then tied on a covering handkerchief. Her sister, Miss Holloway, cut off a curling lock of hair.

On the monitor *Saugus*, lying at anchor in the eastern branch of the Potomac just below the *Montauk*, separate from one another in captain's cabin, coal bunker, chain locker, and head were Lewis Powell, George Atzerodt, and Samuel Arnold and Edman Spangler and Michael O'Laughlen, who had been in on the original plan to kidnap the President, and Dr. Samuel Mudd. Their hands were manacled by handcuffs set on each end of a fourteen-inch-long bar of iron, and the left leg of each was attached by chains to seventy-five-pound balls of iron. They were hooded. The hoods had small openings for the nose and mouth. They were fed through the holes. Mrs. Mary Surratt was in an annex of the Old Capitol prison. Generals Robert E. Lee and Joseph Johnston were free, and Jefferson Davis would serve but a brief term before being freed, but anyone associated with John Wilkes Booth, Secretary of War Stanton was saying, was going to be tried, convicted, and hanged before Abraham Lincoln was buried. A military commission consisting of a lieutenant colonel, a colonel, four brigadier generals, and three major generals would form the prisoners' court. That the prisoners were civilians not subject to military law was beside the point.

Held entirely incommunicado, and soon to be joined by Davy Herold, the prisoners could not know that at about two on the morning of April 27, a tug that had met the *John S. Ide* came up the river past the *Saugus* and toward the *Montauk*. Since midnight, when all hands had been piped to their stations to clear for action, the crew had been standing to, armed with cutlasses and rifles. The tug came alongside, and an object wrapped in a saddle blanket was brought aboard and placed on a carpenter's workbench on the forward deck. Forbidden to ask any questions, the crew was under orders to fire at any boat other than the tug that came near. Secretary Stanton was obsessed with the belief that had seized him the moment he heard the President had been shot: that this was the signal for a reversal of Lee's surrender and the continuance of the rebellion by new means in which the Confederates might make of John Wilkes Booth dead or alive a rallying point for, at least, endless guerrilla warfare that could take the U.S. Army years to put down. The body of the man who killed Lincoln, therefore, must under no circumstances fall into the wrong hands, perhaps to be placed in a grave that might become a shrine.

In the morning three people came aboard the ship, which, like all navy vessels, had been the province of the longtime head of the Senate Committee on Naval Affairs, former senator, now minister-designate John P. Hale. Two of the party were naval officers.

With them was a heavily veiled young woman.

The officers undid the horse blanket shrouding the body on the carpenter's bench and exposed the head. Shrieking, Lucy Hale fell across John Booth. One of the officers cut off a lock of hair for her to take away.

When he found out, Stanton was flung into a frenzy of rage. Orders were issued that nobody could come on board the *Montauk* without a pass signed by both himself and Secretary of the Navy Welles. But news of the incident involving the veiled young lady was getting around, and to counter it the story was given out that the visitor was an assistant of Surgeon General Joseph K. Barnes, who would be conducting an autopsy. Then it was let known that the woman was one of the assassin's mistresses brought to identify him, and then that it was all a misunderstanding: A woman had come on board, but it had nothing to do with the assassin. She was just a visitor to the ship.

Later in the day an official identification of the body was made, with people who had known the dead man in life being brought aboard. The surgeon John F. May was shocked at the corpse laid out for his inspection. Less than two years earlier he had removed a fibroid tumor from the neck of John Booth, who asked him to say if asked that he had removed a bullet. Later Dr. May's patient came to tell him that the actress Charlotte Cushman had ripped open the half-healed incision during a stage embrace. The doctor had told the actor there would be a permanent scar. Now on the *Montauk* he looked down at a haggard cadaver with unkempt and matted hair and yellowed and discolored skin, with a broken leg greatly contused and completely black. "There is no resemblance in that corpse to Booth, nor can I believe it to be that of him," he said.

Then he looked again and asked that the body be propped up in a sitting position, and when it was he recognized it and studied the surgical scar and so identified his former patient. May was a great student of the theater who considered Junius Brutus Booth to be the finest actor who ever stepped on a stage. He left the *Montauk* thinking how stagelike, how theatrical it was that this son of the great tragedian killed Abraham Lincoln in a theater, and then in a blaze of light shouted *"Sic semper tyrannis!"* while waving a dagger. Then, surrounded by fire, standing, proposing as a condition of leaving the Garrett barn a series of single combats in the open field with the men of the 16th New York, he had been shot down. The perfect end, May thought, unequaled as a finisher and the last scene of the final act of the great drama of the war and the death of the American god and the man who slew that deity.

The assassin satisfactorily identified by May and by others, an autopsy was conducted by Surgeon General Barnes. The cause of death was found to be the shot fired by Sergeant Boston Corbett. There would be no penalty imposed for the act, Secretary Stanton decreed, saying that the villain was dead and the patriot lived, and there was no need to go further into the reason why one had killed the other.

The autopsy ended. Barnes cut out and preserved the three vertebrae pierced by Corbett's bullet. It was time for disposal of the decomposing body bruised by the long, bouncing trip in Ned Freeman's wagon and now with the head detached by Barnes's knife. What was done with these remains did not concern him, Stanton told Colonel Baker of the War Department Detective Bureau. But they must be disposed of in such manner that, as he put it, they would not be found until Gabriel blew his trumpet. With his nephew who had with the 16th New York traced the assassin to the Garrett barn, Colonel Baker took away the body in a rowboat and ostentatiously went to Giesborough Point, where for years worn-out government horses and mules had been taken to be shot. The story spread that uncle and nephew had dumped it there, or dropped it with a heavy ball out in the Potomac, and the widely circulated *Frank Leslie's Illustrated Newspaper* devoted its front page to a drawing of a hooded, shrouded form lashed to a board being lowered in the waters in a shameful, secret, by-night burial.

The presumed final resting place did not please everyone in the country. A mass meeting in Dayton, Ohio, voted a resolution that the assassin be thrown into the waters in the middle of the ocean so that he might not desecrate any place of American ownership, and others said that his skeleton should be preserved to be exhibited through all time as the great scoundrel of the nineteenth century, a man who had hunted like a ravening wolf and been shot like a dog to die accursed of mankind. Or perhaps he should be hung up in chains, slowly to decay while on display, or be coated with iron to serve as a horrible sculpture. For brave soldiers, it was said, even the tear of a stranger could fall, and also the tears of later generations, but never for the crawling serpent, vile wretch, deformed vermin, infamous reptile who slew Abraham Lincoln. Printers rushed out *carte de visite* photographs inscribed "J. Wilkes Booth Murderer, Traitor, Scoundrel, Beast, Fiend. That he may be in the lowest depths of Hell. Like a viper he lived—like a dog died—like a dog buried." (That pictures of the assassin were being freely distributed disturbed Stanton and others, and the government issued an edict making it illegal to sell any portrait of John Wilkes Booth. After a couple of weeks the rule was found to be unenforceable and was rescinded.)

Whatever *Leslie's* pictured, and whatever people believed, the Bakers had done nothing with their cargo but sit with it for a time in a silent backwater of Giesborough Point amid the rushes and river weeds. Then in the dark they rowed as noiselessly as possible to where the bulk of what was called the Old Penitentiary loomed against the sky at the foot of Four-and-a-Half Street, S.W. At the beginning of the war the building's convict population had been shipped elsewhere, and it became an arsenal standing amid ord-

nance plants and firing ranges. Lincoln used to like to go there to
see weapons tested on the broad lawns leading down to the Potomac. The Bakers left their rowboat's cargo at the end of a little pier
extending out into the river and holding an open gazebo. There it
stayed under the guard of soldiers told to shoot anyone who approached, as was discovered by Assistant Surgeon George Loring
Porter, a medical officer of the arsenal, when he returned with his
wife from a boating expedition. Only when he pleaded that the
officer of the guard be called, which was done, could he get ashore
and go to his quarters. But as midnight was being called by the post
sentries, Dr. Porter was back at the pier and gazebo, ordered there
with the arsenal's military storekeeper and four soldiers, one of
whom led two horses pulling a wagon.

The only commissioned officer present, Porter was put on his
word of honor never to tell of what he was about to do until the
need for secrecy passed. Forty-six years went by before he spoke.
The body in its blanket was put in the wagon, and the party moved
off. Porter led, carrying a lantern. Two soldiers sat on the wagon
box. One each marched on either side. The storekeeper was in the
rear. They slowly moved up an avenue of the post, nobody saying
a word. On one side were pyramids of cannon balls and dismounted guns of light artillery. The other side had lawns leading
down to the river.

They marched along, challenged from the darkness now and
then by sentries. They reached the series of arsenal buildings still
generally referred to as the Old Penitentiary and about 250 feet
long. There was a middle section with an entranceway large enough
to admit the horses and wagons. The military storekeeper unlocked
massive doors. They went in. He locked the doors behind them.
Porter's lantern flickered over the high walls of a general storage
room of some 40 by 50 feet. There were heavy cedar columns.
There were gun boxes for long rifles, and packing cases. The floor
was unpaved. In it, Porter saw, a shallow hole had been dug. The
excavated earth was piled up.

The body was taken and put into a gun case, which was shut
and lowered into the shallow hole by the flickering light of Porter's
upheld lantern, dim shadows coming and going on the walls. The
excess dirt was shoveled up into the wagon. They left, the room
turned dark again, and the key to the lock, the only one in existence, was taken to Secretary of War Stanton. Early Saturday
morning had come. In a few hours it would be just two weeks since
Lincoln died.

In the silent room the earth settled over the gun case and its occupant: a black, dismal hole, Detective Baker wrote years later. And a bloody and dusty blanket for a winding sheet in an unhonored grave in the floor of what had been a prison. How dark and lonely it was there, Baker reflected. When he thought of John Wilkes Booth, Baker wrote, he did not so much dwell on the man with whom he had negotiated from outside a Virginia tobacco barn and whose last words he had heard, nor of the pity he had then found himself feeling for a paralyzed man dying on a porch, but of the silent grave. This is how I always think of him, Baker wrote.

Two midnights later, joined together by clanking chains, the men hooded, Mrs. Surratt's feet in irons, the prisoners were taken to the Old Penitentiary and individually locked up in old cells restored to their former function. Their trial would be held in a large adjoining room. It would begin on May 9. (Secretary Stanton had abandoned his hope to swing them all before Lincoln was buried.) On that day, their fetters rattling and scraping, they stumbled blindly in to sit blinking and dirty-faced until the hoods were taken off. After that the hoods were removed just before the day's session began, to go back on when it ended.

They were as the cast of a play whose star is offstage, the always heavily veiled Mrs. Surratt an enigmatic leading woman, the trifling Davy Herold as the small-featured juvenile, crude George Atzerodt with his thick German accent the low comedian, hulking and stoical and unblinking-for-hours Lewis Powell as the menacing heavy, Dr. Mudd as the educated interloper-presence at the gathering, the others as utility men, messengers, walk-ons. No one knew that the star lay moldering just three stories below the courtroom.

That the prisoners would all be found guilty to one degree or another was known by anyone who read the newspapers. The only question was who would hang. For Lewis Powell the issue was hardly debatable. The matter did not seem to concern him, and he maintained an impenetrable silence, his verbal and emotional constipation mimicking his physical one, which lasted, his keepers noted, twenty-two days. He said nothing, offered nothing, not even his name, and was tried under one of his aliases, Lewis Payne. Finally he relented and told his court-appointed lawyer, General William Doster, that he was sorry about what he had done to Frederick Seward. As for Frederick's father, Powell considered himself as acting under the orders of the man he called "Cap" and "Captain." The captain told him to do it, and he did.

Along with Powell—or Payne, as they called him—Mrs. Surratt was the defendant people came to see. Here was a motherly-looking boardinghouse-keeper, a fervent Catholic found not in church on Good Friday but instead delivering a package to her country property that the assassin picks up that night. Her property's tenant, John Lloyd, testified that she had used the words "shooting irons"—guns. Would she swing? No woman had ever been hanged by the U.S. government.

The trial went on for seven weeks, the courtroom temperature going up as Washington's brutal summer came, Mary Todd Lincoln rising from the White House bed upon which she had lain for forty days and nights since leaving her husband at the Petersen house. In the heavy black mourning attire with stiff bonnet and large black tulle veil that she would wear for every day but one of the seventeen years of life remaining—once, at Tad's insistence, for his birthday, she took it off—she went back to Illinois. There she seemed unable to speak of anything but what had occurred in the box at the theater. Her powers of speech, a friend said, seemed paralyzed when any other subject was raised. She never again but once wrote a letter on anything but mourning stationery with the widest of black bands. (When that once she sent a note on regular paper, she apologized to the recipient.) The madness the President had always dreaded for her came and fulfilled his fears.

No sign of the resurgence of the rebellion that Stanton had looked for ever appeared, and in late May, two weeks into the proceedings in the Old Penitentiary, the great and final Grand Review of the Union Army was held. Afterward the victorious soldiers would be mustered out to go home to Iowa or New York or Massachusetts to spend the rest of their lives cherishing the sabers and heavy Colts that had licked Johnny Reb. For two days Washington was again bedecked with the flowers, bunting, transparencies of patriotic mottoes that so precipitously had come down on the morning of April 15. Foreign ministers gaped at such a military display as the world had never seen before, infantry parading to thunderous beat, endless cavalry squadrons, rumbling concourses of artillery, the Army of the Potomac marching past on the first day with its tattered old bullet-ridden flags festooned with garlands to be saluted by Grant on a stand at the White House, the Armies of the West coming on the second day with "Marching Through Georgia" booming out again and again for Sherman.

There were those who wondered fearfully if the soldiers in vengeful mass might come to exact a bloody price for what John Wilkes Booth had done. Among them was the imprisoned John T.

Ford. His theater was still set up for the scene where the fortune-seeking harridan and Augusta learn that the American has given his fortune to the sweet heroine. While the hunt for the President's slayer was still going on, the cast of the play had been ordered to put it on for a small group of detectives reconstructing what had happened. Some brought from jail for the occasion, others under orders to report to the authorities each day, the actors went through their parts in the almost empty theater for this grimmest of audiences. They played until the moment when Harry Hawk had paused for the laugh he expected—"Turn you inside out, you sockdologizing old mantrap." Then the theater sat silent, guarded by soldiers, until the officers comprising the Old Penitentiary court came to look at it. It sat silent again until John T. Ford, finally freed, took it back. He announced he would put on a regular schedule of performances, as in the past, and sold some tickets. But before opening night the government seized the theater, paying Ford what it considered a fair monthly rent until it bought it from him at what it considered a fair price, $100,000.

May gave way to June, with temperatures during the day reaching a humid one hundred degrees. It seemed to Assistant Surgeon Porter, who after leading the assassin's burial party had been assigned to provide medical care for the prisoners, that his charges sitting chained for twenty-four hours a day, and hooded for sixteen, might well go out of their minds. He brought in an expert on mental illness who confirmed his fears, and so the hoods were put away and a daily two hours of exercise were permitted under heavy guard. Powell played at quoits with the soldiers. It seemed to his lawyer, William Doster, that his client was scarcely above animal intelligence, and he conceived the idea of attempting to form a defense based upon the influence a John Wilkes Booth would have had upon one of so low an order of intellect and feeling. To this end he subpoenaed Edwin, thinking he could testify to the power of his late brother's personality.

Edwin arrived in Washington perhaps more terrified than he had ever been before. All his life he had found, and would find, that it was almost impossible for him to speak in his own voice. He knew that at social events a gulp was often all he had to contribute, and did not visit colleges for fear he might be asked to offer some remark. He never traveled by trolley car because someone might recognize him and expect him to return greetings. Now he faced a witness stand where he would be asked to speak of the brother whom the world had judged the blackest villain since Judas.

Desperately lying, he told Doster he "knew less of his brother probably than anyone—that he had had nothing to do with him for years." The lawyer could easily have found that John had always stayed with Edwin in New York, had spent the previous Christmas period with him, and had visited him in Boston two weeks before shooting the President, but perhaps Doster took pity or decided such a witness's testimony would do the client no good. He let him go. Edwin fled to his mother and Asia in Philadelphia, never again to set foot in the city where his brother shot Abraham Lincoln, never to board a train that would pass through it.

His career as an actor, he was certain, was over. The public would never permit him to appear on a stage. He had some time earlier formed a most successful partnership with John Sleeper Clarke in which together they managed theaters in New York and Philadelphia; when Clarke was finally released from prison Edwin told him that he should "sever all connection theatrically" with one whose "name and fame were irremediably clouded forever." He was happy that his fiancée, Blanche Hanel, was away, and so spared much of the horror her relationship to him would bring. By September, when they planned to marry, perhaps some of the excitement would have died down. It was the dead Molly in heaven who had sent Blanche to him—" I faithfully believe it." She would be a mother to little Edwina. That her intended's brother had done what he did was not a matter of concern to her—her "great heart" was "faster bound to me than ever," his new "dear angel," he wrote.

Asia was happy for him. But for herself, she knew, all happiness was gone. Such as she, Asia wrote, never again learn to trust in human nature. They "never resume their old place in the world," she wrote, "and forget only in death." When at last her husband was released from the Old Capital prison he said things to her that confirmed her feelings and worked to destroy their marriage. The "secretiveness of the whole Booth race," Clarke told her, using phraseology from their shared theatrical background, "stamped them as Iagos." All her life Asia had tried to protect her family's name from the opprobrium of her bastard birth, and that of Edwin, and that of John, and June, and all of them, which had been put to hang in the air above them. The book on their father that she and Johnny had worked on for years was intended, by gilding the lily and leaving certain things unsaid, and lying about others, to pass his name, and theirs, on to posterity in a favorable guise. In her misery she finished the work alone. It was well written and well received when it came out later in the year—but nothing could save the Booth name now.

She could barely compose herself to write about her dearest brother to her friend Jean Anderson. "I can give you no idea of the desolation which has fallen upon us," she managed to put on paper. "I won't speak of his qualities, you knew him." She mentioned his intended bride. "They were devoted lovers. Their marriage was to have been in a year, when she promised to return from Spain with her father or without him. That was the decision only a few days before this fearful calamity. Some terrible oath hurried him to this wretched end. God help him."

At least he had not lived to be hung. When she received a letter from Boston Corbett she replied that she regarded him as her family's deliverer and told him to have no regrets. For herself: exile. Soon she would leave the United States for England, there to drag out a sad existence until after many long years her body, in accordance with her wish, was returned to lie in Baltimore by that of her father and mother and others of her family, including the dear brother she never ceased to love and whose life she wrote in secret in a book that would never see light until fifty years had passed from the time of her death.

The military judges reached a verdict. For the physician Mudd and the supporting players Arnold, Spangler, and O'Laughlen, terms of hard labor. For Powell, Herold, Atzerodt, and Mrs. Surratt, the gallows. They were told their fates on July 6. Sentence would be carried out the next day.

In the night relatives stayed with them in their cells, save for Powell, who had no one. In the morning, below their windows and those of the courtroom in which they had been tried, a scaffold was erected under the direction of General John F. Hartranft, who had been a Norristown, Pennsylvania, sheriff before the war. When he asked for volunteers to assist in the execution, he was overrun with soldiers who considered it an honor to participate in the punishment of those who had been judged guilty of aiding John Wilkes Booth. The men practiced with strung-up hundred-fifty-pound artillery shells placed on the hinged drops that would swing down to leave the condemned dangling in the air. The sound of the jarring crash of the rehearsals carried clearly to the cells. It was a murderously hot day.

At eight-thirty in the morning, Mrs. Surratt's daughter Anna went to the White House to ask for Presidential pardon. Andrew Johnson refused to see her. She had made a pitiful witness for her mother, losing all composure on the stand to end up brokenly asking, "Where's Ma? Where is Ma?" although her veiled mother sat but a few feet from her. In a different life a few months earlier Anna had liked to write down the name, and put up pictures, of the handsome actor who frequented her home.

When she left the White House, after desperately and hopelessly seeking aid of all she saw, she became stuck in the traffic of people heading for the scheduled execution. General Winfield Scott Hancock, on his way to oversee matters, got her through with the aid of a cavalry squadron. It was noon, or a little after.

She placed a pin through the silk bow of her mother's black dress, and then went to stand by a second-floor window of the Old Penitentiary overlooking the gallows. The lawyer William Doster stood at an adjoining one. At one-fifteen Generals Hancock and Hartranft emerged from the building where the prisoners had been held and the trial conducted. Behind them was Mrs. Surratt, flanked by two priests carrying crosses and reciting the service for the dead. Then Atzerodt, shrinking back from the sight of the dangling nooses, then a bewildered-looking, cringing Herold, and then Powell, who as he walked reached out and took someone's straw hat off the man's head and put it on his own. The temperature had reached a hundred degrees. The tops of the Old Penitentiary walls were jammed with soldiers, and ranks of them were drawn up in front of the scaffold. There were hundreds of civilians, many holding up umbrellas to shield themselves from the blinding sun.

The group climbed up the traditional thirteen steps leading to a gallows. Four armchairs were there, and in plain view on the ground below, four pine coffins. The condemned sat, and General Hartranft read out the warrants and findings, the execution order, in a low voice. An umbrella was held over Mrs. Surratt's head. Most people had never in the world expected she would hang. The evidence against her was purely circumstantial, and the most damning of it from a self-admitted drunkard, John Lloyd, her Surrattsville tenant, who could well have had his own reasons to quote her as speaking of "shooting irons," guns. When he had knotted the four hangman's ropes the previous night, Hartranft had believed that only three would be utilized. Surely President Johnson would extend the woman clemency. After General Hancock had gotten Anna Surratt through the crowds and himself reached the execution grounds he had said to Hartranft that all was ready, proceed, and Hartranft said with a gasp, "My God, the woman too?" "Yes, the woman too."

The clergymen standing before John Wilkes Booth's seated

coconspirators offered prayers. Their recitations seemed interminable to Corporal William Coxhall, standing beneath the gallows as one of four men detailed to knock loose the props that held up the drops. The heat, the waiting, the tension—he took hold of a supporting post, hung on, and threw up. It made him feel slightly better. Above him Mrs. Surratt's black bonnet was being removed and four sets of arms and legs were being securely bound as hoods were drawn down over heads. Ropes were put around the necks. Looking on from the second floor, William Doster saw and heard Anna Surratt at the next window hit the floor, unconscious.

They stood in a line on the drops. Hartranft clapped his hands once, twice, three times, and at the last clap Corporal Coxhall and the other men below swung two horizontally hanging logs forward. The logs knocked away the poles supporting the two drops, one for Powell and Mrs. Surratt, the other for Atzerodt and Herold. The drops crashed down on their hinges, and the four prisoners fell six feet and bounced in the air. Fifteen minutes later, Assistant Surgeon Porter checked for heartbeats. There were none. The bodies were put into the pine coffins.

FIFTEEN

A<small>S THE YEARS</small> passed and the Civil War receded into history, memoirs of generals coming out while the boys who served under them became gray-haired members of the Grand Army of the Republic parading on Decoration Day, or Lost-Cause veterans making do in the impoverished Reconstruction and post-Reconstruction South, those who had known the actor John Booth wondered still how it was conceivable that he had become the Presidential assassin John Wilkes Booth. As late as 1896, when murderer and victim had been in their graves for thirty-one years, the Washington lawyer Seaton Munroe wrote that he continued to find it as impossible to realize now, afterwards, as it would have been to dream before that in this engaging man, his acquaintance Booth, was housed the slayer who awoke two hemispheres to horror.

Munroe had been in the crowd outside Ford's Theatre when Laura Keene had come down from the box, her gown bloody, and her hands, and her cheeks, and heard her gasp when asked if the President lived, "God only knows!" The morning after, a daughter come flying from the Georgetown convent where she was at school found her mother trembling and incoherent. Laura Keene was never entirely to recover. "She never made, or could bear to hear, the slightest allusion to that moment, and the horror and shock of it shortened her days," wrote the actress Catherine Winslow, who once as Juliet was shaken out of her satin shoes by the assassin as Romeo.

Miss Keene's reaction to the events of Good Friday of 1865 was not dissimilar to that of the actor John Mathews, to whom had been entrusted delivery of a letter to the *National Intelligencer* attempting to explain all. Its words burned into his memory, he had destroyed it in his room, later to tell of what it said. Mathews remained in the theater world all his life, ending as an official of an actors' relief fund. His response to any mention of President Lincoln's death made many people believe him insane: He would run out of the room.

Of the insanity of Mary Lincoln there was no doubt. Compulsively speaking about her husband's death, and telling hotel maids, store clerks, and waiters her own life story, she alternated between irrational fear of poverty and extravagant spending frenzies. She was capable of publicly putting up for sale her used clothing while carrying on her person tremendous sums of cash—sometimes more than fifty thousand dollars. She bought furnishings in great quantities for a nonexistent home, went to Europe to live in the most modest of circumstances, and came back. Tad died in 1871, aged seventeen. She said that gas was the invention of the Devil and used only candles for a time, feared that Robert was dying, decided he was out to kill her, and ran from him half-dressed through a hotel corridor. Weeping as he testified to her condition at a sanity hearing, he had her committed to an institution.

She got out, went again to Europe, and came back. People whispered her name when she came into a public place, and stared at her. She went back to Springfield to live with her sister in the house in which she had been married to a lawyer called the plainest-looking man in town. The blinds of the windows of her room were always closed, and when she took a drive the carriage curtains were shut. The end of her broken life came in the summer of 1882. At the funeral the Reverend James A. Reed of Springfield's First Presbyterian Church likened the dead woman and her husband to two stately pines he had seen standing so close together that their roots and branches intertwined. The taller was struck by a flash of lightning and died. The other tree was killed also, but suffered a long, slow decline. "With the one that lingered it was only slow death from the same cause." So it was with the woman being buried. "When Abraham Lincoln died, she died. It seems to me that we are only looking at death placing its seal upon the lingering victim of a past calamity."

Her son Robert, twenty-one when his father died, became the most successful Presidential progeny in history save for John Quincy Adams. Rich from his law practice and the presidency of the Pullman Company, secretary of war, minister to Great Britain, he seemed, however, an unhappy man who suffered several nervous breakdowns. It was his fate to be present at two succeeding Presidential assassinations. He reached Garfield, he estimated, within fifteen seconds of the moment when a disappointed office-seeker fired. It was in Robert Lincoln's carriage that Garfield was taken away from the railroad station where he suffered his death wound. Years later Robert was with McKinley when an anarchist came from a reception line with a gun in his hand. Robert's absence from the first of all Presidential assassinations, that of his father, never ceased to cause him agony. Had he been there, he reasoned, as the junior member of the theater party, he would have taken a seat behind the others and so perhaps have been in a position to deal with the intruder entering the box. That he might have prevented all was "an obsession which he never outgrew," remembered his friend Nicholas Murray Butler, the longtime president of Columbia University.

The same thinking occupied the mind of Henry Rathbone. Recovered from the knife wound he had suffered on Good Friday of 1865, he married the young woman he had escorted to the theater that night. But the assassination preyed on his mind, and he faulted himself for not preventing it. Headaches and stomach upsets plagued him. He resigned from the army and with his wife toured European spas, seeking relief. His health did not improve, and by 1881 Clara Harris Rathbone was telling relatives that in fits of temper her husband threatened her life. She considered a separation or divorce, but ruled it out for the sake of the couple's three children. In Hanover, Germany, before daylight on Christmas morning of 1883, she awoke to find him fully dressed and wandering about her room. He said he wanted to see the children, the oldest of whom was thirteen. She pointed out the earliness of the hour. He produced a revolver and shot her, as once Lincoln had been shot, then took a knife and stabbed himself, as once he had been stabbed. As with Lincoln, she died, and as with his earlier stabbing, he lived—to be, like Mrs. Lincoln, committed to a mental institution. Like Mrs. Lincoln declaring gas to be the invention of the Devil, Rathbone maintained that the walls of his asylum were hollow and contained spray apparatus blowing dust and gas on him and giving him headaches and chest pain. He died in the asylum.

Lucy Hale went with her father and mother and sister to Spain, returned, and eventually married a widower with several children, William E. Chandler. Her husband gave her one son, and also high position in the Washington she had known as a young woman, for he became a U.S. senator and secretary of the navy. In the spring of 1878 newspapers all over the country carried a long article describing her romance with John Wilkes Booth. The article mentioned that Robert Todd Lincoln had been one of her suitors. Shortly the *Chicago Inter-Ocean* printed a rebuttal by Robert saying he had never been romantically involved with her. Then he issued a second rebuttal in the *Chicago Tribune*, saying the earlier statement had been printed without his authority. In the original article the woman who had dined with Lucy and her parents and her fiancé the night Lincoln was shot was quoted as saying of Lucy that if a book were to be written on her existence since the night of the assassination, it should be called *A Dead Woman's Life*. One of her stepchildren, who grew up to be a U.S. Navy admiral, long afterward remembered her as "a thoroughly unpleasant woman, in no way a sensuous woman." At social events, reporters noted, she seemed always to be on the outskirts of the crowd. Even when she gave parties for her young son, she stayed in a hallway, silently looking on. Eventually her widowed sister Elizabeth took over as the Chandler household's hostess. For many years Lucy wore only black, had her coachman outfitted in the same color to drive horses also black, and went about throwing newspaper clippings on the lawns of people she thought would be interested in reading particular stories. She annually contributed small sums to more than one hundred charities.

After leaving the army, Boston Corbett was in demand for speeches to be delivered by the assassin of Lincoln's assassin. But audiences found themselves listening to ranted-out religious tirades of the type that had characterized him for years. Asked for details on what had occurred at Garrett's farm, he would give a brief jerky-sentence description and sit down. The offers to speak ceased. He wandered about the country working as a farmer and at odd jobs, wearing his hair to his shoulders because, he explained, that was what Jesus had done. Perched above was an old army cap.

By 1886 Corbett had located in Kansas, appearing at Sunday farmers' sports events to declare, "It's wicked to play base ball on the Lord's day. Don't do it." A Topeka Grand Army of the Republic post got him an appointment as a doorkeeper in the state legislature, and he was there on a February day in 1887 when some clerks and pages held a mock session, with people jumping up to yell, "Mr. Speaker! Mr. Speaker!" and delivering horseplay speeches. When it was announced that a reverend would invoke a blessing, and a legislative employee rose to do so, Corbett in the balcony took out two revolvers, announced that God demanded the life of the pranksters, and opened fire. This time no one was killed. Corbett was put on trial, the prosecuting attorney being future vice president of the United States Charles Curtis, was found to be insane, and was confined to an institution. He escaped and was never heard of again.

The sanity hearing of Mrs. Lincoln and her death, the Rathbone tragedy, the articles about Robert Todd Lincoln and Lucy Hale, Corbett's outburst, a protracted debate over whether Mrs. Surratt deserved to hang and the allegation that a recommendation for mercy by the military judges had been placed before President Johnson, the trial of Mrs. Surratt's son John, who had been in Elmira, New York, when the fatal shot was fired and who fled the country, to be caught, brought back, tried, and found not guilty— all constituted nationally important stories carried by every newspaper. Each spoke of one common factor: John Wilkes Booth. Such also was the case when President Johnson was impeached and tried, with intimations made that he had been in on Lincoln's slaying: Who else profited, after all? Johnson's enemies asked. Was it not odd that more than two dozen men could not capture alive one trapped cripple? Dead men tell no tales. Congressional investigations went over the assassination in detail, and made headlines doing so. So too did the protracted battles over who deserved what percentage of the reward money, which ultimately had to be decided by a congressional committee. (The largest amount, $15,000, was given to Detective Conger, with diminishing sums down to $1,653.85 for each of the enlisted personnel of the 16th New York Cavalry, and $500 for a maid at the Surratt boardinghouse who told of the assassin's visits there and so directed suspicion at the boardinghouse's mistress.)

There were other stories, in the newspapers and in the minds of the generation that fought the war and the generation that followed. The relics carried on the flight to the Garrett barn, the great revolvers, the compass, the appointment book, gathered dust in a trunk in the War Department attic, and Surrattsville in Maryland was renamed Clinton—but John Wilkes Booth lived on. His ghost was seen, people said, furiously lashing his horse as he fled from the Uniontown—now Anacostia—end of the Eastern Branch Bridge up Good Hope Hill, and seen hurriedly limping across the fields of his escape route, using a crutch as he ran. He was, said the New York World, reported to have been observed playing rouge et noir at Baden-Baden and at the opera in Vienna, sworn to be seen driving in the Bois de Boulogne and visiting St. Peter's in Rome. He was "the only really mysterious personage we have had in our annals," said the paper, like Louis XVIII, son of Louis XVI and Marie Antoinette, the vanished dauphin whose fate was unknown, or the Man in the Iron Mask, or the children in the Tower perhaps slain by the Duke of Gloucester. He was reported to be captain of a pirate vessel that was "the terror of the China seas" and to have played Richard III in a Shanghai production during which people in the audience shouted his name, making him "glare like a tiger" before the curtain was rung down. A St. Louis paper in 1873 carried an extensive interview with a man who told of running into him in the Pelew (now Belaw) Islands carrying a medal presented to Junius Brutus Booth by the citizens of New York City.

In Richmond in the late 1870s and early 1880s the Episcopalian Reverend James G. Armstrong of raven-black hair and dramatic pulpit style, slightly lame and walking with a cane, a lecturer on Shakespeare when he left the ministry, was said to wear his hair long to hide a scar on his neck and to have told his wife: "Never forget you have Wilkes Booth for husband, and Lincoln's blood is still on his hands." The *New York Herald* wrote it up. *The New York Times* reported that in a Calcutta hotel a Southerner had guaranteed that Lincoln's assassin was alive, and had offered to bet five hundred pounds on it. He was said to live in isolation along the Russian River in California, and in a small town near Chattanooga from which, recognized, he at once fled.

He became, he was, a mythical figure, undead, who could not die, who had not died on the Garrett porch. A corner of the collective mind of the American people willed that he wander friendless forever, like a vampire, like *The Flying Dutchman* whose captain for his sins was doomed to sail the seas and make no port until the Day of Judgment, like the Mysterious Huntsman of European legend vainly pursuing forever a phantom deer.

On their deathbeds men averred that they were he, and as late as 1925 five skulls identified as his were on view simultaneously in carnivals and sideshows around the country. Into the late 1930s a mummy advertised as that of John Wilkes Booth was exhibited at country fairs. For the members of his family it was an agony most horrible to know what in death he had become. They dealt with his heritage as best they could, Asia by fleeing to England, Mrs. Booth and Rosalie by living the most secluded of lives, Joseph by retreating into melancholy and by burying himself in long studies aimed at making him a doctor—he finally became one at the age of thirty-nine; June in his practical way by saying that time would set all things right. They dealt with it. Edwin never.

■

For many months, all through the summer and into the fall of 1865, he cooped himself up in his house, never venturing out for a breath of air until darkness had come. Physically worn down, he presented a sad, shamed, grief-stricken appearance. "That introspective look," Asia said. He wrote of his mother to the widow of his friend Richard Cary, killed in the war: "She seems to have still a lingering hope in her heart that all this will prove to be a dream." For himself there were no dreams, at least none of happiness. His fiancée, Blanche Hanel, broke off their engagement. On his deathbed, her father had exacted from her a promise that she would not marry into the family of Lincoln's assassin, perhaps to bear children whose name would be Booth.

He sat, he wrote Mrs. Cary, in "the heavy, aching gloom of my little red room, chewing my heart in solitude." Christmas was coming, Christmas of 1865, and then the first year of peace, 1866, and the North was rich and on its way to becoming richer as the Gilded Age came in; and something of a philosophy asserted itself in his thinking. But it was a sad philosophy. "Life is a great big spelling-book," he told Mrs. Cary, "and on every page we turn the words grow harder to understand the meaning. When the last leaf flops over, we'll know the whole lesson by heart." With the hope of marriage to Blanche gone, she whom he had counted on as sent by Molly in heaven, he had nothing else in life to cling to but what he had always had. He must return to the stage.

"The blood of our martyred President is not yet dry in the memory of our people, and the very name of the assassin is appalling to the public mind," said James Gordon Bennett's *New York Herald*. "Still a Booth is advertised to appear before a New York audience." There were reports that he would be shot when he came onstage. Police were inside and outside the Winter Garden.

But when he was discovered as the second scene of *Hamlet* opened, sitting with bowed head, the audience rose, and cheer after cheer rolled across the footlights, women waving their handkerchiefs, the stage filling up with flung bouquets. When at great length the people quieted and the last shout died down, he found himself unable to begin for long moments. The part of Ophelia was played by Effie Germon.

After that he toured the country to enormous crowds while wondering always if the people paying previously unheard-of prices came to see not Edwin Booth but the brother of the man who shot

Lincoln. By his orders the house lights went on as soon as the play ended. He would not take curtain calls.

For two years he toured the West, and when from unprecedented receipts he had accumulated what he considered sufficient, he built Booth's Theatre. In a day of the construction of great playhouse, with caryatids, fringed curtains, ornate banisters, rococo reliefs, deep pile carpets, sculptures, colonnades, ornamental gold-highlighted plasterwork with scrollwork cascading down from the balconies, his was the most elaborate of all, with towers reaching 120 feet above the sidewalk at New York's Sixth Avenue and Twenty-third Street, with flags flying from the towers and lightning rods adorned with stars and crescents, with a mansard roof and inside lobby faced with marble, with marble winding staircases and a niche at the stair landing holding a statue of his father and with inside in the auditorium busts of Garrick, Talmas, Kean, and overhead paintings of Apollo, the Muses, and the Graces, with the walls below showing Venus in her chariot, Cupid, Lear, Hamlet, Othello, Macbeth. He laid out more than a million dollars. It wasn't enough. He took out loans, repaid them with more loans.

Booth's Theatre opened in early 1869, with its owner playing Romeo to the Juliet of Mary McVicker. He had asked her to marry him. She was the daughter of the owner of Chicago's leading theater, McVicker's, where in 1860 most of the delegates to the Republican Presidential Convention that nominated Abraham Lincoln had gone to see Laura Keene in *Our American Cousin*. She was musical, practical, ambitious, restless, and had a great sense of humor and of the comic and ridiculous that made everybody laugh at her funny stories. (She would be well advised to keep away from Shakespeare, thought the critic William Winter, and play Irish girls in farces.) Tiny and slight of build, she was a discriminating student of the theater who had never known anything else, growing up in an entirely theatrical environment. ("Friend Booth," her father had written to John on Christmas Day of 1864, "What do you say to filling three weeks with me May 29th? There are plenty of little fish but I don't want them if I can help it, so come at the above date." But, of course, when May 29th came the letter's recipient was lying in the earth below the Old Penitentiary.)

Underneath the fun and animation that characterized Mary McVicker there was something else: the germ of a madness that would destroy her. Perhaps it was always destined to grow and overwhelm her, perhaps her solemn and brooding husband so different in temperament unwittingly fed it, or perhaps the death in

a few hours of a child born a year after their marriage. Within a few
years she was under the care of mental specialists and in and out of
institutions. Sometimes she cried for hours as Edwin rocked her in
his arms. Sometimes she screamed and raved, the sounds audible
outside their New York home or rented summer cottages, or the
estate he bought her on the Connecticut shore at Cos Cob.

So he put his soul into Booth's Theatre, staging productions
the splendor of which had never been seen anywhere before. Everything was done with no regard for the enormous bills, and when he
needed money he took out short-term loans at ruinous rates of
interest. He said he wished to put on new plays as well as classics
but was unable ever to find a single one that pleased him. They were
all "smut," he declared. It was the greatest letdown of her life, Julia
Ward Howe told her friends, that he refused to put on a play she
wrote for him. Smut. Like Asia all her life, respectability seized
him. "I never permit my wife or daughter to witness a play," he
wrote The Christian Union, "without previously ascertaining its
character," this because the theater was becoming a "mere shop for
gain open to every huckster of immoral gim-cracks." In that cate-
gory he included Ibsen and, later, Strindberg.

When the bills for interest payments on his loans came due he
went touring to make money. At least on the road production costs
could be laid at someone else's door. He drew great crowds paying
premium prices, sending the money back to New York while doing
nothing beyond going to the theater and then to the hotel and then
to the train, never speaking to reporters beyond "Good evening"
or "Good morning" and seeming to turn into a marble statue if a
stranger approached. He had always been withdrawn, but now he
was ten times more so, his friends sighing to one another that, as
John Ellsler put it, a somber curtain hung before Edwin's eyes with
always sounding behind it that haunting shout on the stage at
Ford's: Sic temper tyrannis.

One night at Booth's Theatre the owner told Garrie Davidson,
his personal attendant, that he wished to be called from his apartment high in the building at 3:00 A.M. At that hour Davidson went
in and found him partially dressed but asleep. Davidson made
coffee over a spirit lamp and then, knowing the sleeper's habit of
awaking in a rage, took from out of range his pipe and a book and
his tobacco jar and all other movables from the night table, and his
boots. Gently shaken awake, he sat up in a daze looking for something to throw and then came to himself quietly to drink two cups
of coffee.

"Still snowing, Garrie?"

"Yes, sir." He helped him into his jacket. "Where shall I go, Mr. Booth?"

"To the furnace room."

With a lantern Davidson led the way down and across the black stage to where the fireman had banked the fires when the night's audience departed. He turned up the gas and saw a large trunk tied with ropes. He was told to get an ax, and with it cut the cords and knocked off the top. The odor of camphor rose in the air. The trunk was packed, Davidson saw, with costumes on top of which sat wigs and theatrical swords. He realized at once whose they had been. Edwin silently put the hairpieces and stage weapons on the trunk cover lying on the floor and took out a costume. It was a steel-blue broadcloth Louis XVI coat. "Claude Melnotte," Davidson said to himself—*The Lady of Lyons*. His employer held it up at arm's length and turned it, trying, Davidson thought, to picture what it had looked like on its owner, and to remember when last it had been worn. "Put it in there." Davidson opened the furnace door and looked at him. It seemed such a shame to do it. Edwin stood, Davidson thought, like a statue.

The coat settled in the flames with a hiss as a bit of lace at the throat caught. The lace of the sleeves caught. There followed a satin waistcoat, knee britches, several pairs of tights. Some of the things had *J.W.B.* on the linings in marking ink. Edwin took out a black-beaded hauberk he turned over in his hands for a while before giving it to Davidson. Silk stockings went in, velvet shoes Davidson thought an Elizabethan type, for Iago perhaps, a cavalier's costume like those used in *The Hunchback* and *The Duke's Motto*, a cut-leather jerkin with slashed green velvet sleeves, a sword belt to match studded with steel nail heads, velvet trunks matching the sleeves, a broad-brimmed hat with ostrich feathers, more cavalier boots.

Roman things for Marc Antony, a velvet coat and gray trousers for Raphael in *The Marble Heart*, Davidson thought, Romeo and Shylock costumes, a gorgeous Othello robe of two East Indian shawls so fine, Davidson saw, that they could have been pulled through a bracelet. It had cost Edwin a good deal of money and effort to get hold of the trunk.

There was a photograph with the trunk's owner in Indian dress dated *Richmond, 1859–60*. Metamora in the play of that name, Davidson knew. By the picture was the costume itself. Both went in, to be joined by a packet of letters wrapped in a handkerchief and tied with an old ribbon. A woman's handwriting, Davidson thought, looking over his employer's shoulder. Edwin took out a long, belted, purple velvet shirt ornamented with stage jewels, and an armhole cloak trimmed in fur, both creased and worn in places. Holding them, he sat down on the trunk with the things on his knees, unmoving. Then he began to cry. "My father's," he said, sobbing. "Garrie, it was my father's Richard III dress. He wore it in Boston on the first night I went on the stage as Tressel."

"Don't you think you ought to save that, Mr. Booth?"

"No, put it with the others."

He returned to handing things to Davidson, sometimes throwing them in himself. The fire scorched Davidson's hands and face as he turned the coals with a furnace poker. Edwin took it from him and did the work himself, then gave it back, then took it again as they continued. "At the bottom of the trunk we found a couple of daggers," Davidson remembered. "They were beauties. Scraps of stage jewelry, some odds and ends, and a pair of women's satin dancing slippers, these were thrown on the coals with the wigs— and even the swords. They would melt and break." At the end Davidson was told to knock up the trunk and toss it and the ropes into the furnace.

They stood and watched the snaky metal rims of the trunk in the ashes. "That's all," Edwin said, very quietly. "We'll go now."

It was nearly six in the morning. A loose shutter was banging against the side of the building and booming through the empty galleries. Crossing the stage Edwin said, "Thank you, Garrie. You needn't come."

"Good morning, sir." Davidson stood at the foot of the stairs with his lantern until he heard the door to the apartment close.

From the very first Mary Ann Booth had wanted to see her son's dead body and to give him a proper burial. He had been, Edwin said, his mother's darling. Her wound would never heal, but that John lay in an unknown and dishonored grave made it ache. Soon after his capture and death, friends prevailed upon the New York political figure Thurlow Weed to inquire of Secretary Stanton the disposition of the remains, or if, as the papers said, there were no remains, they having been torn to pieces, or burned, or flung into the sea. Stanton sent word that when the excitement over Lincoln's death somewhat subsided, the family could have the body. Seven months after the assassination, Edwin wrote to him.

> Mr. Thurlow Weed has delivered to me the message you were kind enough to send, and at the earnest solicitation of my Mother I write to ask if you think the time is

yet arrived for her to have the remains of her unhappy
son. If I am premature in this I hope you will understand
the motive which actuates me, arising purely from a sense
of duty to assuage, if possible, the anguish of an aged
mother. If at your convenience you will acquaint me
when and how I should proceed in this matter you will
relieve her sorrow-stricken heart and bind me ever.

There was no answer. A year and a half passed, and Edwin asked
John T. Ford to see if he could be of assistance in requesting the body.
Ford was still a Washington figure of some prominence, although his
former theater was now a government-owned building housing
among other agencies the surgeon general's office of the War Department, which held the three cervical vertebrae of John Wilkes Booth
removed from his body in the *Montauk* autopsy, showing by the
holes through them the life-ending bullet wound he had suffered.
"Do what you can," Edwin wrote Ford, "whatever you think can be
done. I shall not forget it." To Ford as a friend and business
acquaintance of many years' standing he could speak not so much of
his mother but of himself, and of what the assassination meant to
him. "Any reference to this fearful subject serves to open my
wounds afresh, and God knows the shame and horror heaped upon
my family is enough. Were it not for my child"—Edwina was six—"I
think it would have crushed me long since. As it is I feel more keenly
than the world can know the terrible weight upon me." But Ford was
unable to accomplish much. Two months later, in July 1867, Edwin
tried with the new secretary of war, General Grant:

> Having once received a promise from Mr. Stanton
> that the family of John Wilkes Booth could be permitted
> to receive the body when sufficient time elapsed, I yielded
> to the entreaties of my Mother and applied for it I fear too
> soon, for the letter went unheeded. I now appeal to you,
> on behalf of my heart-broken Mother, that she may re-
> ceive the remains of her son. You, Sir, can understand
> what a consolation it would be to an aged parent to have
> the privilege of visiting the grave of her child, and I feel
> assured that you will, even in the midst of your most
> pressing duties, feel a touch of sympathy for her—one of
> the greatest sufferers living. May I not hope that you will
> listen to our entreaties and send me some encourage-
> ment—some information how and where the remains
> may be obtained? In doing so you will receive the grati-
> tude of a most unhappy family.

Grant did not reply. Edwin tried again in February 1869, writing President Johnson. Almost four years had passed since Boston Corbett had fired what had come to be seen as the last shot of the Civil War. Edwin could not know, for only a tiny handful of people did, that his brother no longer lay under the Old Penitentiary. The section of the building under which he had been put had been razed, and on October 1, 1867, his musket case coffin had been buried in the bottom of a warehouse on the eastern side of the Washington Arsenal grounds. With it were the bodies of the four hanged conspirators, removed from where they had been since the hour of their deaths, the lawn by their gallows.

In a month Johnson would be leaving office to go home to Tennessee, conviction in his impeachment trial avoided by a single vote. One of his last official acts would be to pardon the conspiracy trial defendants who had escaped the scaffold. O'Laughlen, Spangler, Arnold, and Mudd had been condemned to hard labor at the island fortress of Dry Tortugas in the waters of the Gulf of Mexico. O'Laughlen found his death from yellow fever there, as did much of the military garrison and many other prisoners. Dr. Mudd, with the assistance of Spangler and Arnold, helped fight the epidemic. As they were ordered freed, Johnson sent word to Edwin that his brother's body would be given over along with the bodies of the four hanged conspirators.

Edwin retained the services of the Baltimore undertaker John H. Weaver to bury John in the Booth family plot at Greenmount Cemetery, Baltimore. Weaver in turn asked the Washington undertaking firm of Harvey & Marr to be ready to assist him. Their offices were on F Street around the corner from the government building that had once been Ford's Theatre. Calling upon the President, Weaver was told, "I wish this conducted with the utmost secrecy and dispatch, and with the avoidance of all sensationalism and publicity." The undertaker assured Johnson that was very much the wish of the assassin's relatives.

On the afternoon of February 15, 1869, a Harvey & Marr employee, W. R. Speare, told not to use a hearse, which might attract attention, rented a moving van and went with it to the grounds of the Washington Arsenal. The high iron gates of a warehouse opened for him and he went into a room pungent with the odor of freshly dug earth. The coffins of Davy Herold and Mrs. Surratt had been taken away earlier in the day. Soldiers brought up a pine case upon which was written: *Booth*. Four of them lifted it into the moving van. Speare drove to the back entrance of Harvey

& Marr. It opened into the cobblestone alley in the rear of the former Ford's Theatre, a few yards from where Peanut John Burroughs sat on a stone bench holding a little mare on the evening of April 14, 1865.

The coffin was taken inside, then transferred to another wagon, which departed for the seven-thirty to Baltimore. Asked to assist in the matter, John T. Ford telegraphed Edwin at Booth's Theatre: *Successful and in our possession.* The officer commanding the Washington Arsenal sent a memorandum to the War Department's assistant adjutant general: *Sir: I have the honor to report that the body of John Wilkes Booth was, on Monday afternoon the 15th inst., delivered to the person designated in the order of the President of the United States of the same date.*

Two days later a rehearsal at Baltimore's Holliday Street Theatre was interrupted when John T. Ford came onstage and whispered something to the comedian Charles B. Bishop, a close friend of Edwin. The rehearsal was immediately dismissed. Ford took both hands of the actress Blanche Chapman, who would in time marry his brother Harry, and said, "Blanche, I want you to keep your eyes and ears open and your mouth shut." He took her through the stage entrance, her actress-sister Ella walking with Bishop, and her future husband also coming. They went across the street to John Weaver's undertaking establishment at Fayette Street near Gay.

They passed through a large room and into a small one, where Blanche Chapman at once recognized Mary Ann Booth and her daughter Rosalie. Years earlier Blanche had been dismissed with Marion Booth, June's daughter, from the Sisters of the Sacred Heart Convent school in Philadelphia, the sisters ruling they did not desire the attendance of children of people connected with the stage. She greeted mother and daughter and saw that what looked like a mummy was lying partially uncovered on a brown-colored blanket. It had, she saw, wonderful teeth. The lips were gone and the skin shriveled and dark.

Joseph Booth, still pursuing his medical studies, was present. He said, "If this is the body of John Wilkes Booth, it has but one plugged tooth in its head." Blanche noticed that Joe did not use the word "brother." Charles Bishop opened the mouth, took out a filled tooth, and displayed it. John Weaver and Bishop then cut the portion of the blanket that covered the lower legs and showed a broken bone near the ankle.

The head was entirely detached from the body, the result of

the *Montauk* autopsy and removal of the three damaged vertebrae. The hair, everybody saw, was extremely long. So it was true after all, they said to themselves, that hair continues to grow after death. Weaver asked Ella Chapman if she would cut off a lock. She turned away. Blanche did it, taking a large segment from over the forehead. She handed it to Weaver, who gave it to Mrs. Booth. The mother wept as she separated the strands. "And the faint moans coming from her lips. She gave my sister and myself both a strand."

The body had been satisfactorily identified. Edwin had remained in another room throughout. Everybody left. "I could see every feature in that face of John Wilkes Booth," Harry Ford said to his future wife. *Here comes the handsomest man in Washington*, he had said long ago when John walked up to Ford's Theatre on the morning of April 14, 1865, and learned that someone who had once been given a prize for being the ugliest person in creation would be in the audience that night.

Interment was at Greenmount, with a minister visiting Baltimore from New York officiating. Pallbearers from the theatrical profession carried the body, placed in a handsome mahogany coffin with hinged lid and glass plate. Some forty or fifty people were present. The minister had not known until it was time for the services to begin whom he was burying. When word got out he was dismissed from his post by his New York congregation.

In the plot could be seen the names of Junius Brutus Booth and three children who died in infancy. Mrs. Booth, Rosalie, Asia, and Joe would one day join them under stones bearing their names. One grave remained unmarked. Years later the funeral director who took over John Weaver's business asked Edwin if he thought a stone ought to be put up and Edwin said, "Leave that as it is."

SIXTEEN

OWNED AND RUN by a monetary simpleton, Booth's Theatre was probably always destined for financial ruin. The Panic of 1873 settled any doubts about the question. Edwin's bankruptcy took from him his books, pictures, furniture. He still owed. So he toured for years to make money he must immediately hand to others. "I have done great things," he ruefully said, quoting Don Caesar de Bazan in *The Fool's Revenge;* "if you doubt me ask my creditors."

Wherever he went, and he went everywhere, Johnny accompanied him. Every newspaper article mentioned that next week would be appearing, or last night had appeared, the brother of the man who killed Lincoln. Each was a "most brutal ghoul-feast," he wrote the theatrical critic William Winter, "flaunting in my face buried cerements raked up by these hyenas. Each little piddling village has stabbed me through and through." Often the name of John Wilkes Booth appeared in the papers independent of his brother. That did not lessen his brother's reaction. THE WIDOW OF J. WILKES BOOTH, a front-page story in the *New York Tribune* was headlined. It was not generally known, the paper said, that the assassin had left a wife and two children. "A d——nable lie," Edwin wrote his friend Laurence Hutton. "This 'widow' is one of several that wrote to me from different cities. One got hold of poor Rose and robbed her of all the money she had."

The woman had indeed won over Rosalie, who felt her little boy and girl did bear a great resemblance to John, gave them money, called them her children, and was called Aunt Rose by them. The little girl grew up to become an actress who variously billed herself as Ogarita Wilkes and Rita Booth. "Several people who knew Booth claim to have noted in her," said *The New York Times*, "the big ox eyes, the curly hair and high brow of the man who was regarded as the rising actor of his time." Wearing a medallion locket containing John's likeness, she informed people she did not wish to achieve acting eminence because of the notoriety of her late father. When she died young, the reporters who called upon Edwin for a comment were told that Mr. Booth was not at home.

For the second Mrs. Booth he could not feel anything of what he had felt for the first—"Your angel mother," in his letters to Edwina, "who now watches over and prays for us in heaven"—and as her mental condition degenerated he became almost as her keeper. When in Chicago in 1879 a madman rose from the audience at McVicker's Theatre and fired a revolver at him twice, he remained calm, but his wife was devastated and remained prostrated for days, to awake from tortured dreams night after night screaming of bullets and guns. His main concern was for his mother. "Think of her," he wrote to Dave Anderson, the Uncle Davy of California days, "and all the horrid Past reviewed by this event! She cannot rid herself of the sight of my lying dead, while all the miseries of her great sorrow are renewed by memories thus awakened."

The man who shot at him was committed to an asylum, where it became increasingly clear Mary McVicker Booth belonged. She had become "a lunatic who could hardly be controlled." She forbade her husband's dresser to approach him, doing his robing and makeup herself and walking behind him at all times, never letting him go until the cue came for him to go onstage. She could not abide any mention of Mary Devlin, her predecessor. In 1881 she and her husband and Edwina went to England, where he performed to great acclaim, and her mind completely collapsed. Suffering from what doctors called throat and lung consumption—tuberculosis—she told Asia that Edwina shook and pinched her when she tried to sleep, made faces at her, stole from her. "Her violent hatred of the child is the uppermost thought in her mind," Asia said. Mary Booth turned on her husband, marking him as a monster of cruelty and neglect, so writing her parents in Chicago. Then she would forget all, begging that he stay with her when she was too weak to accompany him to the theater. "You can imagine my condition," he wrote Laurence Hutton, "acting every evening and nursing a half-insane dying wife all day and all night too, for that matter. I am scarce sane myself."

He finished up in London. His wife's hallucinations came and went. She told him Uncle Davy had just died, which he had not. She was subject to terrifyingly violent convulsions. Sometimes she cried pitifully when she realized in moments of lucidity what was happening to her. She coughed continuously. They went back to America, where her parents accepted everything she told them in her madness, took her under their care, forbade Edwin to see her, and denounced him in newspapers that were filled with stories about the trial of Charles Guiteau, Garfield's slayer. He told William Winter he was afraid he would go mad, or worse, return to the drinking he gave up on the day he saw Molly lying dead in her bed at Dorchester. On his forty-eighth birthday, November 13, 1881, he was told his second wife was dead.

A year later he again crossed the ocean and went to Germany and Austria to play leads in English while supported by actors speaking their own language. The audience wept for his Hamlet. At the end of his first performance the stage manager-director bent over his hand so deeply as almost to kneel, and kissed it. "*Herr Meister*," he said.

In Berlin he was given a crown of laurel leaves of silver with on it *To the Unrivalled Artist* and in Bremen silver leaves inscribed *To the Great Artist*. In Hamburg there was a delicate sprig of silver bay leaves on a satin cushion, and then, Edwina wrote William Winter, "It fairly took my breath away! A whole bevy of pretty young girls—actresses and otherwise—rushed up with open arms and actually *embraced* and *kissed* Papa as he stood on stage still in Lear's robes!!" The German crown prince came to see him play half a dozen times and declared that for the first time he saw a real prince upon a stage. Living abroad while serving in the diplomatic corps, former general Adam Badeau reflected that sovereigns holding levees or receiving homage or conferring honors had no greater dignity or grace than Edwin.

He returned to the United States and affiliated himself with the actor-impresario Lawrence Barrett, a scholar of the theater and a brilliant producer-businessman. With Barrett making all the plans and attending to all the details, Edwin's income rose to the level of the country's richest men, amounting to as much as a quarter of a million dollars a year at a time when the average laborer earned nine dollars a week, and a skilled craftsman sixteen. He gave away much of it, paying for the funerals of actresses' mothers and buying annuities for aged actors down on their luck. He had always been generous. When he learned that a claim upon the U.S. government by the Garrett family for the replacement of their burned barn had been rejected, he sent money for the construction of a new one. (When he received a letter asking for two free tickets to a play, the writer identifying himself as "the United States soldier that shot your brother who assassinated President Lincoln," he sent them, never knowing if it was really Boston Corbett who had written.)

The Corbett letter came to him in Richmond. The former Confederate capital he would play, but Washington never. When, twenty years after the assassination, President Chester A. Arthur and leading members of Congress wrote asking him to do so, he refused. It was just curiosity to see the brother of Lincoln's slayer, he said. (When he played Baltimore, seats were sold in Washington with to and fro railroad tickets attached.) Christmases he would appear in theaters, New Year's, Thanksgiving Day—but Good Friday, never.

His contact with the Garretts was not yet over. In 1877 a minister who as a child had gotten down from the wall a map for the gentleman he knew as John W. Boyd wrote saying his family still had the lock of hair cut from the head of the man who, dying on their porch, they had learned was John Wilkes Booth. *We have never had an opportunity of telling you before that my mother and sisters did everything in their power to make your brother comfortable in his last hours.* If Edwin wanted the lock of hair, he could have it.

It had been twelve years. *The painful subject is never referred to by any of us, although, of course, everything associated with the unfortunate boy is sacred to his heartbroken mother, and I am sure will be dearly prized by her.* The Reverend Richard Baynham Garrett sent the lock. *I have received and forwarded to our Mother the memento of the misguided boy whose madness wrought so much ill to us. Though his name has never been spoken by us since his untimely end, I desire to express our gratitude to your family for your kindness to him in his last hours, and for this last act which I am sure will do much to sooth and comfort the heartbroken mother.* Years later he was still sending the Reverend Garrett books not affordable on a minister's income.

In 1885 Edwin's mother died. "We know that she is blessed in the reunion with her loved ones gone before. I took her to Baltimore. She looked about forty and very beautiful—as I remember her in my boyhood. To such a weary sufferer the end was a blessing." His own knowledge that one day he too must die, Edwin said, was something for which he daily thanked God. "Why do you not look," he asked William Winter, "at this miserable little life as I do? 'Tis but a scratch, a temporary ill to be soon cured by that dear old doctor, Death." They buried his mother at an earlier hour than that stated in the newspapers so as to avoid sightseers who might come to see her put in the lot where John was. A large number who appeared were disappointed to find her interment completed. The stories of her son's sighting had never ceased in her lifetime: He was spotted in Bombay and Ceylon; a house on Telegraph Hill in San Francisco was shunned because it was said to be haunted by his ghost, but sometimes one saw a figure slip out at night, cloaked, handsome, aloof. It was related as fact that when Edwin was in London riding in a carriage with Asia a man came out of the mist and Edwin cried, "My God, it is John!" and spoke with him and gave him money. What remained of the assassin above ground was moved when the government located the surgeon general's office elsewhere from the former Ford's Theatre, the three vertebrae going along. The Records and Pension Department of the War Department took over the building.

In 1886 Edwin opened a tour that would take him from Buffalo to the West Coast, all arrangements, casting, finances, costumes for the minor players, the rent of railroad cars, advertising, and the prop men and stage assistants, managerial staff, porters, costume masters, and cooks taken care of from New York by Lawrence Barrett. Kitty Molony, eighteen, was signed to play supporting roles. She told Barrett she hesitated to go on tour with Edwin Booth, for she did not wish to lose her reverence for the actor by knowing as a man someone she regarded as the lightning in the clouds, the sun in the sky, the moon in the night, no less Olympian than the statues of Goethe and Schiller she had known in the Germany of her childhood. Her first real introduction to him came when she did herself up as the Bloody Apparition in *Macbeth*. "My God," he said. "You look as if you had been scalped by Indians."

"Shall I take it off?"

"I should hope so." He got a towel and did it himself, then took up a brush, studied her face, and put on the stage blood. "There should be enough skin left exposed to prove it was a human being who was slaughtered," he said. She laughed. It seemed to her that now, so many years on, his great career had piled invisible laurels at his feet saying, "Forget! You are free of your bitter shadow!"

But he was not. "How many brothers and sisters did you have, Mr. Booth?" she asked as he sat smoking and chatting with players in the train. Immediately she hated herself. Her throat ached. But any additional words would make things worse.

"I forget the lot of us," he said. "I'll name them—you count them for me. Junius Brutus—after my father, of course—Rosalie, Henry, Mary, Frederick, Elizabeth—I come in here—Asia, Joe—how many is that?"

"Nine, Mr. Booth."

"What big families they used to raise!" But, "There had leapt from his eyes such a flash of appeal," she wrote, "so beseechingly humble." In New Orleans as they zigzagged all over the country he asked Kitty and two other young actresses, Emma Vaders and Ida Rock, if they would like to take up residency in his private car with their own stateroom along with stage manager Arthur Chase and the dead Molly's brother-in-law Harry Magonigle, his longtime aide and factotum. The food, even the tips for waiters, was at Edwin's expense. It was against all theater etiquette, for the usual destiny of a star was that he live in lonely grandeur while the others of a company were jammed into a Pullman, clubbing together to buy some food for preparation over a spirit lamp or wolfing it down at the station lunch counter during twenty-minute layovers for the locomotive to take on water. Yet, Kitty remembered, "He gave his invitation as if begging a favor. How like him! How very like him!"

He called the three young actresses My Chickens. To Kitty, Emma, who was Amo to her friends, and Ida, Ido to her friends, the trip was a heaven on earth. Bubbly girls, they were in a magnificent private car, the *David Garrick* and later the *Junius Brutus Booth*, eating luscious meals prepared from food bought at choice markets along the way, and sitting at table with Edwin Booth. To him they were gay and happy and cheerful, all that he had never been. "I long to hang from my knees from them," Ido once said of some curtain rods in the private car; and she was fulfilling her desire when unexpectedly he came in. "He *almost* joined in our giggles," Kitty remembered. Almost. For he never laughed. He thanked them, when he went to bed, for helping drive away what he called his vultures, the thoughts that came to him when he lay sleepless.

They were pretty girls destined for no great theatrical futures—and though Kitty would never know it, he was unable greatly to admire her acting. "Miss Molony is not at all capable, even for the parts she has played," he wrote Lawrence Barrett in New York. "I sincerely regret it, for she is a pretty and good little lady. Her case is hopeless. A sweet little lady but I fear she will remain just where she is on the ladder." Her inadequacy presented him with a dilemma, for Barrett had promised Kitty more prominent roles in certain plays as the tour progressed. Rather than "break her aspiring heart" by telling her that others would have to take those parts, Edwin decided not to put on the productions in question. He got out of it by telling Kitty he had neglected to bring along his proper costumes for them.

So she and he and the others went across the country playing to enormous crowds at every stop, with theater managers putting the orchestra backstage so their usual seats could be sold for premium prices. Men came to performances in white tie and swallow tails, and women in hoop skirts and bustles and puffs and frills, carrying mother-of-pearl opera glasses and precipitating hot disputes about their great fruit-tray hats which blocked the view of anyone sitting behind. Very old for someone in his fifties, as always unable to sleep—it was useless for him to try until very late—he sat with his Chickens in the swaying train, told them stories of his travels. Once Kitty asked if he considered himself an authoritative judge of acting. Amo and Ido stared at her as if they believed she had lost her mind. "I hoped . . . there are those . . . well—I acknowledge I am a judge of acting," he said.

"Oh, indeed, Mr. Booth, yes, but you must admit you cannot know as much about acting as I do!"

For once he stopped smoking. He pointed out that he was far older. "What makes me a better judge of acting has nothing to do with age," she said. "It is acting, alone! And you know yourself, Mr. Booth, I have seen the perfection of acting—and you never have!"

They headed West. He allowed no alcohol on board, not even wine or beer, and himself drank milk of Apollinaris. His idea of supreme luxury, he told the girls, was to go to sleep and stay asleep. Usually he could not nod off until dawn had come. He must envy us, his Chickens who turn off the gaslights and are gone, Kitty thought, while he lay fighting his vultures through the wasting hours, the memories who flapped their wings keeping him awake. "Memories are hard upon one in lonely hours," he said, but then added that not all of his memories were vultures: There was one he kept of his guardian angel. "There is another!" he went on. "I must not let it get hold of me, late at night!" She believed she knew of whom both memories were.

Even at such close range and seeing him night after night he tore at her heart in tragedy, and revolted and frightened her when he played villains. It seemed impossible that the same man who was Edwin Booth was the horrid Iago. It appeared to her that only being onstage invigorated him, for tourist-style excursions did not, he doing little but look on while saying he wanted the Chickens to be as young as kittens or puppies, and to play. He took the whole company for a week of relaxation at Monterey on the California coast. All save he amused themselves, and he said, "It takes so little, after all, to rest—only to stop thinking."

"And plenty of money," stage manager Arthur Chase put in. "You are having an expensive outing, Mr. Booth. Closed theaters! Private cars!"

"Money is well spent that buys a week away from myself."

There in California he talked of his youth when he blacked his face and played his banjo as a minstrel, and imitated the way he had boomed around the stage in the Gold Rush melodramas presented on makeshift stages in saloons or dance halls. Now, Kitty thought, the audiences who came to see him in magnificent Gilded Age toilettes, wearing tiaras, were such as to remind her of the court or grand opera crowds she had seen in Germany.

They finished on the Coast and headed back. Approaching Cheyenne, manager Chase told Kitty the citizens of the city were going to have open carriages for the company to ride in, and a brass band. When the star emerged from the train, the band planned to burst into "Lo, the Conquering Hero Comes."

Did Mr. Chase really think, she asked, that this could be done? Did he dream that Mr. Booth would stand for it? Chase explained that Cheyenne meant it as a great honor, a testimonial. They couldn't call it off and insult a whole town. She suggested they send a telegram ahead—"Owing to the lateness of your delightful invitation—" but Chase cut her off by saying the Cheyenne people had been sending letters for weeks. He'd been hopeful something would turn up. Maybe somebody would die or the theater would burn down. But nothing had occurred. Now they were approaching the town. Would Kitty talk to Mr. Booth?

She went to his drawing room, thinking, "Too ridiculous! Mr. Chase could not be serious! He could not be expecting Edwin Booth to parade with a brass band and in an open carriage." Amo and Ido looked happy that she had to go in, not they.

She sat with him, dumb, while he chatted about alcohol rubs. He used to have one after a performance, he remarked, but they seemed to give him slight colds and make his voice husky. The train was slowing down. The sound of a band could be heard. He smiled. Apparently he relished a good brass band. The train halted in the station. Travelers passed under the window. He leaned back so as

not to be seen. She got out that the band was for him, and there was
going to be a parade.

At once he had her out of her seat and through the door. It
banged behind her. She heard the lock snap shut. Chase was waiting outside. Chase knocked. There was no response. Chase con-
fessed that he sent her in knowing that miracles do occur, but that
if one did not, he had an alternative plan. It was a young actor held
in reserve. "Treat him as if he were Mr. Booth, surround him, hang
upon him." They did so, smirking at the impostor, who was Edwin
Milton Royle, the future author of *The Squawman*, one of the first
full-length motion pictures. He wore a cape of the type the star
favored, and had a soft hat pulled down. He entered a carriage
drawn by six white horses, took a seat with his back to them, was
hissed at to sit facing forward. At the hotel he became upset when
shown to the expensive bridal suite, fearful that he was going to
have to pay for it, but Chase told him to sit around a while and then
sneak out the back way. The hotel had raised its rates for the night,
Chase remarked to Kitty, and the railroads were running excursion
trains from outlying districts so people could come to the theater.
At the train all entrances to the *David Garrick* were locked, and the
shades drawn down tight. When Chase went back the cook let him
in through the galley. His star commanded that he be driven to the
hotel through back streets. Young Royle decided he had the right
ever after to say that if he hadn't played Hamlet's role, he'd played
the next thing to it. "He drew all hearts to him, everyone near him
reverenced and loved him," his impersonator said of Edwin. "I
never heard him say a harsh or unkind or sarcastic word."

They finished at Worcester in the spring of 1887. Edwin
would be taking a train alone to Boston. The company came to see
him off, the Chickens standing together. Amo said to him that she
was afraid she had never made clear how she appreciated his patience, the inspiration he offered, his hospitality, what an honor it
was to support him onstage, that she would always take his kindness as her brightest memory. "All my life I shall look back to this
season." She smiled and stepped back.

Ido said, "Oh, Mr. Booth, it's been too wonderful for anything! I can't thank you, but you do know, don't you?"

It was Kitty's turn. She could not speak. She began to cry. The
conductor called "All aboard" and Edwin mounted the train steps
and stood with his hat off. All the company cheered and waved
their handkerchiefs for as long as he could see and hear them.
Chase reminded Kitty that she had said she always feared there

would come a day when the star would do something she could not admire, something that would take him from his pedestal. She replied that day had never come. "I think that is why I cried," she said. "I shall not see another perfect human being very soon."

That summer, 1887, he took a cruise on the steam yacht of his friend the industrialist E. C. Benedict, with Thomas Bailey Aldrich, Laurence Hutton, William Bishram, and Lawrence Barrett coming along. He had it in mind, he told them, to found a club for actors. Actors did not mingle enough with other people, he said, and so the club would have members from outside the profession. Above all, it must exude respectability, decorum. "I do not want my club to be a gathering place of freaks who come to look upon another sort of freak." He would endow it with a building and donate the furnishing of his Chestnut Street house in Boston and his estate in Newport, for Edwina was married now and living with her husband. (One of the last acts of her single life was to have installed in a church at Newport a glass window in honor of the mother she could not remember, the girl-wife, as her father called her, of her father's youth.)

The travelers sailed northern waters. All he would want from the club, he explained, was that a couple of rooms upstairs be allotted to him so he could stay there until he died. At Boothbay Harbor they put in for supplies, and in a druggist's shop he asked after the origin of the town's name to be told it had no connection with "that damned scoundrel who shot Lincoln." He paid the bill and went out with his lips tightly set. Even after so many years no scar had formed on the wound—his friends all knew that. He could not bear to look upon a picture of Abraham Lincoln. When he saw one in the home of his friend the sculptor Launt Thompson, he left the house immediately and did not return until he was told the picture was no longer on view. The author William Dean Howells remembered him picking up the cast of a huge hand in the home of a friend, James Lorrimor Graham. "Whose hand is this, Lorry?" he asked. Graham pretended not to hear. "Whose hand is this?" he repeated. "It's Lincoln's hand," Graham said. Edwin put it down softly without a word.

And, of course, there was the name he never mentioned. Once he did. It was in Boston, on a Christmas night. The veteran actress Eliza Eldridge had played opposite him for years, always revering him, always noting how he never failed to offer a good morning and a good night to a theater's working people, the doorkeeper, carpenter, property man. She and others appearing with him in Boston's Park Theatre gathered in his private sitting room at the Hotel Vendôme that Christmas night. The play had ended hours before. It was very late. He spoke of his father, whom Eliza Eldridge had supported as a child performer. He talked of his boyhood life, cheerfully, and said, "Yes, my brother John and—"

The listeners all looked at each other. He moved his hand slowly and looked straight ahead. He said slowly, "Yes, my unfortunate brother John." He dropped his head so that his face was almost hidden. They saw tears run down his cheek. There was dead silence in the room. He seemed to realize suddenly that he was not alone, pulled himself together, stood up, forced a smile and said, "Come, come, I have displaced the mirth. Let us drink to a merry Christmas." They all stood and drank and then begged to be excused. He shook hands with each, and they went out. Years later Eliza Eldridge wrote that those words, My unfortunate brother John, rang in her ears with the bells of each succeeding Christmas, and that she believed they would for so long as she would live.

See the players well bestowed, Hamlet told Polonius. Edwin named his club The Players. It faced Gramercy Park in New York in a mansion he purchased and had remodeled by Stanford White. He asked Mark Twain and General Sherman to be members and they joined, as would in the years to come Grover Cleveland, George M. Cohan, Ford Madox Ford, Hamlin Garland, Vachel Lindsay, Edgar Lee Masters, Booth Tarkington, Eugene O'Neill, Thornton Wilder, Ernest Hemingway, Herbert Hoover, Walter Lippmann, Humphrey Bogart, Frank Lloyd Wright, Jimmy Cagney, Harry Truman, Gene Tunney, Frank Sinatra, Augustus Saint-Gaudens, Cole Porter, John J. Pershing, J. Pierpont Morgan, Boris Karloff, Clark Gable, Dwight Eisenhower, Walter Cronkite, Bing Crosby, and John Barrymore, who, in 1924, sixty years after the one hundred nights of Hamlet, would break the record despite the appeal of a group of aged men who came asking him not to do so in honor of the Great Master. Barrymore said he had known the Great Master in his childhood—his parents and grandparents had played opposite him—and that he didn't think he would mind.

Downstairs in the great high rooms of The Players hung portraits Edwin had collected over the years of the actors and actresses of the past, and upstairs in the library were his books, including several Shakespeare folios, and all about were mementos of the theater—old playbills, silver cups, props, costumes, swords, busts, statues, paintings by Gilbert Stuart, John Collier, and John Singer Sargent, including a heroic and larger-than-life-size Sargent of the club's founder. On the last night of 1888, as whistles and bells sounded outside to welcome 1889, The Players officially opened as he lifted a vessel of ancient silver and standing beneath his father's portrait said, "Let us drink from this loving cup, from this cup and this souvenir of long ago, my father's flagon, let us now, beneath his portrait, and on the anniversary of this occasion, drink: 'To The Players' perpetual prosperity.' " It was passed from lip to lip, as it would be each New Year's Eve for more than one hundred years into the future on the same spot with the same toast repeated with the addition of: "And to the memory of the finest actor and the greatest gentleman the American theater has ever known."

Meals in the dining room were half a dollar. Soon it was seen that the price was insufficient to meet costs, but he said he would make up the deficit, for he did not want less prosperous members to forgo dining at their club. He had promising young actors sought out for membership, and paid the initiation fee and a year's dues for fifty of them each year.

Upstairs in his suite of two rooms, Molly's portrait the largest adornment on the wall, he read, smoked, lay awake at night, and gazed out at Gramercy Park, where in 1918 his statue would be dedicated with a grandson, Edwina's son, pulling off the covering.

Rosalie died in Joe's house in New Jersey and Asia in England, her long years of self-imposed exile and misery finally over. Both sisters went to lie in Greenmount Cemetery in Baltimore. Soon, he knew, he would also be gone. "I am ready for my cue to quit," he told Lawrence Barrett. Soon the play would be ended, he told Joseph Jefferson, who would in fact succeed him as president of The Players when that occurred. Edwina lived nearby, at 12 West Eighteenth Street. Once when she was away he wrote her to explain how nothing of fame or fortune could compensate for the spiritual suffering some must undergo: "To pass life in a sort of dream where 'nothing is but is not,' a loneliness in the very midst of a constant crowd, especially when the body has to share the penalty of *greatness*, as it is termed. Bosh! I'd rather be an obscure farmer from Way Back, or a cabinet-maker, as my father advised. But nature cast me for the part she found me most fitted for and I have had to play it, and must play it till the curtain falls. But you must not think me sad about it. No, I am used to it and am content."

Edwina understood. She had grown up as a motherless child suddenly alone in his care, her stockings on Christmas filled with toys, his own containing razors and brushes and other toilet articles and nothing else for himself; then he had married his second wife; she had died mad, and Edwina assumed almost a maternal role toward her father. She always thought of him as associated with Hamlet. As a toddler she once heard someone say something about an omelet and piped, "That's Papa!" When she was older it came to her that what she called "his confined nature and pent-up sorrows" found vent in playing the prince. His melancholy he attempted to throw off in her presence, but she always sensed his solitude and always it seemed to her strange and unnatural. At the opening of The Players a wreath of laurel from her had inscribed on it: HAMLET, KING, FATHER.

Not yet sixty, he was old. When he stood up he hung on to something to steady himself for the dizziness. It was difficult for him to conduct board meetings in his capacity as president of The Players, and he had to be prodded on what to say. Occasionally he made theatrical appearances in his old familiar parts. In March 1891 he was told, "Mr. Barrett has gone."

"Where to?" he asked. Then he understood. Larry had taken care of everything for him, all details, had made him rich. Days later he kept a scheduled date to play Hamlet at the Brooklyn Academy of Music. In some mysterious way people sensed that he would never again step on a stage, and so the theater was packed to see him softly go through his part, saying the lines as if speaking to himself, and there were masses outside in Montague Place to cheer him when he came out the stage door. Across the street a building was being repaired, and the scaffold was filled with people waving their hats and handkerchiefs. He recoiled and pulled back before the police cleared a path to his carriage and he drove away. The acting dynasty founded by Junius Brutus Booth when he came to America on the *Two Brothers* from Madeira, and continued by Edwin, and another, was concluded. Asia's children were of the theater, but most prominently as managers, not actors.

After that he largely kept to his two-room suite at The Players, his condition reaching the point where he needed help even to reach the elevator a few feet away which would take him down so that, leaning on somebody's arm, he might take a slow walk around Gramercy Park. In a shaky, old man's hand, he wrote Edwina he hardly did anything but "snooze all day," his meals brought up from the dining room. His mind remained perfectly clear even as his strength ebbed away. He made it a point personally to welcome all new inductees into his club. On the day when that ceremony was scheduled for the famed journalist-author Richard Harding Davis, the new member stepped into a Fourth Avenue bookshop and bought some old playbills, intending to contribute them to The Players holdings, which were rapidly becoming one of the greatest theatrical collections in the world. The playbills were in a packet. Davis did not look through them. At his induction he handed them to the club president, who riffled through them and then staggered into someone's arms and had to be half-carried from the room. Among the playbills was one for *Our American Cousin* on the evening of April 14, 1865. Even here, members told one another sadly, the founder of their club was pursued by the Furies of the past. Then why the picture of Johnny right by his bed? There was no picture of Asia in the room, nor of June, nor of Rosalie or of Joe. He never explained.

He himself sat for his last photograph at the request of *Harper's*, ruling that for it he be in a nondescript chair of the late Pierce or early Buchanan period. The photographer asked if he could not use another, more picturesque one. Edwin hesitated to give a stranger his reasons, but gently declined to change seats. To a few friends he later explained that the chair had been Molly's before he married her, that he associated it with the days when he courted her, that it had gone with him wherever his home had been. So he wanted it in the picture for her sake. She had been gone, then, thirty years.

On April 11, 1893, Edwina and her husband took him to the Lyceum Theatre to see *The Guardsmen*. Eight days later he failed to ring for his breakfast. When a concerned servant went in he was found partially paralyzed and voiceless. A stroke. For weeks he lay in bed, his powers of speech returning, but obviously destined never to arise. On June 5 Edwina came with her little son, who asked, "How are you, dear Grandpa?"

"How are you yourself, old fellow?" was the reply. He never spoke again. The next night a violent electrical storm raged over New York, thunder booming and lightning flashing. Fifty-nine years and seven months earlier he had been born on a similar night of spectacular celestial display, with star-shower rains of meteors shooting through the skies, and the black workers on The Farm had said he would be guided by a lucky star. And gifted to see ghosts.

In the early morning hours, just after one o'clock, there was a tremendous crash of thunder and the lights of The Players went out. "Don't let Father die in the dark!" Edwina screamed. When the lights came on after a moment, he was gone.

The services were on the morning of June 9 at what was

officially the Church of the Transfiguration on Twenty-ninth Street near Fifth Avenue, but what was more generally known as the actors' church, and even more so as The Little Church Around the Corner. It had gotten its nickname in 1870 when the actor George Holland had been refused burial from another church because of his profession, the declining minister telling those who would have arranged it that they had better take the matter up with the people at the little church around the corner. One hundred fifty Players marched together from the club behind the hearse. Among the hundreds of mourners attending the funeral were John Mathews and W. J. Ferguson. To the one, long ago in Washington, had been given a letter for delivery the next day to the *National Intelligencer*. The other's one-line stage debut was opposite the man who wrote the letter. *Towards Chertsey, my Lord? No, to Whitefriars, there to await my coming.*

The rites were very brief. Before eleven o'clock the coffin was scheduled to be loaded into the hearse for the short trip to Grand Central and a Boston train and interment by Molly at Mount Auburn Cemetery, Hamlet leaping into Ophelia's grave after three decades.

Yet even as the services went on there occurred what was mystical, allegorical, baffling, beyond coincidence—Shakespearean. The man being mourned would have understood, for like Abraham Lincoln he believed in omens, visitations, in a whole world that could neither be defined nor understood. As Edwin's funeral progressed, the Records and Pensions Division of the War Department collapsed in Washington. The walls of what had been Ford's Theatre simply caved in, landing on the street and in the alley where Peanut John Burroughs once sat holding a little mare. Twenty-three clerks were killed, twice that number injured. It was the worst accident in Washington's history. There was no warning. Of a sudden the top floor came down, taking the second with it. A woman working where President Lincoln had been sitting when the building was last used as a theater came falling through twisted girders, broken beams, and flying bricks.

The services ended. The coffin was loaded. In Washington every man in the Fire Department and every manual laborer in the employ of the Federal government was sent to dig through the rubble for survivors.

The hearse headed for Grand Central and the Boston train. All cavalry units in Fort Myer outside the capital were ordered to Tenth and F streets to keep sightseers back. The train arrived in

Boston. The broken building would be put back together and then, seventy years into the future, painstakingly reconstituted so it would exactly duplicate its appearance on the night of April 14, 1865, with reproductions of the same chairs, the same adornments. The picture of George Washington that had been with the Treasury Guards flag on that night was put in the place it had held, and the sofa upon which Major Rathbone sat. Across the street the Petersen house where Lincoln died was opened for viewing. From the alley behind what is again called Ford's Theatre, a playhouse again where productions are regularly presented, tours run by the Surratt Society, an organization housed in Mrs. Surratt's old Maryland tavern-post office, leave to trace the route to the Garrett place where the man who shot Lincoln met his final destiny. They are filled months in advance. Much has changed along the way, yet Ford's Theatre looks exactly as it did, and so do, downstairs in the basement museum, the boot Dr. Mudd removed, the carbine Davy Herold carried, the derringer that fired the fatal shot. As in Edwin's suite in The Players, left exactly as it was the day he died, time has stood still.

Twilight had come to Boston when the coffin was interred. Several hundred people were present. In the silence a bird could be heard twittering. The scent of syringa blossoms came from a slope below the grave site next to Molly. Thomas Bailey Aldrich thought of Horatio's farewell to his friend, and repeated it under his breath: Good night, sweet prince. Others thought of the prince's last words: The rest is silence.

NOTES

Page

11   Looked badly weatherbeaten: *Boston Sunday Herald* (December 11, 1881). Signed F.A.B., the article was by Frank A. Burr.
11   "Handsomest man I had ever seen": Ibid.
12   Fifteen years later: *Philadelphia Press* (April 12, 1896).
12   Soldiers were sent to drive them away: *Surratt Society Courier* (April 1987).
13   That each April by the Hudson River: Lewis, pp. 344–45.
13   Spots on the brick pavement: Washington, p. 29.
13   "Get him!": Ibid., p. 95.

Chapter One

17   The Mad Tragedian Has Come to Our City: Kimmel quotes an April 1838 edition of the *Baltimore Sun*, p. 58.
17   "Who the hell are you, sir?": *St. Louis Democrat* (May 3, 1864).
18   "I say, Tom": Asia Booth Clarke, *Junius Brutus Booth*, p. 131.
18   "Ah, Junius, Junius": Dr. A. O. Kellogg, *American Journal of Insanity* (April 1868). Kellogg was a close friend of Edwin Booth and may have gotten the story from him.
18–19   Details on Richard Booth: Moses, pp. 19–20, Forrester, p. 138, and Kimmel, p. 15ff.
19   "Charged by a frail nymph": Anonymous, p. 12.
19   *Necessitated* the stage: Gould, p. 22.
20   Seemed to snap with fire: Jefferson, p. 129.
20   "Then for the first time": Murdoch, p. 183.
20   "I can see again": *Boston Herald* (August 16, 1885).
21   "I'll find you": Winter, *Other Days*, p. 324.
21   "Getting as fat as a great beast": *New York Press* (August 9, 1891).
21   *Grant silence to explain*: Moses, p. 24.
23   "Is it possible this can be . . . ?" Mathews, pp. 125–26.
23   "He was followed as a marvel": Winter, *Vagrant Memories*, p. 149.
23   "An enthusiasm no other could awaken:" Ibid., p. 149.
24   "I can't read": Kimmel, pp. 47–48.
24   "I think you had better come to the hotel": Ellsler, p. 81.

25 "Joined in their worship in the Hebraic tongue": Asia Booth Clarke, *Junius Brutus Booth*, p. 161.

26 "My dear little man": Ellsler, p. 16.

26 "How can you exist in such a wilderness?" Asia Booth Clarke, *Junius Brutus Booth*, p. 104.

27 Wiser to douse the light completely: Kimmel, p. 35.

27 "Which could hardly be reckoned": Lockridge, p. 20.

27 "Murder!": A. O. Kellogg in *American Journal of Insanity* (April 1868).

27 "I only indulge in one kind of flesh": Ibid.

27 "Ride them down!": Ibid.

27 "You're bilious and require physic": Kimmel, p. 46.

28 "Well, you've got me": Mahoney, p. 19.

28 Lay in bed with it, crying and laughing: Barbee, p. 196.

28 Chopping their marble slab stones to bits: Mahoney, p. 52.

28 The fight with Flynn: Kimmel, p. 57.

29 "Their tortuous way in gladsome mood": Allen, p. 574.

29 You damn'd old Scoundrel: Kauffman, p. 14.

30–32 The meeting with the Unitarian clergyman: James Freeman Clarke, p. 266ff.

Chapter Two

33 Tell Junius not to go opossum hunting: Asia Booth Clarke, *Junius Brutus Booth*, p. 101.

35 "My lawyer will fall on his back like a bomb": *New York Press* (August 9, 1891).

35 The Wife of Junius Brutus Booth, Tragedian: Ibid.

36 Gifted to see ghosts and guided by a lucky star: Hutton, p. 11.

36 A show in the basement: Kimmel, pp. 68–69.

38 "Like a giant whirlwind": Moses, p. 170, quotes Louisa Lane, matriarch of the Drew-Barrymore theatrical family.

38 "Father, who is that?" Mathews, p. 103.

39 "Go away, young man, go away!": Winter, *Vagrant Memories*, p. 162.

39 "You shan't go out": Skinner, *The Last Tragedian*, p. 17.

40 On Fontaine: Ellsler, p. 73.

40 On the skull: Asia Booth Clarke, *The Elder and the Younger Booth*, p. 99, and Ellsler, pp. 71–73.

41 "Do you play 'Nellie Bly'?": *Washington Post* (April 5, 1891).

41 "*You* ought to play Tressel": Asia Booth Clarke, *The Elder and the Younger Booth*, p. 125.

41 "Give me my spurs": Ibid., p. 126.

42 "My dearest gratitude": Mathews, p. 99.

42 "It was like a thundershock!": Ibid., p. 104.

43 "Go act it yourself": Asia Booth Clarke, *The Elder and the Younger Booth*, p. 127.

Chapter Three

44 Johnny Booth and his sister Asia: Details are found throughout Asia Booth Clarke, *The Unlocked Book,* and in an original proof copy of Mrs. Clarke's *The Elder and the Younger Booth*, much of which was cut from the published edition of that book. The proof copy, inscribed in 1885 by

Mrs. Clarke to her son Wilfred, is now in the rare book collection of the University of Illinois at Chicago.

44   "Melancholy insanity": *Maryland History Magazine* (Spring 1983).

44   "His mother's darling": In July 1881 Edwin Booth recorded his thoughts about his brother John in a letter to historian Nahum Capen. He did so in the wake of the shooting of President Garfield (who died as a result of his wounds in September 1881). Never before or after did he refer to John in writing. The letter can be found, among other places, in Forrester, pp. 227–28.

44   "Always preferred": Adam Badeau wrote in *McClure's* (August 1893).

44   Played Christopher Columbus: Asia Booth Clarke, *The Unlocked Book*, p. 60.

45   "Self-inflicted torment": Ibid., p. 19.

45   "Oats, peas, beans and barley groves": Ibid., p. 35.

46   "For *great* brains": Ibid., p. 44.

46   "I could have stood anything but that": Ibid., p. 77.

47   "You're not touched": Ibid., p. 96.

47   "Well done, little Booth": Asia Booth Clarke, proof copy *The Elder and the Younger Booth*.

48   The mother's vision: Asia Booth Clarke, *The Unlocked Book*, pp. 42–43.

48   "Tugging at my sleeve": Ibid., p. 57.

49   "Undress Marse Johnny": Ibid., p. 66.

49   "Not merely a habitation": Asia Booth Clarke, proof copy of *The Elder and the Younger Booth*.

50   "What an idea!": Ibid.

50   "Shall I fetch you a mug, sir?": Ibid.

51   "A prostitute": Kimmel, p. 345.

52   Slept with pistols in their hands: Asia Booth Clarke, *The Elder and the Younger Booth*, p. 131.

53   "I'm no flunkey": Mathews, p. 101.

53   "Put a slug in the bottom of your trunk": Asia Booth Clarke, *The Elder and the Younger Booth*, p. 173.

54   Cock-tail Cañon, Shirt-tail Bend: Soliday, pp. 452–53, and Watermeier, p. 36.

54   "I go to save the city from conflagration!": Goodale, p. 148.

54   Rolling behind a piece of scenery: Soliday, p. 222.

55   "There are no more actors!": Moses, p. 39.

56   "Comedian and Ranchero": Dempsey, p. 155.

56   "Kid?" Winter, *Vagrant Memories*, p. 167.

56   "At twenty I was a libertine": Skinner, in *The Last Tragedian*, p. 84, quotes an Edwin Booth letter.

57   Would not eat the pot's contents: Edwin's close friend William Bispham, in *The Century* (November 1893).

57   The Fiery Star: Dempsey, p. 106.

58   Possessed five hundred dollars: Lockridge, p. 63.

58   He looked like a boy still: Asia Booth Clarke, *The Elder and the Younger Booth*, p. 145.

Chapter Four

59   "John is trying to farm": Undated 1854 letter from Asia Booth to Jean Anderson, the Peale Museum, Baltimore.

59   "First find your *ladies*": Asia Booth Clarke, *The Unlocked Book*, p. 100.

60   "I can never be a nimble skip-about": Ibid., p. 108.

61   "Give my respects": *Harford* (Md.) *Gazette and Democratic Ledger* (January 27, 1966) printed the letter when it was sold at auction.

61   "Guess what I've done!": Asia Booth Clarke, *The Unlocked Book*, p. 107.
62   "Madame, I am Pandolfio Pet": Townsend, p. 21.
63   "Get up some sort of impromptu finish": Ellsler, p. 150.
64   "Possessed the faculty of pure tragic power": Winter, *Vagrant Memories*, p. 213.
64   "No actor so completely filled the eye": Skinner, *Footlights and Spotlights*, p. 91.
64   "Sometimes moving in the throng": "Margaret," p. 18.
65   "I am conscious of an interior personality": Winter, *Other Days*, p. 58.
65   "I think I am a little quieter": Skinner, *The Last Tragedian*, p. 8.
65   "Just simple Edwin Booth": *New York Dramatic Mirror* (December 26, 1896).
66   "Oh, Charley, my boy": *The Forum* (July 1893).
66   "A little sweetheart of mine": Shattuck, p. 29.
66   Suffered from a venereal disease: Ibid., p. 28.
66   "I have suffered so much": Grossman, p. 49.
67   "My Prince": Shattuck, p. 29.
67   "But he cared nothing for any of them": Adam Badeau in *McClure's Magazine* (August 1893).
67   So old when young: Ibid.
68   A floating lunatic asylum: Jefferson, p. 47.
68   "Did not expect to be too particular": Helm, pp. 119–20.
68   On Mary Devlin: *Ladies' Home Journal* (September 1904).
68   "He is the greatest actor I have ever known": Ibid.
69   "Almost forget my vow": Ibid.
69   "Father, your blessing": Wilson, *Joseph Jefferson*, p. 146.
69   "I will not write the evil I invoke": Asia Booth, undated 1860 letter to Jean Anderson, the Peale Museum, Baltimore.
70   "I wish to God I had never seen you": Shattuck, p. 29.
70   "He became quite wild": *Ladies' Home Journal* (September 1904).
70   "My heart a happy one": Booth, p. xiii.
70   *I would have written you before this*: Bryan, p. 85.
71   Kidnapped Mary from her bed: *Atlanta Constitution* (December 31, 1887).
71   "He was one of the best exponents of vital beauty": Townsend, p. 26.
71   "Blocked with silly women": Winslow, p. 142.
71   "His head and throat": Clara Morris, *Life on the Stage*, p. 98.
71   "Idol of women": Sir Charles Wyndham interview in the *New York Herald* (June 27, 1909).
71   "Very handsome, lovely": Gilbert, p. 57.
71   "A very handsome man": Jennie Gourlay is quoted in the *Minneapolis Journal* (April 27, 1914).
71   "The handsomest man in Washington": Ford is quoted in the *Washington Star* (December 7, 1887).
72   "We have almost forgotten": *Washington Chronicle* (April 11, 1863).
72   "John has more of the old man's power": Clara Morris in *McClure's Magazine* (February 1901).
72   "A veritable sensation": *New York Herald* (March 18, 1862).
72   "*The* actor of the country": *Boston Daily Advertiser* (May 19, 1862).
72   "The coming man": *Baltimore Sun* (February 12, 1862).
72   "Most talented young man": Barbee quotes a Rochester paper, p. 255.
72   "Very superior genius": *Providence Post* (October 21, 1861).
72   "Genius alone inherits": *Cincinnati Commercial* (November 21, 1861).
72   "It is genius": *Louisville Democrat* (December 8, 1861).
72   "The finest I ever saw": Gilbert, p. 57.
73   "Constantly cut himself": Winslow, p. 141.

73   "The gentlest man I ever knew": Edwin A. Emerson, *The Theatre* (June 1913).
73   "Come on hard!" Clara Morris in *McClure's Magazine* (February 1901).
74   "You satirical little wretch": Clara Morris, *Life on the Stage*, p. 101.
75   "Oh, good Lord!" Clara Morris in *McClure's Magazine* (Feburary 1901).
75   "One of the world's most successful lovers": Wilson, *John Wilkes Booth*, p. 219.
75   "What a dashing, elegant fellow": Clara Morris was interviewed in the *Boston Herald* (January 10, 1890).
75   Traced one of his romances: Townsend, p. 24.
76   "My youth began with my marriage": Skinner quotes an Edwin Booth letter in *The Last Tragedian*, p. 70.

CHAPTER FIVE

77   "Wife, mother, sister, child": Grossman quotes a letter sent to Adam Badeau, p. 141ff.
77   "What more could I wish for": Booth, p. 16.
77   "My head full of": Grossman, p. 131, letter to Richard Cary.
77   "Humble daisy": Booth, p. xiv.
77   "How indignant Mr. Badeau will be": Ibid., p. 23.
78   "Silly batch of whinings": Skinner, *The Last Tragedian*, pp. 84–87, quotes a letter to the Richard Stoddards.
78   "Forget your past life": Booth, p. 15.
79   Hung an American flag over Mary's bed: Goodale, p. 96.
79   He didn't know and didn't care: Samples, p. 40.
80   "Amongst them I notice:" Bryan, p. 87.
80   Philip Whitlock of the Grays saw: Ezekial, p. 153.
80   "A brave old man": Asia Booth Clarke, *The Unlocked Book*, p. 113.
80   "The genius of the Booth family": *Detroit Advertiser* (November 11, 1861).
80   "He would have flashes, passages": Samples, p. 91.
80   "Without having Edwin's culture and grace": *Philadelphia Press* (March 5, 1863).
80   "Edwin has more poetry, John Wilkes more passion": Samples quotes the *Boston Post*, p. 89.
81   I AM MYSELF ALONE: Kimmel, p. 167.

CHAPTER SIX

82   "Of all things I would rather do tonight": *Journal of the Illinois State Historical Society* (December 1940).
82   Left him helpless: Ibid.
83   "Bobbie's lost!": Randall, p. 118.
83   "I was a little bothered": Brooks, pp. 220–22.
84   The threatening letters are found in *The Magazine of History* (1929), p. 36ff.
85   "The first one or two": Carpenter, pp. 62–63.
85   "I am using instead letters from some of those Southern fellows": *The Magazine of History* (1929), p. 36.
86   "Full of genius": *Albany Atlas & Argus* (February 18, 1861).
86   "As tender as love without esteem": Townsend, p. 24.
86   To see *Seven Sisters*: Bryan, p. 24.
87   "I shall blow them to hell": Ibid., p. 17.
88   "Rings with his triumphs": *Harper's* (April 1861).

89   "The seeming standstill": Booth, p. 64.
89   "So very rabid against us": Grossman, p. 137.
89   It came to Adam: *McClure's Magazine* (August 1893).
89   Lie on a black bearskin rug: Aldrich, p. 8.
89   "Starring around the country is sad work": Skinner, *The Last Tragedian*, p. 136.
90   The journey with The Girl: *American Magazine* (January 1909).
90   A hard business: Skinner, *Footlights and Spotlights*, pp. 44–45.
90   "Little B . . . Great B": *New England Magazine* (November 1893).
90   "God Almighty has not yet got so far": Ibid.
90   Mary wore a light silk dress: Ibid.
91   "Lays on the floor and rolls over": Asia Booth Clarke to Jean Anderson (March 3, 1863), the Peale Museum, Baltimore.
91   "Swift and gentle": Clara Morris in *McClure's Magazine* (February 1901).
92   "Greatest tragedian of the age": Samples, p. 93.
92   "Greatest tragedian in the country": Ibid., p. 86.
92   "My goose does indeed hang high": Ibid., p. 95.
92   Coated its base with soot: Ferguson, p. 18.
93   "It's too bad, too bad": Clara Morris interview, *Boston Herald* (January 10, 1890).
93   "He played Pescara": Skinner quotes a letter to Richard Stoddard in *The Last Tragedian*, p. 71.
93   "I have not dared to think": Booth, p. 91.
93   "What is Edwin thinking about?": Lucy S. Pry's letter is in The Players.
93   "Very much pleased with him": Booth, p. 101.
94   "Highly delighted the audience seemed": Ibid., p. 106.
94   "Take me upstairs": Aldrich, p. 34.
94   "Young, handsome, gay": Ibid., p. 34.
94   Never got drunk in the legs: James Shettel in the *New York Dramatic Mirror* (February 26, 1916).
94   "Seldom seen Shakespeare so murdered": Lockridge, p. 121.
94   In such condition that he was unable to negotiate: Lucy S. Pry letter, The Players.
94   "Any undue anxiety": Booth, p. xxiv.
94   Puff of cold air: Grossman quotes a letter to Adam Badeau, p. 143.
95   "Sick or well": Aldrich, p. 35.
95   *This is the fourth telegram*: Ibid., p. 37.
95   "I saw every time I looked from the window Mary dead": Ibid., p. 37.
95   He never touched liquor again: Ibid., p. 38. All who knew him confirm the fact.
95   A Card to the Public: Bryan, p. 91.
96   "One week's illness": Grossman quotes a letter to Adam Badeau, p. 141ff.
96   He held her dresses in his hands: Aldrich, p. 41.
96   Narrow line of insanity: Ibid., p. 42.
96   Borderland of his sanity: Skinner, *The Last Tragedian*, p. 90.
96   "The frightfullest thought": Ibid., p. 100.
96   "Yes, it is right": Ibid., p. 88.
96   "I wish to God I was not an actor": Ibid., p. 87.
96   "A glance at his face and figure": *New England Magazine* (November 1893).
97   "Will this ever be the case with Mary?": Skinner, *The Last Tragedian*, quotes a Stoddard letter, p. 88.
97   "Oh Jesus! Spare me that!": Ibid., p. 103, a Stoddard letter.
97   "Would to God I were there with her": Grossman quotes a letter to Badeau, p. 144.

97 PRIDE OF THE AMERICAN PEOPLE: *Theatre Magazine* (December 1903) reproduces the playbill.

97 "Complete triumph": *Washington National Republican* (April 13, 1863).

97 "A great favorite": Ibid. (April 14, 1863).

97 "Inspired with genius": *Washington National Intelligencer* (May 9, 1863).

98 "A marvelous man": Sir Charles Wyndham interview in the *New York Herald* (June 27, 1909).

98 "Does look pretty sharp at me": Helm, p. 243.

CHAPTER SEVEN

99 Hid him in the basement for days: Badeau in *McClure's Magazine* (August 1893).

100 Pained his host: Brooks, p. 287.

100 Dressed in rags and straw: Ibid., p. 72.

100 "We are coming, Father Abraham": Leonard Grover wrote in *The Century* (April 1909).

100 Made a mistake in his choice of professions: Carpenter, p. 52.

100 Added it to his act: Ibid., p. 161.

100 "Some of Shakespeare's plays I have never read": Moses, p. 160.

101 Thought John gave a "tame" performance: *Lincoln Herald* (Summer 1957).

101 "Claims the most brilliant honors of his art": *Washington Evening Star* (November 9, 1863).

101 "Rapturously" applauded: *Lincoln Herald* (Summer 1957).

101 He failed to do so: *Chicago Inter-Ocean* (June 10, 1901).

102 *In a foreign war I too could say:* Sealed, the composition was left with Asia and her husband. Sandburg prints it on pp. 319–21.

102 "This man's appearance": Asia Booth Clarke, *The Unlocked Book*, p. 124.

102 "A dealer in quinine": Ibid., p. 116.

103 "A man and a cause I hold sacred": Sir Charles Wyndham interview, *New York Herald* (June 27, 1909).

103 *Dear, dear Soul!:* Shattuck, p. 36.

103 "That was a close call, Mr. Booth": William Bispham, *The Century* (November 1893). Robert Todd Lincoln told many people of the incident.

103 "The rush to see the young tragedian": The *Louisville Courier-Journal* (August 26, 1979) quotes the *Louisville Journal* (January 1864).

103 "Far above the capacity of Edwin Booth": Bryan, p. 91.

104 "Mummers, of the quality of skimmed milk": Joseph Hazelton in *Good Housekeeping* (February 1928).

104 "God damned spad": James Shettel in the *New York Dramatic Mirror* (February 26, 1916).

104 "Look down in horror!": Ellsler, p. 127.

104 Pretty cozy after all: Ibid., p. 128.

105 So they could play together: Miller, p. 30.

105 Simply a family quarrel on an immense scale: June's statement is in the David Rankin Barbee Papers, Vol. III, in Georgetown University's Special Collections.

105 Edwin had trembled for his laurels: Asia Booth Clarke, *The Unlocked Book*, p. 122.

106 In other roles: *McClure's Magazine* (August 1893).

106 "His playing throughout has an exquisite tone": *Harper's* (April 1865).

106 "He *is* Hamlet": Clara Morris, *McClure's Magazine* (February 1901).

Chapter Eight

107   "Noble band of patriotic heroes": Sandburg, pp. 319–21.
107   *Abe Lincoln departed this life:* The Century (April 1896).
107   "I will never allow": *Pennsylvania Heritage* (Summer 1981).
107   "The old feeling aroused by our loving brother": Kimmel, p. 197.
108   A fibroid tumor on his neck: *Records of the Columbia Historical Society,* Vol. XIII (1910).
108   Led the two to the President's carriage: *The Century* (April 1909).
109   "I have a proposition to submit to you": Laughlin, p. 285, reprints the single lecture Surratt gave on his experiences.
109   "No time on record": Teillard, p. 368.
110   *I regret that you do not appreciate:* Ibid., pp. 274–75.
110   "What does anyone want to harm me for?": Keckley, p. 121.
112   "His most intimate acquaintances": Buckingham, p. 31.
112   "A little blab": Thomas Eckert testimony, *House Reports.* After holding his silence for weeks, Powell opened somewhat to Major Eckert during his imprisonment.
112   "Highly distinguishing marks": Arnold, p. 37.
112   "I want to tell you what this speculation is": Chester's April 28, 1865, interrogation is in the Barbee Papers.
113   "I am all raw with riding this old horse": Oldroyd, p. 92.
113   "Are you crazy?" Ibid., p. 93.
114   "I have just taken a peep in the parlour": Laughlin reprints the letter on p. 35.
114   Addressing him as "Pet": *The Century* (April 1896).
114   "A perfect fool": Doster, p. 267.
114   "Such sticks": Moore, p. 99.
114   "What perfect acting!": *Washington National Intelligencer* (January 22, 1865).
115   He fell asleep on the bed smoking his host's pipe: Asia Booth Clarke, *The Unlocked Book,* p. 176.
115   Her dreams were "fearful": Arnold, p. 21.
115   "No matter how far apart they were": Gilbert, pp. 57–58.
115   Say they belonged, rather, to Sam: Arnold, p. 21.
115   "Virginia, Virginia": Asia Booth Clarke, *The Unlocked Book,* p. 119.
115   "A dictionary": Ibid., p. 120.
116   Details on Hale are found throughout Sewell.
117   "So cross": *American Heritage* (October 1970).
117   "I came back from the station": Ibid.
118   "With or without her father": Asia Booth Clarke to Jean Anderson, May 22, 1865, the Peale Museum, Baltimore.
119   "The secret you have told me": Starr, *Further Light on Lincoln's Last Day,* pp. 33–34.
119   If only he weren't an actor: Chester interrogation, Barbee Papers, Georgetown University Library Special Collections, and the *Philadelphia Press* (December 8, 1881).
121   "The height of madness": Arnold, p. 45.
122   "Who's in the house?": Kimmel, p. 205.
122   "Have you come to hear the great Lincoln speak?" *Boston Globe* (June 17, 1878).
123   Such intensity and passion: Weichmann, p. 119.
123   "Fresh vision of beauty": *Harper's* (April 1865).

123 "Even physically finer than Edwin": *McClure's Magazine* (August 1893).

123 "Very beautiful and accomplished lady": McClure, p. 249.

123 "It's an awful thing": Grossman, p. 168. The letter was to Emma Cary (January 10, 1865).

124 "Our news is indeed glorious": Ibid., p. 171. The letter was to Emma Cary (March 19, 1865).

124 A bitter song he sang: Asia Booth Clarke, *The Unlocked Book*, p. 123.

124 "What are you going to do?" Henry Clay Ford statement, War Department Archives, a copy of which can be found in Barbee, Vol. III.

124 "I was dreadfully shamefaced": Asia Booth Clarke, *The Unlocked Book*, p. 112.

124 Could not get used to her actually being a mother: Asia Booth Clarke to Jean Anderson (March 3, 1863), the Peale Museum, Baltimore.

124 "I hope you will keep well and get stronger": Asia Booth Clarke, *The Unlocked Book*, pp. 126–27.

124 "Remember me, babies": Ibid., p. 110.

125 What a splendid chance I had to kill the "President": Chester interrogation, Barbee Papers, Georgetown University.

125 *My Darling Boy:* William G. Shepherd was given permission to look through the possessions of John Wilkes Booth, then kept in a War Department attic, and wrote of them in *Collier's* (December 17, 1924).

126 Mrs. Lincoln at City Point: Smith, *Lee and Grant*, p. 241ff.

128 "Well, Jim, Richmond has fallen at last": Chester statement, Barbee Papers, Vol. III.

127 He recited the lines a second time: Chambrun, p. 83.

129 "Never again must we repeat that word": Ibid., p. 84.

CHAPTER NINE

130 "He seemed to me positively handsome": Doster, p. 16.

131 "Anything to drive away the blues": Barbee ms., p. 663.

131 "That old scoundrel": Edwin A. Emerson in the *Literary Digest* (March 6, 1926).

131 "We are all slaves now": Barbee ms., p. 677.

132 "That means nigger citizenship!": Jesse W. Weik in *The Century* (February 1913).

132 "By Christ, I'll put him through": Ibid.

132 "Quart of brandy in less than two hours": *New York Sunday Telegraph*, May 23, 1909.

132 "What do you want with more candles?": Mrs. William A. Brown, *The Century* (February 1913).

133 *Dearest Mother:* Bryan, p. 148.

133 *I have never doubted your love: Collier's* (December 17, 1924).

135 "I had this strange dream again last night": Seward, p. 225, and Navy Secretary Welles in *The Galaxy*, April, 1872.

137 "How do you do, Mr. Booth?": *St. Louis Democrat* (May 3, 1864).

137 "I stood in my gate and looked right wishful at him:" Bryan, p. 153.

138 "Your friends Lincoln and Grant": Laughlin, p. 63.

139 "When I went in to my lunch today": Porter, p. 498.

139 "An act of clemency and kindness": Sewell, p. 222.

140 "I believe there are men who want to take my life?": Crook, p. 66.

140 "Stanton, it is useless": Thomas Reed Turner, p. 71.

140 "With that firm conviction": Teillard, p. 113.

140   "There are, I think": Ibid., p. 114ff.
141   "That is horrid!": Ibid., p. 117.
142   "Good-bye, Crook": Crook, pp. 67–68.
142   "Have you seen the prisoners?" Mathews testimony, *House Reports*.
143   "Not wishing to hurt the feelings": Chambrun, p. 92.
143   "I wish to ask you a favor": Mathews testimony, *House Reports*.
143   "That is the man who looked at me": Porter, p. 499.
144   His stage debut had come a year earlier: Ferguson, p. 13.
144   "I think I'll reconsider": Ibid., p. 46.
144   To be seen by a woman guest: *Chicago Daily Inter-Ocean* (June 18, 1878).
145   *I am engaged to go to the theater:* Former senator Stewart wrote in *The Saturday Evening Post* (February 15, 1908).
145   *Allow Mr. Ashmun & friend:* Starr, *Further Light on Lincoln's Last Day*, p. 125.
146   "Two very fat bundles of hair": *American Heritage* (October 1959).
147   "I am glad to form your acquaintance": *Good Housekeeping* (February 1928).
147   Flinging goldfish around the room.: Sothern, p. 172.
149   The spurs on his heels . . . were the ones Junius Brutus Booth had lent to Edwin: Ferguson, p. 21.
149   He took hold of two fingers of Buckingham's hand: Buckingham, p. 13.
150   Extreme paleness of his face: *Minneapolis Journal* (April 27, 1914).
150   "What will Miss Harris think . . . ?": Randall, p. 382.
151   Fanny read aloud from *Legends of Charlemagne: American Heritage* (October 1959).
151   Another guest at the hotel: Smith, *High Crimes and Misdemeanors*, p. 75.

CHAPTER TEN

153   Rathbone thought, "Freedom!": Rathbone's affidavit is in Buckingham, p. 75.
153   "My God, that's John Booth!": Eisenschiml, *Why Was Lincoln Murdered?*, p. 69.
153   Looked at the stage when he heard the unexpected explosion: Buckingham, p. 13.
154   Looked through a window facing the stage: Ford was interviewed in the *New York Evening Post* (July 8, 1884).
154   Heard a popping sound: Edwin A. Emerson in *The Theatre* (June 1913).
154   "Done for the purpose of frightening Dundreary": Mathews testimony, *House Reports*.
154   She started when someone dropped a book: Helm, pp. 206–7.
154   She seemed in a daze: W. J. Ferguson in *The Saturday Evening Post* (February 12, 1927).
154   They had played at billiards the night before: *Atlantic Monthly* (January 1930).
155   "What is it?" Helm, p. 258.
155   A friend who was there: Thomas Reed Turner, p. 25.
155   "Turned the house into an inferno of noise": *New York World* (February 17, 1924).
155   "Order, order!": Mrs. William A. Brown, *The Century* (February 1913).
156   She went down on the floor in a faint: Edwin A. Emerson in *The Theatre* (June 1913).
156   Seemed to quiver with fear: Mrs. William A. Brown, *The Century* (February 1913).
156   Seen a man lifting aloft a dagger: Dr. Charles Leale, Address before Com-

mandery of the State of New York Military Order of the Loyal Legion of the United States (February 1909).

157 "You shan't go!" Bryan, p. 182.

158 "His dream was prophetic": Teillard, p. 120.

158 "Clear the passage!" Leale address, op. cit.

158 "You sons of bitches!": Whitman, pp. 310–313.

158 Ran with a purpose: Smith, *High Crimes and Misdemeanors*, pp. 76–77.

159 "Where is my husband?": *The Saturday Evening Post* (February 12, 1944).

159 "Blood, my hands and face": Clara Harris's April 29, 1865, letter is in the New-York Historical Society.

160 "I refused to let you see Mr. Seward": Seward, p. 259.

160 Fanny thought: *American Heritage* (October 1959).

160 Thought his father had become delirious: Laughlin, p. 107.

Chapter Eleven

163 "Mr. Seward is murdered": Smith, *High Crimes and Misdemeanors*, p. 78.

163 Too terrified to handle the horse: Buckingham, p. 21.

163 It came into Welles's mind: Smith, *High Crimes and Misdemeanors*, p. 77.

164 Stanton looked down: Ibid., p. 79.

164 "Oh, my husband's blood": Clara Harris letter (April 29, 1865), New-York Historical Society.

164 "Oh, why didn't he kill me?": Laughlin, p. 304.

165 "Do live!": Dr. Charles Sabin Taft, *The Century* (February 1893).

165 "They've killed Papa dead!": Pendel, p. 44.

165 THANK GOD IT WASN'T OURS: Leonard Grover in *The Century* (April 1909).

165 Did not know who had shot the President: *Lincoln Herald* (Winter 1980).

165 "In 15 minutes": *Schoharie County (N.Y.) Historical Review* (Fall–Winter 1967).

166 Sumner had been sitting at home: Smith, *High Crimes and Misdemeanors*, p. 77.

166 "Have you heard the news?": Pendel, p. 41.

166 "It's no use, Mr. Sumner": Smith, *High Crimes and Misdemeanors*, p. 78.

167 "Doors were slamming all over": *Chicago Daily Inter-Ocean* (June 18, 1878).

167 "We all laughed": *Washington Star* (January 24, 1909).

167 Lucy fell prone on the floor: *Chicago Daily Inter-Ocean* (June 18, 1878).

167 "A message from Captain Robert Lincoln": Mrs. Dixon's May 1, 1865, letter is printed in *The Surratt Society News* (March 1982).

168 "Have I given my husband to die?" *Schoharie County (N.Y.) Historical Review* (Fall–Winter 1967).

168 The soldiers everywhere seemed intensely dangerous: Chambrun, pp. 95–96.

169 "In touch with humanity and had a friend": Leale address, op. cit.

169 "Oh, that dreadful house!": Taft, *The Century* (February 1893).

170 Unable to move or speak: Ellsler, p. 130.

170 Bought black cotton and were tacking it on: *McClure's Magazine* (February 1901).

171 "Are you sure?": Fowler, p. 29.

171 He could not halt her cries: Barbee ms., p. 1051.

171 "The name we would have enwreathed with laurels": Asia Booth Clarke, *Junius Brutus Booth*, p. vii.

171 June did not understand: Oldroyd, pp. 96–97.

172   "If this be true, let him shoot himself": Aldrich, p. 72.

172   Presented with a gold ring: *Surratt Society News* (September 1985).

172   "You never could guess what has happened!": Aldrich, p. 71.

CHAPTER TWELVE

174   "Make haste and get those things!": *Blue and Gray Magazine* (June 1990).

174   Never got a good look at him: Both Mudds vigorously emphasized this and their story is continued by their descendants, who maintain a museum in what was the doctor's home. It is however alleged elsewhere that in later life Dr. Mudd told intimates he did indeed recognize his visitor.

175   No work makes Jack a bad boy: Mudd, p. 31.

175   Remembered the piercing wail: Doster, p. 36.

175   Terrible convulsion of grief: Keckley, pp. 191–92.

176   "My back hurts me dreadfully": Mudd, p. 32.

177   "Edwin Booth is in Boston": John T. Ford testimony, *House Reports*.

177   *A fearful calamity*: Wilson, *John Wilkes Booth*, p. 281.

177   *With deepest sorrow*: Ibid., p. 282.

177   Orlando Tomkins accompanied him: Quincy Kilby Papers, Princeton University Library.

178   The only one not to cry: Aldrich, p. 73.

178   In actual danger of losing his mind: *The Century* (November 1893).

178   Life-sized portrait of John: Aldrich, p. 75.

179   "I had visitors this morning": Jones, p. 68.

179   "What the world thought of his deed": Ibid., p. 80.

180   Reminded of a pistol shot: Baker, pp. 247–48.

180   Did not thank them for saving her life: Bryan, p. 244.

180   Went out to offer assurances: Leech, p. 399.

181   *The unhappy lady*: New York Tribune (April 22, 1865).

181   *You are advised to leave this city*: Skinner, *The Last Tragedian*, p. 142.

181   "Oh, how little did I dream": Lockridge, p. 155.

181   *My fellow Citizens*: A copy of the statement is in The Players.

182   "If those men enter below the spot": *The Century* p. 000.

182   "I will give one hundred thousand dollars": Jones, p. 93.

182   Attracted the policeman's attention: Ibid., p. 95.

183   "That is a large sum of money": Ibid., p. 93.

183   Come-to-the-Lord-and-be-saved expression: Buckingham, p. 63.

183   "I felt shakier than ever": Ibid., p. 68.

183   When he and Williams met again: Ibid., pp. 63ff.

184   From inside the top of the Capitol: Brooks, p. 266.

184   "Revolted with horror": Barbee, p. 1076.

184   Expressions of sympathy and horror: *The Assassination of Abraham Lincoln and the Attempted Assassination of William H. Seward and Frederick W. Seward*.

185   "The heaviest blow": *Richmond Whig* (April 17, 1865).

185   "This terrible deed": *The World's Work* (February 1908).

185   "Our expression of disgust": Barbee, p. 1101.

186   "Our heart stands almost still": *Baltimore Intelligencer* (April 17, 1865).

186   Nothing could stop the soldiers: Chambrun, p. 121.

186   So sobbingly overwhelmed: Putnam, p. 431.

186   Little appointment book: *Illinois State Journal of History* (February 1979). It is now in the basement museum of Ford's Theatre.

187   Troops came thrusting swords: Mahoney, p. 50.

187 "Great God!": Mathews testimony, *House Reports.*
188 Things far more complex and personal: *The Century* (August, 1893).
188 "This seemed impossible": *New York Herald* (June 27, 1909).
189 "The madman!": *Lincoln Herald* (Summer 1957).
190 "No news yet of Joe": *Maryland Historical Magazine* (Spring 1983).
190 "I did not think anything of that": Ibid.
190 "But a crack that way": Ibid.
190 Lincoln's trip set him off: Asia Booth Clarke, *The Unlocked Book*, p. 139.
190 "I would not distress these people": Smith, *Lee and Grant*, p. 280.
190 To go at such a time: Asia Booth Clarke, *The Unlocked Book*, p. 139.
191 "Think no more of him as your brother": Ibid., p. 130.
191 "I have had a heartbroken letter": Ibid., p. 130.
191 *Dear Madam:* Ibid., p 132.
191 Said a Detroit pastor: Lewis, p. 104.
192 "Out of God's jurisdiction": Ibid., p. 104.
192 Taken from her finger by her parents: Barbee, pp. 1071ff.
192 Never be able to go before the public: *Philadelphia Press* (April 24, 1865).
192 Hancock published an appeal: Washington, p. 254.

CHAPTER THIRTEEN

194 "Friends, this is your only chance": *The Century* (April 1884).
196 Worst blow the South had ever been struck: Buckingham, p. 64.
198 "I don't want to know anything about you": *Blue and Gray Magazine* (June
     1990).
199 "I am a colored man and have no right": Roscoe quotes War Department
     interrogations, pp. 364–65.
200 *Forgive me, but I have some little pride:* The original copy of the note mention-
     ing payment of $5 was found in the slain fugitive's appointment book; the
     second copy was sent to Stuart.
201 "We are the assassinators of the President": *Blue and Gray Magazine* (June
     1990).
201 His suit appeared seamed: Bainbridge's remembrances are in *The Century* for
     January 1890.
202 "I'll be with you soon, John": Ibid.
202 Such calmness and savoir-faire was almost unearthly: Ibid.
202 "I suppose you hardly remember me": *Virginia Magazine of History and
     Biography* (October 1963) has a copy of the address the Rev. Richard Bayn-
     ham Garrett delivered at colleges and churches.
202 Asked if his wound pained him: Ibid.
203 Sitting on a park bench opposite the White House: *The Century* (January
     1890).
203 "Those who have all sorts of excuses": Doherty testimony, *House Reports.*
203 Corbett's life is described in Lewis, pp. 246ff and by a Kansas neighbor,
     Albert Reid, in *Scribner's Magazine* (July 1929).
205 The talk with Rollins: *The Century* (January 1890) contains Doherty's
     remembrances; *McClure's Magazine* (May 1897) has Baker's recollections as
     recorded by a relative, the famed journalist Ray Stannard Baker.
205 Saw two enormous revolvers: *Virginia Magazine of History and Biography*
     (October 1963).
205 Man who decided to commit suicide: Barbee, p. 899.
205 Seemed strange to Richard: *Virginia Magazine of History and Biography*
     (October 1963).

206   "Would you do such a thing?": *Blue and Gray Magazine* (June 1990).
206   "Jett has a lady-love": *McClure's Magazine* (May 1897).
206   "Town is full of Yankees in search of Booth": *The Century* (January 1890).
207   "Do as you say, boys": Ibid.
207   Showed impressive calm and courage while facing great peril: Ibid.
207   "I will tell you the truth": *Virginia Magazine of History and Biography* (October 1963).
208   "What do you want?": An article by L. B. Baker is reprinted in *The Journal of the Illinois State Historical Society* (December 1946).
209   "Open the door": *McClure's Magazine* (May 1897).
209   "Damn the women": Townsend, p. 31.
209   "Bring a rope": *Virginia Magazine of History and Biography* (October 1963).
210   "Oh, Captain!": Former Lieutenant Doherty was interviewed for *The Century* (January 1890).
211   "Draw up your men": *McClure's Magazine* (May 1897).
211   The clear and ringing-toned words carried clearly: Ibid.
212   Was surprised by the appearance of the man: Townsend, p. 36.
212   "Standing under and within an arch of fire": Baker in *The Journal of the Illinois State Historical Society* (December 1946).
212   "As beautiful as the statue of a Greek god": *Virginia Magazine of History and Biography* (October 1963).
212   It was that of God Almighty: *McClure's Magazine* (May 1897).
213   "Useless": Doherty is quoted in *The Century* (January 1890); Baker in *McClure's Magazine* (May 1897).

CHAPTER FOURTEEN

214   Endeavored to smother by loud and incessant talk: Aldrich, p. 76.
214   "Is it over?": Asia Booth Clarke, *The Unlocked Book*, p. 130.
215   "A dead Yank?": *McClure's Magazine* (May 1897).
215   Cut off a lock of curling hair: *Virginia Magazine of History and Biography* (October 1963).
216   Shrieking, Lucy Hale fell across John Booth: Barbee, p. 1016.
217   "There is no resemblance in that corpse to Booth": *Records of the Columbia Historical Society* (Vol. 13, 1910).
218   Mass meeting in Dayton: Barbee, p. 1002.
218   Done nothing with their cargo: *McClure's Magazine* (May 1897).
219   Returned with his wife from a boating expedition: *Columbian Magazine* (April 1911).
220   Black, dismal hole: *The Journal of the Illinois State Historical Society* (December 1946).
220   Lasted 22 days: *New York World* (June 9, 1865).
222   Grimmest of audiences: *The Century* (February 1913).
223   "Knew less of his brother probably than anyone": Doster, p. 275.
223   "Sever all connection theatrically": Asia Booth Clarke, *The Unlocked Book*, p. 133.
223   "I faithfully believe it": Grossman, pp. 172–73.
223   "Never resume their old place in the world": Asia Booth Clarke, *The Unlocked Book*, p. 131.
223   "Secretiveness of the whole Booth race": Ibid., p. 138.
224   "I can give you no idea of the desolation": Asia Booth Clarke to Jean Anderson, May 22, 1865, the Peale Museum, Baltimore.
225   "My God, the woman too?": *Surratt Society Courier* (September 1986).

226   Took hold of a supporting post: Hoyt, pp. 148ff.
226   Hit the floor unconscious: Doster, p. 276.

CHAPTER FIFTEEN

227   As late as 1896: *North American Review* (April 1896).
227   "The horror and shock of it shortened her days": Winslow, p. 78.
228   He would run out of the room: Bryan, p. 202.
228   Details on Mrs. Lincoln are found in *Collier's Weekly* (December 25, 1926); in Baker, Ross, and Randall.
228   "A past calamity": Ross, p. 334.
229   "Obsession which he never outgrew": *The Saturday Evening Post* (February 11, 1939).
229   On the Rathbone tragedy: *Lincoln Herald* (Winter 1944); Oldroyd, p. 98, and *Surratt Society News* (July 1982). Rathbone lived until 1911; he was 74 at the time of his death.
229   On Lucy Hale: Professor Terry Alford in a publication of the Alexandria Historical Society (1990) discusses the matter. Additionally, Richmond Morcum permitted the author access to his collection of Lucy Hale memorabilia. Mr. Morcum's purchase of Lucy Hale Chandler's home brought him into possession of trunkfuls of her papers. His mother had known her son and told him stories of an aged lady considered eccentric by the children of the neighborhood. She was generally known to have been "John Wilkes Booth's girl friend," Mr. Morcum's mother told her son.
230   "In no way a sensuous woman": The stepson's letter of October 9, 1944, is in the Barbee Papers at Georgetown University.
230   "Wicked to play base ball": Albert Reid, a onetime neighbor, in *Scribner's Magazine* (July 1929).
231   Prosecuting attorney Charles Curtis: Ibid.
231   Distribution of reward money: Oldroyd, pp. 87–88.
231   Lashing his horse as he fled: Washington, p. 146.
231   Playing *rouge et noir*: *New York World* (August 17, 1867).
232   "Terror of the China seas": Ibid.
232   "Glare like a tiger": Bryan, p. 325.
232   In the Pelew Islands: Ibid.
232   "You have Wilkes Booth for husband": *New York Herald* (April 26, 1903).
232   Finally became one at the age of 39: John C. Brennan in *Maryland Historical Magazine* (Spring 1983).
233   "Introspective look": Asia Booth Clarke, *The Elder and the Younger Booth*, p. 163.
233   "She seems still to have a lingering hope": Grossman quotes from a letter to Mrs. Emma Cary, p. 174.
233   "Heavy, aching gloom": Ibid., to Emma Cary on December 20, 1865.
233   "A great big spelling-book": Ibid., p. 174.
233   "Blood of our martyred President": Lockridge, pp. 168–69.
234   Well advised to keep away from Shakespeare: Winter, *The Life and Art of Edwin Booth*, p. 54.
234   "Friend Booth": The Barbee Papers, Georgetown University, Box IV, contain a copy of a Judge Advocate General report quoting the December 25, 1864, letter.
235   "I never permit my wife or daughter": Winter, *The Life and Art of Edwin Booth*, p. 80.
235   A somber curtain: Ellsler, p. 154.

236   The burning of the costumes: Skinner, *The Last Tragedian*, pp. 143–47.
237   *Mr. Thurlow Weed*: Barbee, p. 1258.
238   "Do what you can": Kincaid, p. 38.
238   *Having once received a promise*: Bryan, p. 304.
239   "I wish this conducted with the utmost secrecy": *Baltimore Sun* (February 17, 1869).
239   Told not to use a hearse: Speare was interviewed in the *Washington Evening Star* (January 5, 1907).
240   *Successful and in our possession*: Bryan, p. 309.
240   *I have the honor to report*: Ibid., p. 309.
240   "Keep your eyes and ears open": Wilson, *John Wilkes Booth*, p. 294.
241   "And the faint moans": Ibid., p. 295.
241   Dismissed from his post: *Maryland Historical Magazine* (Vol. VIII, 1913).

CHAPTER SIXTEEN

242   "If you doubt me": *The Century* (November 1893).
242   "Most brutal ghoul-feast": Watermeir, p. 58.
242   THE WIDOW OF J. WILKES BOOTH: *New York Tribune* (December 5, 1885).
242   "A d—nable lie": Bryan quotes a letter to Laurence Hutton, pp. 363–64.
242   "Several people who knew Booth": Forrester, p. 82.
242   "Your angel mother": Grossman, pp. 44–45.
243   "Think of her": Ibid., pp 198–99.
243   "Lunatic who can hardly be controlled": Lockridge, p. 278.
243   "Her violent hatred of the child": Skinner, *The Last Tragedian*, p. 52.
243   "You can imagine my condition": Isabel Moore quotes a letter to Laurence Hutton, p. 70.
244   Afraid he would go mad: Watermeir, p. 195.
244   *"Herr Meister"*: Goodale, pp. 132–33.
244   "Fairly took my breath away": Watermeir, pp. 234–35.
244   No greater dignity or grace than Edwin: Badeau in *McClure's Magazine* (August 1893).
245   "The United States soldier that shot your brother": Kimmel, p. 292.
245   *We have never had an opportunity of telling you*: Bryan, p. 269.
245   "We know that she is blessed": Skinner, *The Last Tragedian*, quotes a letter to Lawrence Barrett, p. 209.
245   "Why do you not look": Skinner, *The Last Tragedian*, quotes a letter to William Winter, p. 211.
246   "My God, it is John!": Forrester, p. 406.
246   "Shall I take it off?": Goodale, pp. 28–29.
247   "How very like him!" Ibid., p. 104.
247   Unable greatly to admire her acting: Soliday, pp. XII–XIII.
248   "Oh, indeed, Mr. Booth, yes": Goodale, p. 125.
250   Had the right ever after: Royle, p. 20.
250   "It's been too wonderful for anything!": Goodale, p. 298.
251   "A gathering place of freaks": Goodale, p. 256.
251   "That damned scoundrel who shot Lincoln": Kimmel, p. 332.
251   Picking up the cast of a huge hand: Howells, p. 107.
251   In Boston, on a Christmas night: Louisia Eldridge in *The New York Dramatic Mirror* (December 26, 1896).
252   In honor of the Great Master: Fowler, p. 217.
253   "Let us drink": The Players Club has an elaborately done-up copy of the toast.

253 "I am ready for my cue": Skinner, *The Last Tragedian*, p. 201.

253 "In a sort of dream": Grossman, pp. 109–10.

254 "That's Papa!": Ruggles, p. 208.

254 "Mr. Barrett has gone": Ibid., p. 357.

254 Scaffold was filled: *Boston Journal* (April 17, 1893).

254 "Snooze all day": Grossman, p. 123.

255 Had to be half-carried from the room: *New York Express* (June 8, 1893).

255 It had been Molly's: Isabel Moore, p. 71.

255 "How are you, dear Grandpa?": Grossman, p. 22.

255 "Don't let Father die in the dark!": Lockridge, p. 328.

256 Ford's Theatre simply caved in: All newspapers carried lengthy descriptions the following day.

257 Horatio's farewell to his friend: Winter, *Life and Art of Edwin Booth*, p. 156.

BIBLIOGRAPHY

Aldrich, Mrs. Thomas Bailey. *Crowding Memories*. Boston: Houghton Mifflin, 1920.

Allen, Hervey. *Israfel: The Life and Times of Edgar Allan Poe*. New York: George H. Doran, 1927.

Anonymous. *Memoirs of Junius Brutus Booth*. London: Chapple et al., 1817.

Arnold, Samuel B. *Defence and Prison Experiences of a Lincoln Conspirator*. Hatties-burg, Miss.: The Book Farm, 1943.

Baker, Jean H. *Mary Todd Lincoln*. New York: W. W. Norton, 1987.

Barbee, David Rankin. "Lincoln and Booth." Unpublished manuscript.

Bishop, Jim. *The Day Lincoln Was Shot*. New York: Harper & Brothers, 1955.

Booth, Mary Devlin. *Letters and Notebooks*, ed. L. Terry Oggel. Westport, Conn.: Greenwood Press, 1987.

Brooks, Noah. *Washington in Lincoln's Time*. New York: Century, 1896.

Bryan, George S. *The Great American Myth*. New York: Carrick & Evans, 1940.

Buckingham, J. E. *Reminiscences and Souveniers of the Assassination of Abraham Lincoln*. Washington, D.C.: Rufus H. Darby, 1894.

Carpenter, F. B. *Six Months at the White House with Abraham Lincoln*. New York: Hurd and Houghton, 1866.

Carter, Samuel. *The Riddle of Dr. Mudd*. New York: G. P. Putnam's Sons, 1974.

Chambrun, the Marquis Adolph de. *Impressions of Lincoln and the Civil War*. New York: Random House, 1952.

Chamlee, Roy. *Lincoln's Assassins*. Jefferson, N.C.: McFarland, 1990.

Clarke, Asia Booth. *Junius Brutus Booth*. New York: Carleton, 1865.

———. *The Elder and the Younger Booth*. Boston: James R. Osgood, 1882.

———. *The Unlocked Book*. New York: G. P. Putnam's Sons, 1938.

Clarke, James Freeman. *Memorial and Biographical Sketches*. Boston: Houghton, Osgood, 1878.

Cottrell, John. *Anatomy of an Assassination*. London: Frederick Muller, 1966.

Cowell, Joe. *Thirty Years Passed Among The Players in England and America*. New York: Harper, 1844.

Crawford, Mary Caroline. *The Romance of the American Theatre*. Boston: Little, Brown, 1925.

Crook, William H. *Through Five Administrations*. New York: Harper & Brothers, 1910.

Dempsey, David. *The Triumphs and Trials of Lotta Crabtree*. New York: William Morrow, 1968.

De Witt, David Miller. *The Assassination of Abraham Lincoln.* New York: Macmillan, 1909.

Doster, William E. *Lincoln and Episodes of the Civil War.* New York: G. P. Putnam's Sons, 1915.

Eisenschiml, Otto. *Why Was Lincoln Murdered?* Boston: Little, Brown, 1937.
————. *In the Shadow of Lincoln's Death.* New York: Wilfred Funk, 1940.

Ellsler, John E. *Stage Memoirs.* Cleveland: The Rowfant Club, 1950.

Ezekiel, Herbert, and Gaston Lichtenstein. *The History of the Jews of Richmond.* Richmond, Va.: Herbert Ezekiel, 1917.

Ferguson, W. J. *I Saw Booth Shoot Lincoln.* Boston and New York: Houghton Mifflin, 1930.

Ford, George D. *These Were Actors.* New York: Library Publishers, 1955.

Forrester, Izola. *This One Mad Act.* Boston: Hale, Cushman and Flint, 1937.

Fowler, Gene. *Good Night, Sweet Prince.* New York: The Viking Press, 1944.

Furtwangler, Albert. *Assassin on Stage.* Urbana: University of Illinois Press, 1991.

Gilbert, Anne Hartley. *Stage Reminiscences.* New York: Charles Scribner's Sons, 1901.

Goff, John S. *Robert Todd Lincoln.* Norman: University of Oklahoma Press, 1969.

Goodale, Katherine. *Behind the Scenes with Edwin Booth.* Boston: Houghton Mifflin, 1931.

Gould, Thomas R. *The Tragedian.* New York: Hurd and Houghton, 1868.

Greenslet, Ferris. *The Life of Thomas Bailey Aldrich.* Boston: Houghton Mifflin, 1910.

Grossman, Edwina Booth. *Edwin Booth.* New York: The Century Company, 1894.

Gutman, Richard and Kellie O. *John Wilkes Booth Himself.* Dover, Mass.: Hired Hand Press, 1979.

Hall, James O. *John Wilkes Booth's Escape Route.* Clinton, Md.: The Surratt Society, 1990.

Helm, Katherine. *The True Story of Mary, Wife of Lincoln.* New York: Harper & Brothers, 1920.

Howells, William Dean. *Literary Friends and Acquaintances.* New York: Harper & Brothers, 1902.

Hoyt, Harlowe. *Townhall Tonight.* New York: Bramhall House, 1955.

Hutton, Laurence. *Edwin Booth.* New York: Harper & Brothers, 1893.

Jefferson, Joseph. *Autobiography.* New York: The Century Company, 1889.

Jennings, John J. *Theatrical and Circus Life.* Brandon, Vt.: Sidney M. Southard, 1884.

Jones, Thomas A. *J. Wilkes Booth.* Chicago: Laird & Lee, 1893.

Kauffman, Michael W. "Booth, Republicanism, and the Lincoln Assassination." Special scholars thesis, University of Virginia, 1989.

Keckley, Elizabeth. *Behind the Scenes.* New York: G. W. Carlton, 1968.

Kimmel, Stanley. *The Mad Booths of Maryland.* Indianapolis, Ind.: Bobbs-Merrill, 1940.

Kincaid, Arthur, ed. *John Wilkes Booth, Actor.* North Leigh, Oxfordshire, Eng.: Arthur Kincaid, 1989.

Kunhardt, Dorothy Meserve and Philip B., Jr. *Twenty Days.* New York: Castle Books, 1965.

Lanier, Henry Wysham, ed. *The Players' Book.* New York: The Players, 1938.

Lattimer, John K. *Kennedy and Lincoln.* New York: Harcourt Brace Jovanovich, 1980.

Laughlin, Clara E. *The Death of Lincoln.* New York: Doubleday, Page, 1909.

Leech, Margaret. *Reveille in Washington.* New York: Harper & Brothers, 1941.

Lewis, Lloyd. *Myths After Lincoln.* New York: The Readers Club, 1941.

Lockridge, Richard. *Darling of Misfortune: Edwin Booth.* New York: The Century Company, 1932.

McClure, Alexander. *Abraham Lincoln and Men of War-times.* Philadelphia: Times Publishing, 1892.

Mahoney, Ella V. *Sketches of Tudor Hall and the Booth Family.* Belair, Md.: Ella V. Mahoney, 1925.

"Margaret" [Margaret Townshend]. *Theatrical Sketches.* New York: The Merriam Company, 1894.

Mathews, Brander, and Laurence Hutton, eds. *Kean and Booth and Their Contemporaries.* Boston: L. C. Page, 1886.

Millet, Ernest. *John Wilkes Booth, Oilman.* New York: The Exposition Press, 1947.

Modjeska, Helena. *Memories and Impressions.* New York: Macmillan, 1910.

Moore, Guy W. *The Case of Mrs. Surratt.* Norman: University of Oklahoma Press, 1954.

Moore, Isabel. *Talks in the Library with Laurence Hutton.* New York: G. P. Putnam's Sons, 1905.

Morris, Clara. *Life on the Stage.* New York: McClure, Phillips, 1901.

———. *Stage Confidences.* Boston: Lothrop, 1902.

Moses, Montrose J. *Famous Actor-Families in America.* New York: Thomas D. Crowell, 1906.

Mudd, Nettie, ed. *The Life of Dr. Samuel J. Mudd.* New York: Neale, 1906.

Murdoch, James E. *The Stage.* Philadelphia: J. M. Stoddart, 1880.

Oldroyd, Osborn H. *The Assassination of Abraham Lincoln.* Washington: O. H. Oldroyd, 1901.

Pendel, Thomas F. *Thirty-six Years in the White House.* Washington, D.C.: Neale, 1902.

Pierce, Edward L. *Memoir and Letters of Charles Sumner,* Vol. IV. Boston: Roberts Brothers, 1894.

Porter, Horace. *Campaigning with Grant.* Bloomington: Indiana University Press, 1961 (originally published 1897).

Putnam, George Haven. *Memories of My Youth.* New York: G. P. Putnam's Sons, 1914.

Randall, Ruth Painter. *Mary Lincoln.* Boston: Little, Brown, 1953.

Reuter, William L. *The King Can Do No Wrong.* New York: Pageant Press, 1958.

Richardson, Elmo R., and Alan W. Farley. *John Palmer Usher.* Lawrence: University of Kansas Press, 1960.

Robins, Edward. *Twelve Great Actors.* New York: G. P. Putnam's Sons, 1900.

Roscoe, Theodore. *The Web of Conspiracy.* Englewood Cliffs, N.J.: Prentice-Hall, 1959.

Ross, Ishbel. *The President's Wife.* New York: G. P. Putnam's Sons, 1973.

Rourke, Constance. *Troupers of the Gold Coast, Or the Rise of Lotta Crabtree.* New York: Harcourt, Brace, 1928.

Royle, Edwin Milton. *Edwin Booth as I Knew Him.* New York: The Players, 1933.

Ruggles, Eleanor. *Prince of Players.* New York: W. W. Norton, 1953.

Samples, Gordon. *Lust for Fame.* Jefferson, N.C.: McFarland, 1982.

Sandburg, Carl. *Abraham Lincoln: The War Years,* Vol. IV. New York: Harcourt, Brace, 1939.

Seward, Frederick W. *Reminiscences of a War-Time Statesman and Diplomat.* New York: G. P. Putnam's Sons, 1916.

Sewell, Richard H. *John P. Hale and the Politics of Abolition.* Cambridge, Mass.: Harvard University Press, 1965.

Shattuck, Charles H. *The Hamlet of Edwin Booth.* Urbana: University of Illinois Press, 1969.

Skinner, Otis. *Footlights and Spotlights.* Indianapolis, Ind.: Bobbs-Merrill, 1924.

———. *The Last Tragedian.* New York: Dodd, Mead, 1939.

Smith, Gene. *High Crimes and Misdemeanors.* New York: William Morrow, 1977.

———. *Lee and Grant.* New York: McGraw-Hill, 1984.

Soliday, John Chase. "The 'Joint Star' Tours of Edwin Booth and Lawrence Barrett." Ph.D. thesis, University of Minnesota, 1974.

Sothern, Edward H. *The Melancholy Tale of "M."* London: Cassell, 1917.

Starr, John W., Jr. *Further Light on Lincoln's Last Day.* Harrisburg, P.A.: Privately printed, 1930.

————. *Lincoln's Last Day.* New York: Frederick A. Stokes, 1922.

Steers, Edward, Jr., and Joan L. Chaconas. *The Escape and Capture of John Wilkes Booth.* Washington, D.C.: Marker Tours, 1989.

Stern, Philip Van Doren. *The Man Who Killed Lincoln.* New York: Random House, 1939.

Tebbel, John. *A Certain Club.* New York: The Hampden/Booth Theatre Library, 1989.

Teillard, Dorothy Lamon. *Recollections of Abraham Lincoln by Ward Hill Lamon.* Washington, D.C.: Dorothy Lamon Teillard, 1911.

Townsend, George Alfred. *The Life, Crime, and Capture of John Wilkes Booth.* New York: Dick & Fitzgerald, 1865.

Turner, Justin G., and Linda Levitt. *Mary Todd Lincoln.* New York: Alfred A. Knopf, 1972.

Turner, Thomas Reed. *Beware the People Weeping.* Baton Rouge: Louisiana State University Press, 1982.

U.S. Government Printing Office. *The Assassination of Abraham Lincoln and the Attempted Assassination of William H. Seward and Frederick W. Seward: Expressions of Condolence and Sympathy Inspired by These Events.* Washington, D.C.: 1866.

————. *Reports of Committees of the House of Representatives, 40th Congress, First Session,* 1867.

Washington, John E. *They Knew Lincoln.* New York: E. P. Dutton, 1942.

Watermeier, Daniel J. *Between Actor and Critic: Selected Letters of Edwin Booth and William Winter.* Princeton, N.J.: Princeton University Press, 1971.

Weichmann, Louis J. *A True History of the Assassination of Abraham Lincoln and of the Conspiracy of 1865.* New York: Vintage Books, 1977.

Whitman, Walt. *Specimen Days and Collect.* Philadelphia: The Author, 1888.

Wilson, Francis. *Joseph Jefferson.* New York: Charles Scribner's Sons, 1906.

————. *John Wilkes Booth.* Boston: Houghton Mifflin, 1929.

Winslow, Catherine. *Yesterdays with Actors.* Boston: Cupples and Hurd, 1887.

Winter, William. *The Life and Art of Edwin Booth.* New York: Macmillan, 1893.

————. *Other Days.* New York: Moffatt, Yard, 1908.

————. *Vagrant Memories.* New York: George H. Doran, 1915.

Withers, Nan. "The Acting Style and Career of John Wilkes Booth." Ph.D. thesis, University of Wisconsin at Madison, 1979.

INDEX